Fodor's InFocus

SANTA FE

Welcome to Santa Fe

On a plateau at the base of the Sangre de Cristo Mountains—at an elevation of 7,000 feet—Santa Fe brims with reminders of four centuries of Spanish and Mexican rule, and of the Pueblo cultures that have been here for hundreds of years more. With a vibrant diversity seen in its food, art, and shopping scenes, Santa Fe remains a magical place for visitors looking for that Southwestern flair. Not too far from Santa Fe, the cities of Albuquerque and Taos beckon with their own fascinating histories and artistic flairs. As you plan your upcoming travels to Santa Fe, please confirm that places are still open and let us know when we need to make updates by writing to us at editors@fodors.com.

TOP REASONS TO GO

■ **Food:** From enchiladas to blue-corn pancakes, Santa Fe is an exceptional dining town with a diverse culinary history.

■ **Art:** See why Georgia O'Keeffe was so inspired here, or check out the modern-day galleries lining Canyon Road.

■ **Markets:** From weekly farmers' markets to the yearly Indian Market, the city delivers with its local goods.

■ **Outdoor adventures:** Hike the incredible, and surprisingly lush, mountains that rise out of Santa Fe; raft the Rio Grande; snowboard; snowshoe; or try mountain biking.

■ **Native American history:** Learn the history of the region's Pueblo cultures that still influence the landscape today.

Contents

MAPS

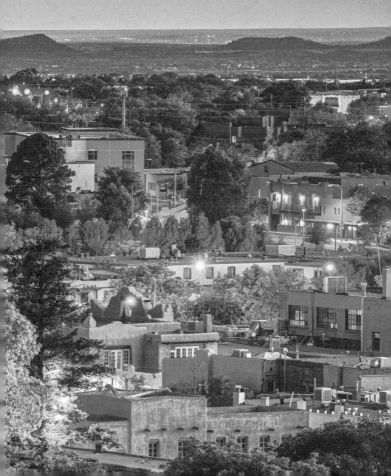

EXPERIENCE
SANTA FE

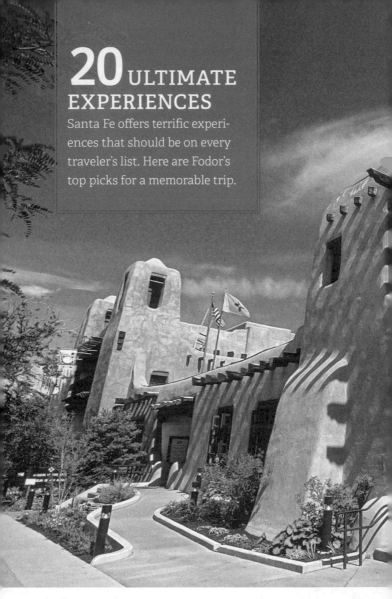

20 ULTIMATE EXPERIENCES

Santa Fe offers terrific experiences that should be on every traveler's list. Here are Fodor's top picks for a memorable trip.

1 Museums

Learn about local and regional art and culture at the excellent attractions on Santa Fe's Museum Hill, including the Museum of Indian Arts and Culture. *(Ch. 4)*

2 Dining

A rising national culinary destination, the city has superb restaurants that offer both traditional and contemporary New Mexican fare as well as more eclectic global cuisine. *(Ch. 3–6)*

3 Railyard District

A popular indoor-outdoor farmers' market, a fun urban park, and hip restaurants, galleries, and indie shops keep things bustling in this redeveloped historic neighborhood. *(Ch. 5)*

4 Albuquerque Balloon Festival

More than 600 hot air balloons ascend over the Rio Grande Valley during this colorful October gathering, the largest ballooning festival in the world. *(Ch. 8)*

5 Santa Fe Trail

This nearly 900-mile, 19th-century trade route passes through historic Las Vegas and crosses the Sangre de Cristo Mountains at Pecos National Historical Park en route to downtown Santa Fe. *(Ch. 7)*

6 The Turquoise Trail

A scenic alternative route to Interstate 25, this 70-mile road starts in Santa Fe and plunges through offbeat villages like Madrid and the dramatic highlands of Sandia Crest. *(Ch. 7)*

7 Canyon Road

Meandering about 3 miles from downtown Santa Fe, this narrow road is lined with colorfully preserved adobe houses, many of which now contain highly regarded art galleries. *(Ch. 4)*

8 Intimate Inns

Unwind in a Southwestern-style abode or one of the city's intimate inns and bed-and-breakfasts, many featuring original artwork and handcrafted furnishings. *(Ch. 3–6)*

9 Meow Wolf

Spend a few hours wandering through this madly imaginative and completely immersive 33,000-square-foot collaborative art installation. *(Ch. 6)*

10 Bandelier National Monument

Climb inside cliff dwellings and ceremonial kivas of ancestral Puebloans within this 33,600-acre natural and archaeological wonder. *(Ch. 7)*

11 Art Galleries

The city's more than 250 galleries tempt with ceramics, paintings, photography, and sculptures, especially during First Friday Night Art Walk. *(Ch. 3–6)*

12 The High Road to Taos

For a scenic adventure, drive between Taos and Santa Fe via this breathtaking alpine route through quaint Spanish-colonial villages and past sweeping vistas. *(Ch. 7)*

13 Santa Fe Plaza

Soak up the energy and take in the culture of the city's lively and historic central plaza, which is lined with stellar museums and colorful shops and restaurants. *(Ch. 3)*

14 Georgia O'Keeffe

Connect with the work of this iconic American Modernist artist, who drew inspiration from the area's landscape, at the exceptional Georgia O'Keeffe Museum downtown and her house in Abiquiú. *(Ch. 3, 7)*

15 Rafting on the Rio Grande

From peaceful floats to rollicking rafting trips, the nation's fourth-longest river is one of the region's top destinations for outdoor recreation. *(Ch. 7–9)*

16 Santa Fe Opera

Simply stunning, this internationally acclaimed opera's indoor-outdoor amphitheater is carved into a hillside and presents five works during its annual eight-week summer season. *(Ch. 6)*

17 Markets

Annual market weekends like the Santa Fe Indian Market and Traditional Spanish Market offer incredible opportunities for shopping and art collecting. *(Ch. 1)*

18 Taos Pueblo

Continuously occupied for more than 1,000 years, this rambling, carefully preserved adobe-walled pueblo looks much as it has for centuries. Fascinating guided tours are offered. *(Ch. 9)*

19 Native American Culture

Santa Fe celebrates Native culture at historic monuments and museums throughout the city, including Native American dances and jewelry-making demonstrations in Milner Plaza. *(Ch. 3–7)*

20 Kasha Katuwe Tent Rocks National Monument

Known for bizarre sandstone rock formations that look like stacked tepees, this dramatic box canyon and lofty promontory is a memorable hiking getaway about 40 miles southwest of Santa Fe. *(Ch. 7)*

WHAT'S WHERE

1 The Plaza and Downtown Santa Fe. The heart of historic Santa Fe is the Plaza. The Old Santa Fe Trail is a historic section of the city that joins the Plaza from north of Museum Hill after passing the state capitol and some of the area's oldest neighborhoods.

2 East Side with Canyon Road and Museum Hill. Taking in some of the city's prettiest and most historic streets, the East Side is bisected by charming Canyon Road, which is lined with galleries, shops, and restaurants housed in adobe compounds. To the south, Museum Hill is home to four excellent museums and the Santa Fe Botanical Garden.

3 The Railyard District. A model for urban green space, this colorful district just south-west of Downtown contains a vibrant farmers' market, inviting restaurants, shops, art galleries, and the SITE Santa Fe contemporary art museum.

4 Greater Santa Fe. West of the city center are several historic, mostly residential neighborhoods with a few notable restaurants and shops on Guadalupe Street. North, a scenic expanse of the Sangre de Cristo foothills is home to the Santa Fe Opera House and some high-profile resorts. South, you'll find the more modern and suburban parts of the city, along with the city's hottest arts attraction, Meow Wolf.

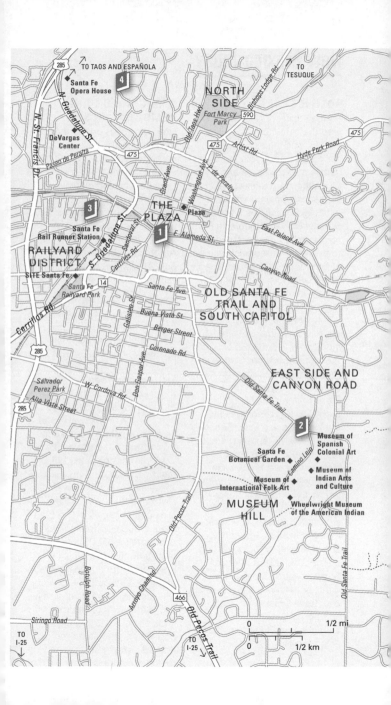

TO TAOS AND ESPAÑOLA

NORTH SIDE

TO TESUQUE

Santa Fe Opera House

4

285

N. Guadalupe St.

DeVargas Center

Paseo de Peralta

N. St. Francis Dr.

Fort Marcy Park

590

Bishops Lodge Rd.

Artist Rd.

475

Hyde Park Road

475

Grant Ave.

Washington Ave.

P. de Peralta

Old Taos Hwy.

THE PLAZA

Plaza

1

East Palace Ave.

E. Alameda St.

3

Santa Fe Rail Runner Station

RAILROAD DISTRICT

SITE Santa Fe

Santa Fe Railyard Park

Sandoval St.

S. Guadalupe St.

Cerrillos Rd.

14

Santa Fe Ave.

Cerrillos Rd.

285

Galisteo St.

Buena Vista St.

Berger Street

Coronado Rd.

Canyon Road

OLD SANTA FE TRAIL AND SOUTH CAPITOL

Don Gaspar Ave.

Salvador Perez Park

Alta Vista Street

285

W. Cordova Rd.

Old Santa Fe Trail

EAST SIDE AND CANYON ROAD

2

Museum of Spanish Colonial Art

Santa Fe Botanical Garden

Camino Lejo

Museum of Indian Arts and Culture

Museum of International Folk Art

MUSEUM HILL

Wheelwright Museum of the American Indian

Old Pecos Trail

Botulph Road

Arroyo Chamisa

466

Old Pecos Trail

Old Santa Fe Trail

Siringo Road

TO I-25

TO I-25

0   1/2 mi

0   1/2 km

New Mexico Today

POLITICS

As the capital of New Mexico (and the oldest capital city in the United States), Santa Fe plays an outsized role in the state's political scene and when the state legislature is in session, Downtown hums with elected officials and other political workers. Ideologically, the state has moved steadily to the left over the past couple of decades—New Mexico has voted Democrat in every U.S. Presidential election since 1988 with the exception of 2004, when George W. Bush edged John Kerry by less than a percentage point. As of 2023, the state's governor, both senators, and all three members of congress are Democrats, and Team Blue maintains 27 to 15 and 45 to 25 advantages in the New Mexico State Senate and House of Representatives, respectively. Moreover, the state's northern Rio Grande corridor hews especially to the left, with Santa Fe and Taos (and to only a slightly lesser extent, Albuquerque) embracing progressive elected officials and agendas, including racial, gender, and LGBTQ+ equality, gun control, reproductive rights, conservation initiatives, and the like. Santa Fe, Taos, and Bernalillo (Albuquerque) counties are also all sanctuary jurisdictions.

IMMIGRATION AND DEMOGRAPHICS

New Mexico is one of the most ethnically diverse states in the nation—as of the 2020 census, nearly 47.7% of the population identifies as Hispanic (of any race), by far the highest percentage of any U.S. state. About 12.5% of residents identify as Native American; New Mexico trails only Alaska and Oklahoma in this regard.

At the very southern end of New Mexico, about a five-hour drive south of Santa Fe, the state has a desolate and relatively short (about 180 miles long) international border with Mexico. There are just three border crossings, none of them connected to large cities or major highways, and so they generally do not see a lot of traffic. However, many who immigrate via the busier nearby border crossings in Texas and Arizona do eventually make their way to New Mexico, which, as of 2021, had around 200,000 foreign-born residents (about 9% of the state's population, which is lower than the national average of 14.3%). About 72% of New Mexico's immigrants originally hail from Mexico, and roughly 40% of the state's foreign-born population are naturalized U.S. citizens. Immigrants play a vital role in the state's economy and cultural fabric, making up about 12% of the workforce. The state also has nearly 6,000 active DACA recipients.

New Mexico also claims the highest number of U.S. residents (around 340,000) who identify as Hispano, meaning they're descended from the Spanish settlers who inhabited this land when it was part of the Spanish Empire (1598–1821) and then Mexico (1821–48).

WILDFIRES

With its dry climate and abundance of grasslands and coniferous forests, New Mexico has always been a region prone to wildfires, especially from May through early July, which is typically the hottest and driest time of year. By mid-July, the frequent late-afternoon rains of the "monsoon" season usually help to quell fires. Extended droughts and the significant effects of climate change, however, have created especially severe and long wildfire seasons in recent years, and experts warn fire danger is increasingly likely in North-Central New Mexico from March through October, and can even be a possibility during the winter months. And even when fires aren't present locally, smoky skies from fires elsewhere in the West can cause burning eyes and respiratory challenges from spring through fall.

You can do your part to help prevent fires by always checking the official government websites of state and federal parks and wilderness areas for wildfire advisories and even temporary closures, and also keeping an eye out for road signs throughout the region that indicate the potential for fires on a given day. The New Mexico Fire Information website (⊕ nmfireinfo.com) provides updates on fires around the state as well as restrictions and tips on safety.

Public lands in New Mexico all have stringent campfire restrictions—some prohibit fires of any kind, while others limit fires to designated grills and pits. Observe these restrictions, don't drive or park cars where grasses and plants can come into contact with the underside of your vehicle, and never toss cigarettes from a car or anywhere outdoors. If you see an unattended fire or smoke in the wilderness, report it immediately by calling ☎ 911. And in the relatively unlikely event that authorities issue an evacuation order in the area in which you're staying, follow these orders immediately.

What to Eat and Drink in Santa Fe

CHOCOLATE

Archaeologists have traced the consumption of chocolate in this part of the world to AD 900 Chacoan culture. These days, you'll find a bounty of artisan chocolatiers in Santa Fe.

CHILES

New Mexico's famous hot chiles are featured in countless traditional New Mexican dishes, from tamales to cheeseburgers, served with either green or red chiles (or "Christmas" for both).

POSOLE

What might look to the uninitiated like popcorn soup is actually a sublime marriage of hominy, lime, pork, garlic, and spices. It's a regional staple of Mexico that's also hugely popular throughout New Mexico.

CRAFT BEER

The beer scenes in Santa Fe, Taos, and especially Albuquerque—which has among the highest number of beer producers per capita in the country—are impressive and innovative. Breweries like Bosque and Le Cumbre earn raves for their distinctive creations.

SOPAIPILLAS

Puffy, deep-fried bread that's similar to Navajo fry bread (which is native to Arizona and western New Mexico), sopaipillas are served either as a dessert drizzled with honey or as a savory dish stuffed with pinto beans or meat and smothered with chile sauce.

ENCHILADAS

Among burritos, tacos, tostadas, chiles rellenos, and New Mexico's many other comfort-food standards, enchiladas are perhaps the most celebrated here.

Posole

BLUE-CORN PANCAKES

The Southwest's Puebloan and Hopi tribes popularized the cultivation of blue-corn meal, which these days appears on New Mexico menus in just about anything flour-based, from enchiladas to corn chips. But blue corn's slightly sweet personality makes it especially delicious in breakfast foods, namely pancakes but also waffles.

COFFEE

A distinct regional take on this beverage is New Mexico Piñon Coffee, a company begun in the late '90s that infuses its beans with natural piñon flavoring during the roasting process, giving the coffee a nutty, slightly sweet quality—it's sold in most grocery stores around the state.

FRITO PIE

Said to be originally from Texas—although some New Mexicans claim it comes from Santa Fe—the Frito pie is also extremely popular in New Mexican diners and short-order restaurants. This savory, humble casserole consists of Fritos corn chips layered with chile, cheese, green onions, and pinto beans.

MARGARITAS

Originally invented just over the border in either Tijuana or Ciudad Juárez, depending on which origin story you believe, these sweet-and-sour cocktails consisting of tequila, lime juice, and either Triple Sec or Cointreau have been a mainstay of northern New Mexico bar culture for decades.

What to Buy in Santa Fe

WEAVINGS AND TEXTILES
Hand-woven goods rank among the region's most prized shopping finds, including priceless antique Navajo rugs and Spanish-colonial blankets.

TURQUOISE JEWELRY
Dazzling, hand-crafted turquoise jewelry has been a symbol of Santa Fe and nearby pueblos for generations. Note that authentic Southwest-mined turquoise is increasingly hard to find. If you're seeking top-quality turquoise jewelry crafted by local Native American artists, stick with a reputable gallery or the certified vendors working in front of the Palace of the Governors.

ART AND CRAFTS FROM ANNUAL MARKETS
Santa Fe's legendary summer exhibitions—including the International Folk Art Market in July—are great opportunities to find hand-woven and hand-crafted items, and to meet the talented makers.

COWBOY BOOTS AND HATS
O'Farrell Hat Company has produced custom cowboy hats since 1979 while colorful, bespoke cowboy boots fashioned from alligator, ostrich, and other precious skins are another favorite local good.

PUEBLO POTTERY
From the Navajo Nation to the state's many pueblos, native artisans in New Mexico have a centuries-old tradition of producing intricate pottery with striking, complex designs and in a breathtaking range of colors and styles that are often specific to a particular tribe.

Pueblo Pottery

FETISHES
These small and often fanciful stone carvings for which New Mexico's Zuni tribe is famous are said to bring out the characteristics of whomever possesses them.

FOLK FURNITURE
The often brightly hued, hand-carved furniture you see all around Santa Fe—from massive dining tables to smaller *equipale* (pigskin) chairs and punched-tin lamps and frames—make terrific additions to any home.

LOCAL ARTWORK
Santa Fe boasts one of the world's most impressive art scenes, with more than 250 galleries, from international showcases like the sprawling Gerald Peters Gallery to other renowned spaces like Peyton Wright, Nedra Matteucci, LewAllen, and Monroe Gallery. Although traditional artwork, such as regional landscape paintings, proliferates here, the city also supports an edgy contemporary arts scene.

LOCAL SALSAS AND ROASTED CHILES
Looking to bring New Mexico's inimitable green- and red-chile salsas home with you? Several companies sell flavorful sauces by the jar along with bags of flash-frozen roasted chiles. Powdered chiles, strings of dried chiles (*ristras*), and chile-inflected candies, honey, jams, and other gourmet items are also popular.

Best Outdoor Adventures in North-Central New Mexico

ASPEN VISTA TRAIL

This winding alpine hike takes in breathtaking fall foliage scenery, but also makes for an enjoyable trek in spring and summer, too. In winter, it's a popular spot for snowshoeing.

VALLES CALDERA NATIONAL PRESERVE

A spectacular expanse anchored by one of the world's largest volcanic calderas, this 89,000-acre preserve in the Jémez Mountains is popular for hiking, skiing, and mountain biking.

RANDALL DAVEY AUDUBON CENTER

This 135-acre nature center offers a couple of fairly short but wonderfully scenic trails for observing wildlife, especially local and migrating birds, of which more than 200 have been spotted.

THE DALE BALL TRAIL NETWORK

This 24-mile complex of hiking and mountain-biking trails winds through the eastern foothills of Santa Fe and is easily accessed from several areas, including Hyde Park and the end of Canyon Road.

TAOS SKI VALLEY

One of the West's preeminent ski areas, this dramatic valley famed for its vertiginous slopes and sunny conditions draws serious skiers and snowboarders from late November through early April.

WHEELER PEAK

One of the more strenuous hiking challenges in the area, the 8-mile round-trip trek to New Mexico's highest point (elevation 13,161 feet) rewards visitors with stunning views in all directions.

Taos Ski Valley

RIO GRANDE NATURE CENTER STATE PARK

A 166-acre urban oasis just north of downtown Albuquerque, this peaceful park contains the country's largest forest of cottonwood trees.

RIO GRANDE DEL NORTE NATIONAL MONUMENT

The signature feature of this 242,555-acre national monument is its stunning stretch of the Rio Grande. It's best viewed from the Rio Grande Gorge Bridge, which soars 650 feet above the river.

KASHA-KATUWE TENT ROCKS NATIONAL MONUMENT

This stunning geological wonder is named for its bizarre rock formations, which look like tepees rising over a narrow box canyon. The hike here is relatively short and only moderately challenging.

PETROGLYPH NATIONAL MONUMENT

The several trails through this expanse of extinct volcanoes on Albuquerque's west side pass by hundreds of well-preserved petroglyphs that date from as far back as 3,000 years ago.

BANDELIER NATIONAL MONUMENT

More than 70 miles of trails traverse this remarkable 33,600-acre wilderness near Los Alamos, the most popular of which wind past wooden ladders that lead into centuries-old cliff dwellings.

What to Read and Watch

BLESS ME, ULTIMA
BY RUDOLFO ANAYA

Written in 1972 and widely considered one of the most important and impressive works of Chicano literature, this coming-of-age novel set in a small, largely Hispano New Mexican community shortly after World War II is based partly on the writer's early life in the town of Santa Rosa. Anaya, who passed away in 2020, continued to write about New Mexico throughout his life. A 2013 movie adaptation was filmed around Albuquerque and Santa Fe.

BREAKING BAD AND BETTER CALL SAUL

High school teacher–turned–meth-dealing antihero Walter White might just be New Mexico's most infamous resident, fictional or otherwise (with apologies to Billy the Kid). *Breaking Bad* and its similarly acclaimed prequel *Better Call Saul* were both set and filmed in Albuquerque, where an entire cottage industry of tours that visit the shows' noted locations has sprung up in recent years.

CITY SLICKERS

This classic 1991 Billy Crystal comedy about friends in New York City who confront their respective midlife crises by embarking on a two-week cattle drive through New Mexico and Colorado packs plenty of laughs and shows off the stunning landscapes of Abiquiú, the Nambé and Santa Clara pueblos, and Santa Fe.

DANCE HALL OF THE DEAD BY TONY HILLERMAN

One of the state's most treasured fiction writers, the late Albuquerquean Tony Hillerman set 18 detective novels on and around the Native American reservations of the Four Corners region of New Mexico and Arizona. It's hard to pick a favorite among his many gripping page turners, but *Dance Hall of the Dead*—which won a coveted Edgar Award in 1974—is one of the best.

DEATH COMES FOR THE ARCHBISHOP BY WILLA CATHER

The great American novelist Willa Cather—who spent time with D. H. Lawrence, Witter Bynner, and other notables of New Mexico's early-20th-century literary and arts scene—penned this tale of the attempts by Catholic Archbishop Jean-Baptiste Lamy to establish a diocese in Santa Fe. Although it's a fictionalized account, it does touch on a number of real events and actual characters who played an important role in northern New Mexico history during the late 19th century.

EASY RIDER

With key scenes in Santa Fe, Taos, and Las Vegas, this ode to road-tripping, bikers, and counterculture brought international fame to Peter Fonda, Dennis Hopper, and Jack Nicholson, and also the mesmerizing scenery of New Mexico.

GODLESS

Netflix's 1880s-period Western consists of just seven episodes, but earned critical acclaim for its gripping portrayal of an outlaw on the run and the proprietress of a ranch who takes him in. Like another stellar TV Western, *Longmire,* the show was filmed entirely in and around Santa Fe, but *Godless* stands out for having also been set in a New Mexico mining town, the fictional community of La Belle.

THE MILAGRO BEANFIELD WAR BY JOHN NICHOLS

This humorous, poignant 1970s novel about a small-town New Mexico farmer taking on soulless government bureaucracy and deep-pocketed developers in order to save his humble beanfield was adapted into an entertaining movie in 1988. Directed by Robert Redford, the film was shot primarily in the beautiful village of Truchas, located along the High Road to Taos.

THE MYTH OF SANTA FE BY CHRIS WILSON

This rich and thorough study explains how and why Santa Fe came to look as it does today. The legacy of the city's earliest Native American and then Spanish settlers is explored, as are the conscious efforts by enterprising business owners in the early 20th century to turn the city into a bona fide international tourist destination.

OPPENHEIMER

Significant portions of this Christopher Nolan biopic about the eponymous "father of the atomic bomb" were filmed in and around Los Alamos and Santa Fe. The big-budget 2023 thriller traces J. Robert Oppenheimer's years working on the Manhattan Project and stars Cillian Murphy in the lead, along with Emily Blunt, Matt Damon, and Robert Downey Jr. The 2014–2015 TV series *Manhattan* also depicted the lives of scientists and their families living in Los Alamos during the Manhattan Project and was filmed almost entirely in the area.

PUEBLO NATIONS: EIGHT CENTURIES OF PUEBLO INDIAN HISTORY BY JOE S. SANDO

One of the most definitive and engrossing histories of New Mexico's 19 Indian Pueblos was written by the late Joe S.

Sando, who was born—and
later served as an elder—on
Jémez Pueblo.

TRUE GRIT

Countless Westerns have
been filmed in north-central
New Mexico, including *All the
Pretty Horses, A Million Ways
to Die in the West,* and the
remakes of *3:10 to Yuma* and
The Magnificent Seven, but
this Coen Brothers revisionist
adaptation of the John Wayne
classic stands out for the way
it captures the breathtaking
landscape around Santa Fe.
The Coen Brothers are fans
of shooting in the Land of
Enchantment, having also
filmed parts of *No Country for
Old Men* and *The Ballad of
Buster Scruggs* here.

TRAVEL SMART

Updated by
Andrew Collins

★ **STATE CAPITAL:**
Santa Fe

👥 **POPULATION:**
89,220

💬 **LANGUAGE:**
English

$ **CURRENCY:**
U.S. dollar

☎ **AREA CODE:**
505

⚠ **EMERGENCIES:**
911

🚗 **DRIVING:**
On the right side of
the road

⚡ **ELECTRICITY:**
120–240 v/60 cycles;
plugs have two or
three rectangular
prongs

🕐 **TIME.**
Two hours behind
New York

🌐 **WEB
RESOURCES:**
www.newmexico.org
www.santafe.org

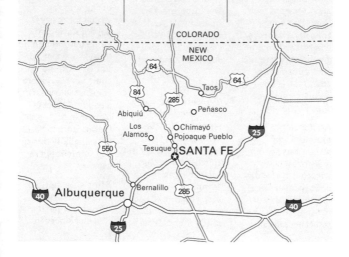

Know Before You Go

As one of the American Southwest's most popular destinations, Santa Fe and the surrounding region have dozens of notable attractions and can even be a little overwhelming for a first-time visitor. Here are some key tips to help you navigate your trip, whether it's your first time visiting or your twentieth.

HOURS OF OPERATION

Although hours differ little in New Mexico from other parts of the United States, some businesses do keep shorter hours here than in more densely populated parts of the country. Within the state, businesses in Santa Fe, Albuquerque, and Taos tend to keep later hours than in rural areas, where it's always a good idea to confirm that a business or attraction is open before you make a special trip.

Most major museums and attractions are open daily or six days a week (with Monday or Tuesday being the most likely day of closing). Hours are sometimes shorter on Saturday and especially Sunday, and a handful of museums in the region stay open late one night a week, usually Friday. In Santa Fe and Albuquerque—and to a lesser extent in Taos—you can find some convenience stores and drugstores open 24 hours, and quite a few supermarkets open until 10 or 11 at night. Bars and nightclubs stay open until 1 or 2 am.

PACKING

Typical of the Southwest and southern Rockies, temperatures can vary considerably in north-central New Mexico from sunup to sundown. Generally, you should pack for warm days and chilly nights from late spring through early fall, and for genuinely cold days and freezing nights in winter if you're headed to Taos and Santa Fe (Albuquerque runs about 6 to 12 degrees warmer). Any time of year you should pack at least a few warm outfits and a jacket or sweater (along with gloves and a hat from September through April); in winter pack very warm clothes—coats, parkas, and whatever else your body's thermostat and your ultimate destination dictate. And bring comfortable shoes; you're likely to be doing a lot of walking.

New Mexico is one of the most informal and laid-back areas of the country, which for many is part of its appeal. Dress codes, even for dinner, are virtually unheard of, though some may feel more comfortable wearing a collared shirt or a dress in high-end restaurants in Santa Fe, especially during the summer opera season.

Bring skin moisturizer: even people who rarely need this elsewhere in the country can suffer from dry and itchy skin in New Mexico. Sunscreen is an absolute must, even on cold winter days. And bring sunglasses to protect your eyes from the glare of lakes or ski slopes, not to mention the brightness present everywhere. The high altitude (around 7,000–7,200 feet in Santa Fe and Taos and 5,300 feet in Albuquerque) can cause headaches and dizziness for some, especially if you're unaccustomed to these conditions, so at a minimum drink at least half your body weight in ounces in water each day (150-pound person equals 75 ounces, or a little over 2 liters). When planning even a short day trip, especially if there's hiking or exercise involved, always pack 1 or 2 liters of water per person—it's very easy to become dehydrated in New Mexico.

VISITOR ETIQUETTE

The Albuquerque–Santa Fe–Taos corridor contains a number of smaller, sometimes quite insular, Indigenous or predominantly Hispanic villages. Tread lightly and behave respectfully as you travel in these areas, and never take pictures of locals or enter private property without first receiving permission. Many members of the state's 23 Indigenous communities—usually called pueblos—refer to themselves as Indians more commonly than Native Americans, but the best practice is to refer to persons who reside in a particular community by their tribal name. Many pueblos welcome visitors and have museums, galleries, hiking trails, and other attractions, and some are open for guided tours or allow outsiders to attend feast days and other events. Always check tribal office websites or call ahead to be sure a community is welcoming visitors on the day you plan to visit. Photography, sketching, and video recording are typically not allowed at pueblos; occasionally permission is granted for a fee, but you should always ask first.

THE ART SCENE

In contrast with its more traditional artistic past, increasing numbers of galleries in the area now specialize in abstract, contemporary, and often international works. One of the first major forces in the city's artistic evolution, the acclaimed SITE Santa Fe museum, opened in 1995 and has since undergone a dramatic redesign and expansion. The surrounding Railyard District has seen an emergence of provocative, modern galleries in recent decades, as have Downtown and Canyon Road. But the biggest artistic development in Santa Fe has been the opening and growing popularity of a permanent multimillion-dollar art complex by Santa Fe's edgy Meow Wolf collective. The organization has since added new locations in Las Vegas, Denver, and Grapevine, Texas, and plans are underway for a Houston branch.

Getting Here and Around

A car is the best way to take in Santa Fe and the surrounding region. City buses are available in Santa Fe, Albuquerque, and Taos, as are Lyft and Uber, but buses are not very convenient for visitors and the costs of ride-sharing services can quickly exceed that of a rental car, especially if you're staying outside the city centers. You can get around Santa Fe's Plaza area as well as some Taos and Albuquerque neighborhoods on foot, but a car is essential for roaming farther afield and visiting many of north-central New Mexico's most prominent attractions and scenic byways.

Air

Most visitors to the area fly into Albuquerque, home of the region's main airport, but Santa Fe also has a charmingly small and handily located airport with daily nonstop service to a few key hubs. From Albuquerque, ground transportation is available to both Santa Fe (65 miles away) and Taos (130 miles), although most visitors rent a car.

Albuquerque's airport is served by all major U.S. airlines and has direct flights from most major West Coast and Midwest cities and a few cities on the East Coast (JFK in New York City on JetBlue, Atlanta on Delta, and Baltimore-Washington and Orlando on Southwest). Santa Fe Regional Airport has direct flights on American Airlines from Dallas and Phoenix and United Airlines from Denver. Flights into Santa Fe tend to cost a bit more than those to Albuquerque, but the convenience can be well worth the extra expense. If you're venturing north from Santa Fe up to Taos, you might also consider flying into Denver, which is 2½ hours farther than Albuquerque (the drive is stunning) but offers a huge selection of direct domestic and international flights.

Flying time between Albuquerque and Dallas is 1 hour and 45 minutes; Los Angeles, 2 hours; Chicago, 2 hours and 45 minutes; New York, 4 to 4½ hours (direct, which is available only on JetBlue; factor in another hour if connecting).

GROUND TRANSPORTATION

From the terminal at Albuquerque's airport, Groome Transportation provides scheduled van service to hotels, bed-and-breakfasts, and several other locations around Santa Fe; the cost per person is $46 each way. RoadRunneR offers private rides in vans and SUVs from both the Albuquerque and Santa Fe airports to locations throughout Santa Fe and the surrounding area (including Albuquerque, Los Alamos, and Española)—for a price, you can charter a shuttle to just about any town in the state. This option is most cost-effective if you're in a group of four or more passengers. The Taos Rides shuttle service provides scheduled van service from Albuquerque and Santa Fe to Taos, and Santa Fe and Taos to Taos Ski Valley; fares range from $85 to $145 each way.

🚌 Bus

The city's bus system, Santa Fe Trails, covers 10 major routes through town and is useful for getting from the Plaza to some of the outlying attractions. Route M is most useful for visitors, as it runs from Downtown to the museums on Old Santa Fe Trail south of town, and Route 2 is handy if you're staying at one of the hotels on Cerrillos Road and need to get into town (if time is a factor for your visit, a car is a much more practical way to get around). Individual rides cost $1, and a daily pass costs $2. Buses run from early morning to midevening about every 30 minutes on weekdays, every hour on weekends.

There's no intercity bus service to Santa Fe, but you can get to Albuquerque from a number of cities throughout the Southwest and Rocky Mountain regions, and then catch a Rail Runner commuter train from Albuquerque's bus station to Santa Fe. This strategy really only makes sense if you're unable or unwilling to drive or fly; bus travel in this part of the world is relatively economical but quite time-consuming.

🚗 Car

A car is a basic necessity in New Mexico, as even the few cities are challenging to get around solely using public transportation. Distances are considerable, but you can make excellent time on long stretches of interstate and other four-lane highways with speed limits of up to 75 mph. If you wander off major thoroughfares, slow down. Speed limits here are generally only 55 mph, and for good reason. Many such roadways have no shoulders and are frequently crossed by wildlife; on many twisting and turning mountain roads speed limits dip to 25 mph. For the most part, the scenery on rural highways makes the drive a form of sightseeing in itself.

Interstate 25 runs north from the state line at El Paso through Albuquerque and

Getting Here and Around

Santa Fe, then angles northeast into Colorado and up to Denver. Interstate 40 crosses the state from Arizona to Texas, intersecting with Interstate 25 in Albuquerque, from which it's an hour's drive to Santa Fe. Although it's a long journey from big cities like Los Angeles, Dallas, and Chicago, plenty of visitors drive considerable distances to visit Santa Fe, which makes a great stop on a multiday road trip around the Four Corners region, or across the Southwest.

U.S. and state highways connect Santa Fe, Albuquerque, and Taos with a number of key towns elsewhere in New Mexico and in neighboring states. Many of these highways, including large stretches of U.S. 285 and U.S. 550, have four lanes and high speed limits. You can make nearly as good time on these roads as you can on interstates. Throughout the region, you're likely to encounter some unpaved surface streets. Santa Fe has a higher percentage of unpaved roads than any other state capital in the nation.

Morning and evening rush-hour traffic is light in Santa Fe. It can get a bit heavy in Albuquerque. Keep in mind that there are only a couple of main routes from Santa Fe to Albuquerque, so if you encounter an accident or some other obstacle, you can expect significant delays. It's a big reason to leave early and give yourself extra time when driving to Albuquerque to catch a plane.

Parking is plentiful and either free or inexpensive in Santa Fe, Albuquerque, and Taos. During the busy summer weekends, however, parking in Santa Fe's most popular neighborhoods—the Plaza, Canyon Road, and the Railyard District—can be a bit more challenging. There are pay lots both Downtown and in the Railyard District.

Here are some common distances and approximate travel times between Santa Fe and several popular destinations, assuming no lengthy stops and averaging the 65 to 75 mph speed limits: Albuquerque is 65 miles and about an hour; Taos is 70 miles and 90 minutes; Denver is 400 miles and 6 hours; Phoenix is 480 miles and 7 to 8 hours; Las Vegas is 630 miles and 9 to 10 hours; Dallas is 650 miles and 10 to 11 hours; and Los Angeles is 850 miles and 12 to 14 hours.

GASOLINE

Once you leave Santa Fe or other larger communities in the region, there's a lot of high, dry, lonesome country in New Mexico—it's possible to go 50 or 60 miles in some of the less-populated areas between gas stations. For a safe trip, keep your gas tank full. Self-service gas stations are the norm in New Mexico. The cost of unleaded gas in New Mexico is close to the U.S. average, but it's usually a bit higher in small out-of-the-way communities, and significantly cheaper on some Indian reservations—on the drive between Santa Fe and Albuquerque, the gas stations just off Interstate 25 at Santo Domingo Pueblo (Exit 259), San Felipe Pueblo (Exit 252), and Sandia Pueblo (Exit 234) all have lower-priced gas.

RENTAL CARS

All the major car-rental agencies are represented at Albuquerque's airport, and several of them have branches at Santa Fe airport (Avis and Hertz) or in Downtown Santa Fe (Avis, Budget, Enterprise, Hertz).

Rates at the airports in Albuquerque and Santa Fe can vary greatly depending on the season (the highest rates are usually in summer) but typically begin at around $35 a day and $200 a week for an economy car with unlimited mileage.

If you want to explore the backcountry, consider renting an SUV, which will cost you about $45 to $60 per day and $250 to $400 per week, depending on the size of the SUV and the

time of year. You can save money by renting at a nonairport location, as you then are able to avoid the hefty (roughly) 10% in extra taxes charged at airports.

ROAD CONDITIONS

Arroyos (dry washes or gullies) are bridged on major roads, but lesser roads often dip down through them. These can be a hazard during the rainy season, late June to early September. Even if it looks shallow, don't try to cross an arroyo filled with water. Wait a little while, as it's likely to drain off almost as quickly as it filled. If you stall in a flooded arroyo, get out of the car and onto high ground if possible. In the backcountry, never drive (or walk) in a dry arroyo bed if the sky is dark anywhere in the vicinity. A sudden thunderstorm 15 miles away can send a raging flash flood down a wash in a matter of minutes.

Unless they are well graded and graveled, avoid unpaved roads in New Mexico when they are wet. The soil contains a lot of caliche, or clay, which gets slick when mixed with water. During winter storms roads may be shut down entirely; check with the State Highway Department for road conditions.

At certain times in fall, winter, and spring, New Mexico

Getting Here and Around

winds can be vicious for large vehicles like RVs. Driving conditions can be particularly treacherous in passages through foothills or mountains where wind gusts and ice are concentrated.

New Mexico has a high incidence of drunk driving and uninsured motorists. Factor in the state's high speed limits, many winding and steep roads, and eye-popping scenery, and you can see how important it is to drive as alertly and defensively as possible.

Taxi

Santa Fe has no taxi company, but the city is well served by Lyft and Uber, which are also widely available in Taos and Albuquerque.

Train

Amtrak's Southwest Chief, from Chicago to Los Angeles via Kansas City, stops in Las Vegas, Lamy (near Santa Fe), and Albuquerque.

The state's commuter train line, the New Mexico Rail Runner Express, runs from Santa Fe south through Bernalillo and into the city of Albuquerque, continuing south through Los Lunas to the suburb of Belén, covering a distance of about 100 miles and stopping at 15 stations. The Rail Runner offers an inexpensive and scenic alternative to getting to and from the Albuquerque airport to Santa Fe (shuttle buses run from the airport to the Rail Runner stop in Downtown Albuquerque).

The New Mexico Rail Runner Express runs numerous times on weekdays from early morning until late evening, and less often (about six times a day) on weekends. Tickets cost $2 to $10 one way, depending on the distance traveled; it costs just $1 more for an all-day pass (and it's the same price as a one-way ticket if you purchase it online).

Essentials

🏃 Activities

When it comes to outdoor adventure, Santa Fe—along with Taos and Albuquerque—are four-season destinations. Low humidity and year-round cool temperatures (thanks to the high elevation) make north-central New Mexico a mecca for hiking, biking, wildlife viewing, rafting, and golfing from late spring through autumn. During the winter months, snow sports dominate in the mountains above the city and at renowned ski areas like Taos and Angel Fire, which are both within day-tripping distance (although better suited to overnight excursions).

Santa Fe National Forest lies right in the city's backyard and includes the Dome Wilderness (more than 5,000 acres in the volcanically formed Jémez Mountains) and the Pecos Wilderness (about 225,000 acres of high mountains, forests, and meadows at the southern end of the Rocky Mountains chain). The 12,500-foot Sangre de Cristo Mountains (the name translates as "Blood of Christ," for the red glow they radiate at sunset) fringe the city's east side. To the south and west, several less formidable mountain ranges punctuate the sweeping high desert. From the Plaza in the center of the city, you're within a 10-minute drive of truly rugged and breathtakingly beautiful wilderness.

🍴 Dining

Dining out is a major pastime in Santa Fe as well as in Taos, Albuquerque, and even many of the small towns throughout the region. Although Santa Fe in particular has a reputation for upscale dining at restaurants with several high-profile chefs where dinner for two can easily set you back more than $200, the region also offers plenty of low-key, affordable spots, from mom-and-pop taquerias and diners to hip coffeehouses and gastropubs.

Waits for tables are common during the busy summer season, so it's a good idea to call ahead even when reservations aren't accepted, if only to get a sense of the waiting time. Reservations for dinner at the better restaurants are a must in summer and on weekends the rest of the year. In cities like Santa Fe and Albuquerque, you'll find at least a few restaurants that serve food (sometimes from a bar menu) late, until 10 or 11, and sometimes a bit later on weekends. In smaller communities, including Taos, many kitchens stop serving around 8 pm. It's smart to call first and confirm closing hours

Essentials

if you're looking forward to a leisurely or late dinner.

Many of the region's top eateries embrace a farm-to-table approach to cuisine, sourcing heavily from local farms and ranches, while also frequently incorporating Latin American, Mediterranean, and East Asian influences. Yet plenty of traditional, old-school restaurants still serve authentic New Mexican fare, which combines both Indigenous and Hispanic traditions and is quite distinct from other Americanized as well as regional Mexican cooking. Most longtime residents like their chile sauces and salsas with some fire—throughout the state, chile is sometimes celebrated for its ability to set off smoke alarms. Most restaurants offer a choice of red or green chile with one type typically being milder than the other (ask your server, as this can vary considerably). If you want both kinds with your meal, when your server asks you if you'd like "red or green," reply "Christmas." If you're not used to spicy foods, you may find even the house salsa served with chips to be hotter than back home so proceed with caution or ask for chile sauces on the side. Excellent barbecue and steaks are also served throughout northern New Mexico, with other specialties being local game

(especially elk and bison) and trout.

Santa Fe's culinary reputation continues to grow not just in terms of restaurants but also in businesses that produce or sell specialty foods and beverages, from fine chocolates and local honeys and jams to increasingly acclaimed New Mexico wines, beers, and spirits (which you'll find on many local menus). To find many of these products in one place, don't miss the Santa Fe Farmers' Market, one of the best in the Southwest.

⇨ *Prices in the restaurant reviews are the average cost of a main course at dinner or, if dinner is not served, at lunch.*

What It Costs in U.S. Dollars			
$	$$	$$$	$$$$
RESTAURANTS			
under $17	$17–$25	$26–$35	over $35

 ## Lodging

Although New Mexico itself has relatively affordable hotel prices, tourist-driven Santa Fe (and to a slightly lesser extent Taos) can be fairly pricey, especially during high season from spring through fall, with rates particularly steep during major Santa Fe festivals (such as the

Indian, International Folk Art, and Spanish markets). Generally, you'll pay the most at hotels within walking distance of the Plaza and those located in some of the more scenic and mountainous areas north and east of the city; B&Bs usually cost a bit less, and you can find some especially reasonable deals on Airbnb, which has extensive listings throughout the region.

The least expensive Santa Fe accommodations are south and west of town, particularly along drab and traffic-clogged Cerrillos Road, on the south side of town. The best of these, from roughly most to least expensive, are the DoubleTree, Holiday Inn Express, Hyatt Place, Fairfield Inn & Suites, Hampton Inn, Coyote South, Best Western Plus, Comfort Inn, the Mystic Santa Fe, and Econolodge. Rates in Albuquerque, just an hour away, can be half as expensive (sometimes even less), except during busy festivals, particularly the Balloon Fiesta in early October. In Taos and the smaller towns near Santa Fe, expect to pay somewhere between what you would in Albuquerque and Santa Fe.

⇨ *Prices are for a standard double room in high season, excluding 12%–14% tax.*

What It Costs in U.S. Dollars			
$	$$	$$$	$$$$
HOTELS			
under $150	$150–$250	$251–$400	over $400

Nightlife

Culturally endowed though it is, Santa Fe has a pretty mellow nightlife scene. The city does have a decent, and steadily improving, crop of bars, many specializing in craft beers and artisan cocktails, but evening carousing tends to wind down early, and this is not a destination for clubbing and dancing. When popular acts do occasionally come to town, the whole community shows up and dances like there's no tomorrow. Taos is even quieter in terms of nightlife but does have a few notable spots, while Albuquerque has emerged in recent years as one of the top craft-beer cities in the country and also has a handful of scene-y cocktail bars.

Performing Arts

Few small cities in America can claim an arts scene as thriving as Santa Fe's—with opera, symphony, and theater in splendid abundance. The music

Essentials

acts here tend to be high caliber, but a bit sporadic. A wonderful three-month series of free concerts and movies, known as the Santa Fe Summer Scene, takes place several nights a week at different venues, including the downtown Plaza, the Railyard District, and Swan Park. Gallery openings, poetry readings, plays, and dance concerts take place year-round, plus you have the city's famed opera and chamber-music festivals. Check the arts and entertainment listings in Santa Fe's daily newspaper, the *New Mexican* (⊕ *www. santafenewmexican.com*), particularly on Friday, when the arts and entertainment section, "Pasatiempo," is included, or the weekly *Santa Fe Reporter* (⊕ *www.sfreporter.com*) for shows and events. As you might suspect, activities peak in the summer.

🛍 Shopping

Santa Fe has been a trading post for eons. Nearly a thousand years ago the great pueblos of the Chacoan civilizations were strategically located between the buffalo-hunting tribes of the Great Plains and the Indigenous people of Mexico. Native Americans in New Mexico traded turquoise and other valuables with Mexican tribes for metals, shells, parrots, and other regional items. After the arrival of the Spanish and the West's subsequent development, Santa Fe became the place to exchange silver from Mexico and natural resources from New Mexico for manufactured goods, whiskey, and greenbacks from the United States. The construction of the railroad in 1880 brought Santa Fe access to all kinds of manufactured goods.

The trading legacy remains, but now Downtown Santa Fe caters increasingly to those looking for handmade furniture and crafts, and bespoke apparel and accessories. Sure, a few chains have moved in and a handful of fairly tatty souvenir shops still proliferate, but shopping in Santa Fe consists mostly of high-quality, one-of-a-kind independent stores. Canyon Road, packed with internationally acclaimed galleries, is the perfect place to browse for art and collectibles. The Downtown blocks around the Plaza have unusual gift and curio shops, as well as clothiers and shoe stores that range from theatrical to conventional. You'll find quite a few art galleries here, too. The revitalized Railyard District (sometimes referred to as the Guadalupe District), less touristy than the Plaza, is on Downtown's southwest perimeter and includes a wide-ranging mix of hipster boutiques, gift shops, and avant-garde contemporary art galleries—it's arguably the most eclectic of Santa Fe's shopping areas.

○ Visitor Information

The New Mexico Department of Tourism provides general information on the state, but you'll find more specific and useful information by consulting the local tourism offices in Santa Fe as well as in other cities and towns throughout north-central New Mexico.

Check out the New Mexico Tourism site (⊕ *www.newmexico.org*) for information and tips on visiting and even living in the Land of Enchantment. Monthly *New Mexico Magazine* (⊕ *www.newmexico.org/nmmagazine*) is a long-running publication with regular stories on culture and travel throughout the state. An excellent source of information on the state's recreation pursuits is the New Mexico Outdoor Sports Guide (⊕ *nmosg.com*).

📅 When to Go

Santa Fe has four distinct seasons, and the sun shines brightly during all of them (about 300 days a year). In June through August temperatures typically hit the high 80s to low 90s during the day and the low- to mid-50s at night, with afternoon rain showers often cooling the air. These sudden rain showers can come unexpectedly and quickly drench you so pay attention to weather forecasts and have an umbrella and jacket with you, even if it looks sunny in the morning or early afternoon. September and October bring beautiful weather and a marked reduction in crowds. Temperatures—and prices—drop significantly after Halloween. December through March is ski season, but even nonskiers can appreciate this quieter time when the air smells of piñon burning in fireplaces, and the mountains and even the Plaza at times can be draped in powdery snow. Spring comes late at this elevation. March and April are blustery, with warmer weather finally arriving in May and June, but keep in mind that these two typically very dry months are also peak wildfire season (although fires are a distinct possibility from mid-April through October).

Great Itineraries

3 Days in Santa Fe

One helpful strategy for exploring Santa Fe over the course of three days is to devote roughly a full day to one neighborhood. For example, you could devote one day to the Plaza and environs, another to Museum Hill and the East Side, and your final day to the Railroad District and points south.

DAY 1

Plan on spending a full day wandering around Santa Fe Plaza, strolling down the narrow lanes, under portals, and along ancient adobe-lined streets. Sip coffee on the tree-shaded Plaza, take in a museum or two (or three), and at some point be sure to marvel at the late 19th-century cathedral. The Palace of the Governors and adjoining New Mexico History Museum are great places to start to gain a sense of the history and cultures that influence this area. It's well-worth taking one of the free docent-led tours offered by the museums—these are a great way to gain invaluable insight into the collections.

Break for lunch, perhaps at casual and historic Tia Sophia's (a terrific spot for breakfast, too). In the afternoon, take a walk through the exceptional New Mexico Museum of Art and singularly fascinating Georgia O'Keeffe Museum. Be sure to set aside some time to visit the many galleries and curio shops lining the streets near the Plaza. A good way to wrap up your adventure is with a cocktail at Secreto Lounge, on the inviting covered patio of the historic Hotel St. Francis.

DAY 2

A few miles south of the Plaza on Museum Hill, you'll find four world-class museums, all quite different and all highly relevant to the culture of Santa Fe and northern New Mexico. There's also the Santa Fe Botanical Garden, which offers a lovely open-air break from touring these mostly indoor attractions. Start at the intimate gem, the Museum of Spanish Colonial Art, where you'll gain a real sense of the Spanish empire's influence on the world beyond Spain. The Museum of International Folk Art is thoroughly engaging for both young and old. Next enjoy the creative lunch fare at the bright and airy Museum Hill Café, before visiting the Museum of Indian Arts and Culture and finally—if time and energy permit—the Wheelwright Museum of the American Indian. There is a path linking all these museums together, and the walk is easy. A tip for arts, crafts, and books collectors: the museum shops are all outstanding.

From Museum Hill, it's a pleasant 10-minute drive or 25-minute walk through a historic residential neighborhood to one of the nation's most impressive gallery districts, Canyon Road, which winds downhill to the eastern edge of downtown and should definitely be explored on foot. Most galleries here are open daily 10–5, so consider heading over early in the afternoon if you're keen on doing a lot of art browsing. On Friday nights, you can also attend the Canyon Road Art Walk, during which galleries stay open until 7 and often offer refreshments and present special exhibits.

As you're wandering through, take any of the side streets and stroll among the historical homes and ancient *acequias* (irrigation ditches). For a more extensive adventure, keep going up the road past Cristo Rey Church, where the street gets even narrower and is lined with residential compounds. At the top is the Randall Davey Audubon Center, which draws bird-watchers and has a few beautiful, relatively easy hiking trails. For dinner, the venerable El Farol has been going strong since 1835 and offers an extensive menu of tasty tapas and Spanish fare.

DAY 3

You can spend your final day exploring the lively Railyard District, which bursts with energy and development from bustling Railyard Park and the many galleries and boutiques that surround it. The Santuario de Guadalupe is a great place to start. Head south from there and enjoy the shops, cafés, art galleries, farmers' market (open Saturday year-round and Tuesday May through December), and Railyard Park. The expanded and impressively redesigned SITE Santa Fe is also here, with its cutting-edge modern art installations, making it a must for art aficionados. Among the many lunch options in the Railyard District, bustling La Choza is a long-time favorite for classic New Mexican fare.

In the afternoon, you can hop into your car and venture out to one of the city's attractions located a bit farther afield, perhaps El Rancho de las Golondrinas or even the Turquoise Trail if you're feeling ambitious. But of all the places you might explore outside Santa Fe's central core, the absolute must-see is Meow Wolf, the electrifyingly imaginative interactive arts space. Drinks and/or a bite to eat in Meow Wolf's inspiring Float Café & Bar make for a great end to your visit.

Great Itineraries

Albuquerque to Taos

You only need a week (although 10 days will give you a bit more breathing room) to take in the region's three best cities, along with plenty of outdoor adventures along the way.

DAY 1: ALBUQUERQUE

Start out by strolling through the shops of Old Town Plaza, then visit the New Mexico Museum of Natural History and Science and the Albuquerque Museum. For lunch, stop by the Indian Pueblo Cultural Center to sample the hearty Indigenous-inspired fare at Indian Pueblo Kitchen.

In the afternoon, drive east a couple of miles along Central to reach the University of New Mexico's main campus—with its gracious adobe buildings and outstanding Maxwell Museum of Anthropology—and the nearby Nob Hill District, a hip bastion of offbeat shops and noteworthy restaurants. If it's summer, meaning that you still have some time before the sun sets, it's worth detouring from Old Town to Far Northeast Heights (a 15-minute drive), where you can take the Sandia Peak Aerial Tramway 2.7 miles up to Sandia Peak for spectacular sunset views of the city. Either way, plan to have dinner back in Nob Hill, perhaps at Bosque Brewing Co. Public House.

DAYS 2 AND 3: SANTA FE

On Day 2, head to Santa Fe early in the morning by driving up the scenic Turquoise Trail; once you arrive in town, explore the adobe charms of the Downtown central Plaza. Visit the Palace of the Governors and check out the adjacent New Mexico History Museum. A short drive away at the nearby Museum of Indian Arts and Culture you can see works by talented members of the state's pueblos, and across the courtyard at the Museum of International Folk Art, you can see how different cultures in New Mexico and elsewhere in the world have expressed themselves artistically. Return Downtown and give yourself time to stroll its narrow, adobe-lined streets, and treat yourself to some delicious New Mexican cuisine in the evening, perhaps with a traditional meal at The Shed or a fancier dinner at Sazón.

On your second day in town, plan to walk a bit. Head east from the Plaza up to Canyon Road and peruse the galleries. If you're up for some exercise, hike the foothills—there are trails beginning at the Randall Davey Audubon Center and also from the free parking area leading into the Dale Ball Trail Network, both a short drive from the Plaza. And it's worth it to make the detour slightly out of town to visit Meow Wolf, an immersive art installation that's one of the highlights of Santa Fe. You might want to try one of Santa Fe's truly stellar, upscale restaurants, like Geronimo, your final night in town.

DAYS 5 AND 6: TAOS

Begin by strolling around Taos Plaza, taking in the galleries and crafts shops. Head south two blocks to visit the Harwood Museum of Art. Then walk north on Paseo del Pueblo to the Taos Art Museum at Fechin House. In the afternoon, drive out to the Rio Grande Gorge Bridge. Return the way you came to see the Millicent Rogers Museum on your way back to town. In the evening, stop in at the Adobe Bar at the Taos Inn and plan for dinner at the Love Apple. On the second day, drive out to Taos Pueblo in the morning and tour the ancient village while the day is fresh. Afterwards, head to one of the excellent restaurants in El Prado, just north, for a bite to eat, maybe the Farmhouse Cafe. After lunch drive out to La Hacienda de los Martinez for a look at early life in Taos and then to Ranchos de Taos to see the San Francisco de Asís Church.

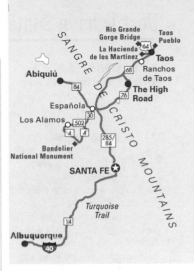

DAY 4: ABIQUIÚ

From Santa Fe, drive north up U.S. 285/84 through Española en route to Abiquiú, the fabled community where Georgia O'Keeffe lived and painted for much of the final five decades of her life. On your way up, make the detour toward Los Alamos and spend the morning exploring the fascinating Bandelier National Monument. In Abiquiú, plan to tour Georgia O'Keeffe's home (open early March through late November)—advance reservations are required.

DAY 7: THE HIGH ROAD

On your final day, drive back down toward Albuquerque and Santa Fe via the famed High Road, which twists through a series of soaring vistas and tiny, historic villages.

Best Tours in Santa Fe

BIKE TOURS

Routes Bicycle Tours. A full-service bike repair and rental shop based in Albuquerque's Old Town and with a seasonal (March–November) satellite location at Santa Fe's La Fonda Hotel, Routes offers a wide range of guided bike tours. In Santa Fe (which doesn't offer rentals or repairs), excursions include daily two-hour treks focused on the city's art and history as well as weekly tours geared around food and brewpubs. ⊠ Albuquerque ☎ 505/933–5667 ⊕ www.routesrentals.com.

GUIDED TOURS

Food Tour New Mexico. Savor some of Santa Fe and Albuquerque's tastiest posole, blue-corn enchiladas, margaritas, craft beers, and sweets on lunch and dinner excursions—some offered with wine pairings—which make three to five stops at locally revered hot spots. ☎ 505/465–9474 ⊕ www.foodtournewmexico.com.

Great Southwest Adventures. This reliable group-oriented company conducts guided tours via vans and buses (typically with a minimum of four guests) to Bandelier, Pecos National Historical Park, Taos (via the "Low Road" through the Gorge), O'Keeffe country, Pecos National Historical Park, Taos, and elsewhere in the region. The company can also arrange single- and multiday custom trips throughout the region for groups of any size. ⊠ Santa Fe ☎ 505/455–2700 ⊕ www.swadventures.com.

Heritage Inspirations. This team of highly knowledgeable, friendly guides offers nearly two dozen engaging, culturally immersive driving, walking, e-biking, and hiking tours throughout northern New Mexico. Excursions include hikes through Bandelier and Kasha-Katuwe Tent Rocks, a highly popular Santa Fe architecture and wine walk, Taos and Chaco Canyon glamping trips, and agricultural adventures in Albuquerque's Rio Grande Valley. ☎ 888/344–8687 ⊕ www.heritageinspirations.com.

Historic Walks of Santa Fe. Get to know the fascinating stories behind many of Santa Fe's most storied landmarks on these engaging strolls through Downtown and along Canyon Road. Other walks focus on ghosts, galleries, shopping, and food; Bandelier, Chimayó, and Taos excursions are also offered. ☎ 505/986–8388 ⊕ www.historicwalksofsantafe.com.

Santa Fe Tour Guides Association. To find an experienced local to lead you on a personal tour, visit the website of this member-based organization of about 25 reliable and vetted independent tour guides, many of whom specialize in specific topics, from art history to hiking. ⊕ santafetourguides.org.

Wander New Mexico. Run by passionate locals with extensive culinary backgrounds, this Santa Fe–based outfitters is best known for its four-hour Historic Plaza Food Tour, which has a history focus and includes tastings at four different venues. There are also a pair of Railyard District tours, one focused on the farmers' market and one on off-the-beaten-path eateries. Wander is also a great option for arranging private custom food tours, including curated progressive meals. ⊠ Santa Fe ☎ 505/395–0552 ⊕ www.wandernewmexico.com.

RIVER RAFTING TOURS
Bureau of Land Management (BLM), Taos Field Office. For a list of outfitters who guide trips on the Rio Grande and the Rio Chama, contact the Bureau of Land Management (BLM), Taos Resource Area Office, or stop by the Rio Grande Gorge Visitor Center along NM 68 (on the "Low Road" to Taos), 16 miles south of Taos in the small village of Pilar, the launching point for many rafting trips on the Rio Grande.

⊠ 1024 Paseo del Pueblo Sur, Taos ☎ 575/758–8851 Taos field office, 575/751–4899 Rio Grande Gorge Visitor Center ⊕ www.blm.gov/office/taos-field-office.

Kokopelli Rafting Adventures. This respected outfitter offers half-day, full-day, and multi-day river trips—both relaxing floats and more exhilarating rapids excursions—down the Rio Grande and Rio Chama. ⊠ South Side ☎ 505/983–3734 ⊕ www.kokopelliraft.com.

New Wave Rafting. Look to this company founded in 1980 for full-day, half-day, and overnight river trips on the Rio Chama and Rio Grande, as well as fly-fishing trips, from its riverside location in Embudo, on the Low Road to Taos. You can also rent funyaks and paddle easier stretches of rapids yourself. ⊠ 2110 NM 68, mile marker 21, Embudo ☎ 800/984–1444 ⊕ www.newwaverafting.com.

Santa Fe Rafting Company. This well-known tour company leads day trips down the Rio Grande and the Chama River and customizes rafting tours. Tell them what you want—they'll figure out a way to do it. ⊠ South Side ☎ 505/988–4914 ⊕ www.santaferafting.com.

On the Calendar

SUMMER

Contemporary Hispanic Market.
A companion piece to the famed Traditional Spanish Market (which takes place the same July weekend), this showcase of contemporary art and crafts featuring local and regional works of painting, photography, jewelry, ceramics, textiles, and more is held on the Plaza. ⊕ *www.contemporaryhispanicmarket.org*.

International Folk Art Market.
Held the second full weekend in July, this three-day market (the world's largest folk art market) sprawls across Railyard Park in the Santa Fe's lively Railyard District. More than 160 master folk artists from every corner of the planet—over 60 countries in total—come together to sell their work amid a festive array of huge tents, colorful banners, music, food, and delighted crowds. ⊕ *www.folkartmarket.org*.

Rodeo de Santa Fe. One of the West's premier rodeo events since 1949, this four-day event in late June takes place at the city's rodeo grounds and offers a full line-up that includes barrel racing, bull riding, calf roping, and top-name entertainment. ⊕ *www.rodeodesantafe.org*.

Santa Fe Summer Scene Concerts and Movies. The newer and bigger incarnation of the city's long-running Bandstand Concert series is now presented by Lensic 360, an extension of the Lensic Performing Arts Center. From early June through August, outstanding local and nationally known musicians from a variety of genres (blues, country, folk, Latin, rock) perform for free most nights of the week, typically either at Downtown's festive and historic Plaza or at the lively Railyard Plaza. Free movie screenings are also part of this superb mix of programming. ⊕ *www.lensic360.org*.

Santa Fe Indian Market. This world-class showcase of Indigenous art features some 600 booths set up over 14 blocks in the heart of Santa Fe. Taking place over a weekend in mid-August, the market features works by nearly 1,000 Indigenous artists from some 250 tribes throughout the United States and Canada. Other events over this exciting weekend include fashion shows, films, readings, music performances, and a hugely attended Best of Show Ceremony. A smaller but still outstanding Winter Indian Market is held in Santa Fe in mid-December. ⊕ *www.swaia.org*.

Traditional Spanish Market.
Begun in 1926 and administered by the esteemed Spanish Colonial Arts Society, one of

the country's most popular arts festivals takes place on the Plaza in late July and features an astounding selection of traditional Spanish-colonial works, including woodcarving, straw appliqué, metalwork, furniture, pottery, and colcha embroidery. A smaller Winter Spanish Market takes place in Albuquerque each December. ⊕ *www. spanishcolonial.org*.

FALL

Albuquerque International Balloon Fiesta. The most popular festival in Albuquerque, the balloon fiesta draws some 850,000 visitors over nine days in October to watch a variety of events during which hot-air balloons of all shapes and sizes take to the skies. Held in what's considered the world's hot-air ballooning capital, it's a wonderful event for kids and adults, especially the "mass ascensions" that feature hundreds of balloons. ⊕ *www. balloonfiesta.com*.

Fiesta de Santa Fe. Billed the longest continuously running festival in the country, Fiesta de Santa Fe started in 1712 and remains one of the city's top events, drawing thousands over a week in mid-September. It features a mariachi extravaganza, pet parade, concerts, and the famed Burning of Zozobra (the burning of a giant

50-foot-tall effigy of Old Man Gloom). ⊕ *www.balloonfiesta. com*.

Santa Fe Wine & Chile Fiesta. One of the most popular culinary events in the Southwest, this five-day celebration in late September features special food-and-wine events at dozens of local restaurants. There's also a special Grand Tasting celebration at the Santa Fe Opera grounds, during which top wineries and restaurants serve delicious food and beverages. ⊕ *www.santafewineandchile.org*.

WINTER

Christmas in Santa Fe. Santa Fe is a magical destination during the December holiday period, with dozens of events, concerts, and celebrations held throughout the month, including feast days and dances at several of the area's Indian Pueblos and the famous Farolito Walk along Canyon Road on Christmas Eve.

Santa Fe Film Festival. With the film industry booming in New Mexico, this five-day event held in mid-February has become increasingly well attended, and film screenings, workshops, and discussion panels take place at venues around the city. ⊕ *www.santafefilmfestival.com*.

Contacts

Air

AIRPORT INFORMATION Albuquerque International Sunport.
⊠ *2200 Sunport Blvd. SE, Albuquerque* ☎ *505/244–7700* ⊕ *www.abqsunport.com.*
Denver International Airport.
⊠ *8500 Peña Blvd., Denver* ☎ *303/342–2000* ⊕ *www.flydenver.com.* **Santa Fe Regional Airport (SAF).** ☎ *505/955–2900* ⊕ *flysantafe.com.*

SHUTTLE CONTACTS Groome Transportation. ☎ *505/474–5696* ⊕ *www.groometransportation.com/santa-fe.* **RoadRunneR.** ☎ *505/424–3367* ⊕ *www.rideroadrunner.com.* **Taos Rides.** ☎ *575/613–3256* ⊕ *www.taosrides.com.*

Bus

CONTACTS Greyhound.
☎ *800/231–2222* ⊕ *www.greyhound.com.* **Santa Fe Trails.** ☎ *505/955–2001* ⊕ *santafenm.gov/transit.*

Car

CONTACTS New Mexico Department of Transportation Road Advisory Hotline. ☎ *800/432–4269* ⊕ *www.nmroads.com.*

🛏 Lodging

CONTACTS New Mexico Bed and Breakfast Association. ⊕ *www.nmbba.org.*

🚆 Train

CONTACTS Amtrak. ☎ *800/872–7245* ⊕ *www.amtrak.com.*
New Mexico Rail Runner Express. ☎ *866/795–7245* ⊕ *www.riometro.org.*

📍 Visitor Information

CONTACTS Indian Pueblo Center. ☎ *505/843–7270, 866/855–7902* ⊕ *www.indian-pueblo.org.* **New Mexico Tourism Department Visitor Center.**
⊠ *Lamy Bldg., 491 Old Santa Fe Trail, Old Santa Fe Trail and South Capitol* ☎ *505/795–0343* ⊕ *www.newmexico.org.*
Tourism Santa Fe. ⊠ *Santa Fe Community Convention Center, 201 W. Marcy St., The Plaza* ☎ *505/955–6200, 800/777–2489* ⊕ *www.santafe.org.*

Chapter 3

THE PLAZA AND DOWNTOWN SANTA FE

Updated by
Natalie Bovis

⦿ Sights   🍴 Restaurants   🛏 Hotels   🛍 Shopping   🍸 Nightlife

★★★★★   ★★★★★   ★★★★★   ★★★★★   ★★★★★

NEIGHBORHOOD SNAPSHOT

TOP EXPERIENCES

■ **Shop at the Inn of the Governors:** Meet Native American artists and craftspeople selling their wares under the portal of the Inn of the Governors, one of the oldest buildings in town and where Lew Wallace penned parts of *Ben Hur*.

■ **Attend a festival:** Santa Fe loves its festivals and the Plaza is host to many special gatherings, especially in summer with free concerts on the bandstand. Other highlights include TACO WARS in early summer, the Traditional Spanish Market in July, the famed Indian Market in August, and the Wine & Chile Fiesta in September.

■ **Appreciate art:** Public art abounds in Santa Fe—as if the historic buildings weren't enough. Keep your eyes open for street-side sculptures all around downtown, and don't miss the "Santa Fe Current" bronze fish outside the Convention Center on Marcy Street.

■ **Snap photos:** Visiting Santa Fe means stepping into history with picturesque corners everywhere you turn. The area's famous golden light, which has attracted artists for decades, changes the town's facade not just with the seasons but by the hour.

VIEWFINDER

Tourists love meandering down historic Burro Alley, a short thoroughfare connecting San Francisco Street and Palace Avenue, where popular eateries abound. But perhaps best of all is the fun photo-op with the life-sized *burro* (donkey) sculpture found in the alley.

GETTING HERE AND AROUND

■ Getting to Downtown Santa Fe is easiest by car. There is metered street parking (which is free on Sunday and federal holidays), and there are also convenient municipal parking garages that allow for longer parking periods than the two-hour street meters. Those traveling from Albuquerque can also take the Rail Runner train from downtown Albuquerque to the Santa Fe Railyard. Once here, the neighborhood is easily navigable by foot.

You haven't been to Santa Fe if you haven't discovered the wonders of its historic Downtown. From territorial Spanish-Pueblo architecture and towering churches to Native jewelry artists and one-of-a-kind museums, Santa Fe's Downtown offers visitors a taste of what makes it "the City Different."

There is no other city like it in the world and its unique blend of art, imagination, and culture has earned it an official Creative City designation from UNESCO and solidified its standing as a favorite filming location for various television shows and movies. To top things off, downtown Santa Fe is home to some of the region's finest restaurants and people-watching, all thanks to its unique local flavor.

Much of the history of Santa Fe, New Mexico, the Southwest, and even the West has some association with Santa Fe's central Plaza, which New Mexico governor Don Pedro de Peralta laid out in 1610. The Plaza was already well established by the time of the Pueblo revolt in 1680. Freight wagons unloaded here after completing their arduous journey across the Santa Fe Trail. The American flag was raised over the Plaza in 1846, during the Mexican War, which resulted in Mexico's loss of all its territories in the present Southwestern United States. For a time the Plaza was a tree-shaded park with a white picket fence. In the 1890s it was an expanse of lawn where uniformed bands played in an ornate gazebo. Particularly festive times on the Plaza are the weekend after Labor Day, during Las Fiestas de Santa Fe, on Indigenous Peoples' Day in October (which brings dance celebrations), and during the winter holidays, when all the trees are filled with lights and rooftops are outlined with *farolitos,* votive candles lit within paper-bag lanterns.

It was along the Old Santa Fe Trail that wagon trains from Missouri rolled into town in the 1820s, forever changing Santa Fe's destiny. This street, off the south corner of the Plaza, is one of Santa Fe's most historic and is dotted with houses, shops, markets, and the (relatively modern) state capitol several blocks down.

Though Santa Fe is the oldest capital city in the United States, many considered it little more than a pass-through town of mud and livestock corrals until the early 1900s, when a group of anthropologists, archaeologists, and artists formed a powerful community alliance to lead Santa Fe into a new era of tourism. These scholars and political influencers, which included archaeologists Adolf Bandelier and Kenneth Chapman, led the charge to preserve and promote Santa Fe's characteristic adobe architecture as a way to attract tourists interested in northern New Mexico's unique cultural and historical treasures. This group, also responsible for the founding of the Museum of New Mexico, paved the way for the "City Different" of today.

With its eclectic mix of museums, shops, galleries, restaurants, and more, downtown Santa Fe can take days to explore thoroughly. A good way to plan for a visit is to start in the historic central Plaza and work your way out from there or, plan one day for museums, another for sights, and another for shopping. Downtown Santa Fe is lively both day and night so it's easy to start exploring in the morning and still be going as night falls. To ensure you get a real "taste" of the area, make reservations for dinner as restaurants tend to fill up quickly with both locals and visitors—one of the reasons some call Santa Fe "the city that never stops eating."

The Plaza

 Sights

★ Cathedral Basilica of St. Francis of Assisi

CHURCH | This iconic cathedral, a block east of the Plaza, is one of the rare significant departures from the city's nearly ubiquitous Pueblo architecture. Construction was begun in 1869 by Jean Baptiste Lamy, Santa Fe's first archbishop, who worked with French architects and Italian stonemasons. The Romanesque style was popular in Lamy's native home in southwest France. The cleric was sent by the Catholic Church to the Southwest to influence the religious practices of its native population and is buried in the crypt beneath the church's high altar. He was the inspiration behind Willa Cather's novel *Death Comes for the Archbishop* (1927). In 2005 Pope Benedict XVI declared St. Francis the "cradle of Catholicism" in the Southwestern United States, and upgraded the status of the building from mere cathedral to cathedral basilica—one of just 36 in the country.

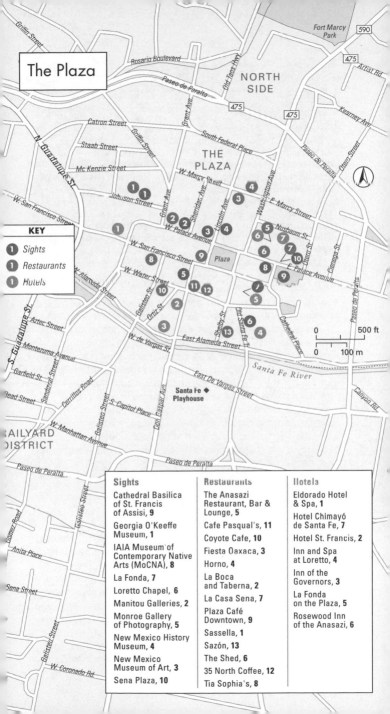

The Plaza

Griffin Street
Fort Marcy Park
590
Rosario Boulevard
Paseo de Peralta
Old Taos Hwy
NORTH SIDE
475
475
Artist Rd
Kearney Ave
Catron Street
South Federal Place
475
475
Staab Street
THE PLAZA
Paseo de Peralta
Cerro Street
Mc Kenzie Street
Griffin Street
Grant Ave
W. Marcy Street
4
Washington Ave
E. Marcy Street
N. Guadalupe St
Johnson Street
1 1
3
W. San Francisco Street
Sheridan Ave
Lincoln Ave
2 2
Nusbaum St.
W. Palace Avenue
4
5
6 6 7 7
Grant Ave
Cienega St.
KEY
1
8
W. San Francisco Street
9 Plaza
6 10
1 Sights
W. Water Street
8 9
E. Palace Avenue
1 Restaurants
10
5
1 Hotels
11 12
7
W. Alameda Street
2
5
Ortiz St.
Old Santa Fe
Galisteo St.
S. Guadalupe St
Aztec Street
3
6
Montezuma Avenue
W. de Vargas St.
13 4
Shelby St.
Garfield St.
East Alameda Street
Cathedral Place
Sandoval St.
Read Street
Cerrillos Road
East De Vargas Street
Santa Fe River
Paseo de Peralta
0   500 ft
0   100 m
S. Capitol Place
Don Gaspar Ave
W. Manhattan Avenue
Santa Fe Playhouse
Canyon Rd
RAILYARD DISTRICT
Paseo de Peralta
Galisteo Street
W. Coronado Rd
Bonney Road
Anita Place
Sena Street
Paseo de Peralta

Sights

Cathedral Basilica of St. Francis of Assisi, **9**

Georgia O'Keeffe Museum, **1**

IAIA Museum of Contemporary Native Arts (MoCNA), **8**

La Fonda, **7**

Loretto Chapel, **6**

Manitou Galleries, **2**

Monroe Gallery of Photography, **5**

New Mexico History Museum, **4**

New Mexico Museum of Art, **3**

Sena Plaza, **10**

Restaurants

The Anasazi Restaurant, Bar & Lounge, **5**

Cafe Pasqual's, **11**

Coyote Cafe, **10**

Fiesta Oaxaca, **3**

Horno, **4**

La Boca and Taberna, **2**

La Casa Sena, **7**

Plaza Café Downtown, **9**

Sassella, **1**

Sazón, **13**

The Shed, **6**

35 North Coffee, **12**

Tia Sophia's, **8**

Hotels

Eldorado Hotel & Spa, **1**

Hotel Chimayó de Santa Fe, **7**

Hotel St. Francis, **2**

Inn and Spa at Loretto, **4**

Inn of the Governors, **3**

La Fonda on the Plaza, **5**

Rosewood Inn of the Anasazi, **6**

New Mexico Culture Pass

You can purchase a New Mexico Culture Pass (⊕ www.newmexicoculture.org) for $30 online or at any participating museum, and gain admission to each of the 15 state museums and monuments once over a 12-month period. These include a number of attractions elsewhere in the state (Albuquerque's National Hispanic Center and New Mexico Museum of Natural History and Science, the state monuments in Jémez, Coronado, and several other places) as well as the following Santa Fe museums: New Mexico History Museum/Palace of the Governors, New Mexico Museum of Art, Museum of Indian Arts & Culture, and Museum of International Folk Art. Note that the first Sunday of each month, these four museums offer free admission.

A small adobe chapel on the northeast side of the cathedral, the remnant of an earlier church, embodies the Hispanic architectural influence absent from the cathedral itself. The chapel's *Nuestra Señora de la Paz* (Our Lady of Peace), popularly known as *La Conquistadora,* the oldest Madonna statue in the United States, accompanied Don Diego de Vargas on his reconquest of Santa Fe in 1692, a feat attributed to the statue's spiritual intervention. Each new season, the faithful adorn the statue with a new dress. Take a close look at the keystone in the main doorway arch: it has a Hebrew tetragrammaton on it. It's widely speculated that Bishop Lamy had this carved and placed to honor the Jewish merchants of Santa Fe who helped provide necessary funds for the construction of the church. ⊠ *131 Cathedral Pl., The Plaza* ☎ *505/982–5619* ⊕ *www.cbsfa.org.*

★ Georgia O'Keeffe Museum

ART MUSEUM | One of many East Coast artists who visited New Mexico in the first half of the 20th century, Georgia O'Keeffe, today known as the "Mother of American Modernism," returned to live and paint in northern New Mexico for the last half of her life, eventually emerging as the demigoddess of Southwestern art. At this intimate museum dedicated to her work, you'll find how O'Keeffe's innovative view of the landscape is captured in *From the Plains,* inspired by her memory of the Texas plains, and in *Jimson Weed,* a study of one of her favorite plants; additional highlights include selections from O'Keeffe's early days as an illustrator, abstract pieces from her time in New York City, and iconic works featuring floating skulls, flowers, and bones. Special exhibitions with O'Keeffe's modernist peers, as well as contemporary artists, are on view throughout the year—many of these are exceptional, and just as interesting as the museum's permanent collection, which numbers some 3,000 works (although not all are on display as the museum is surprisingly small). The museum also manages a visitor center and tours of O'Keeffe's famous home and studio in Abiquiú, about an hour north of Santa Fe. ⊠ *217 Johnson St., The Plaza* ☎ *505/946–1000* ⊕ *www.okeeffemuseum. org* ⊠ *$20* ⊘ *Closed Tues. and Wed.*

★ IAIA Museum of Contemporary Native Arts (MoCNA)

ART MUSEUM | Sitting just a block from the Plaza, this fascinating museum is part of the esteemed Institute of American Indian Arts (IAIA) and contains the largest collection—some 7,500 works—of contemporary Native American art in the United States. The paintings, photography, sculptures, prints, and traditional crafts were created by past and present students and teachers. In the 1960s and 1970s, it blossomed into the nation's premier center for Native American arts and its alumni represent almost 600 tribes around the country. The museum continues to showcase the cultural and artistic vibrancy of Indigenous people, helping to expand what is still an often limited public perception of what "Indian" art is and can be. Be sure to step out back to the beautiful sculpture garden. Artist Fritz Scholder taught here, as did sculptor Allan Houser. Among their disciples were the painter T. C. Cannon and celebrated local sculptor and painter Dan Namingha. ⊠ *108 Cathedral Pl., The Plaza* ☎ *505/983–8900, 888/922–4242* ⊕ *www. iaia.edu* ⊠ *$10* ⊘ *Closed Tues.*

La Fonda

HOTEL | **FAMILY** | A *fonda* (inn) has stood on this site southeast of the Plaza for centuries, and architect Isaac Hamilton Rapp built the area landmark that stands there today in 1922. The hotel was sold to the Santa Fe Railway in 1926 and remained a Harvey House hotel until 1968. The property completed its latest major renovation in 2013, its guest rooms receiving a smart but still classic makeover, but the historic public areas retain their original design elements. Because of its proximity to the Plaza and its history as a gathering place for everyone from cowboys to movie stars (Errol Flynn stayed here), it's referred to as "The Inn at the End of the Trail." Free docent tours, which touch on the hotel's rich history and detail key pieces in the astounding public art collection, are offered Wednesday through Saturday morning at 10:30. Step inside to browse the shops on the main floor or to eat at one of the restaurants, including the impressive greenhouse glass-topped La Plazuela. The lobby bar often has live music. In warm

Many of Santa Fe's art galleries, like the Manitou Galleries, are housed in traditional adobe buildings.

months, enjoy a drink at the fifth-floor Bell Tower Bar which offers tremendous sunset views. ⊠ *100 E. San Francisco St., at Old Santa Fe Trail, The Plaza* ☎ *505/982–5511* ⊕ *www.lafondasantafe.com.*

Loretto Chapel

CHURCH | A delicate Gothic church modeled after Sainte-Chapelle in Paris, Loretto was built in 1878 by the same French architects and Italian stonemasons who built St. Francis Cathedral, and is known for the "Miraculous Staircase" that leads to the choir loft. Legend has it that the chapel was almost complete when it became obvious that there wasn't room to build a staircase to the choir loft. In answer to the prayers of the cathedral's nuns, a mysterious carpenter arrived on a donkey, built a 20-foot staircase (using only a square, a saw, and a tub of water to season the non-native wood) and then disappeared as quickly as he came. Many of the faithful believed it was St. Joseph himself. The staircase contains two complete 360-degree turns with no central support; no nails were used in its construction. Adjoining the chapel are a small museum and gift shop. ⊠ *207 Old Santa Fe Trail, The Plaza* ☎ *505/982–0092* ⊕ *www.lorettochapel.com* ✎ *$5* ☉ *May close without advance notice for special events.*

Manitou Galleries

ART GALLERY | This respected gallery near the Plaza carries mostly contemporary representational paintings and sculptures by world-renowned artists as well as impressive works by local and Native artists including Nocona Burgess and B. C. Nowlin. The gallery also features bronze statues and interesting photographs. In 2021, Manitou was sold to gallery owners from Arizona who now run this location and its sister gallery at 225 Canyon Road. Both Manitou showrooms are hard to miss thanks to the beautiful bronze sculptures outside. ✉ *123 W. Palace Ave., The Plaza* ☎ *505/986–0440* ⊕ *legacygallery.com.*

Monroe Gallery of Photography

ART GALLERY | In this attractive storefront space a couple of blocks from the Plaza, you can admire works by the most celebrated black-and-white photographers of the 20th century. The focus is on humanist and photojournalist-style photography, and many classic images are available for purchase. ✉ *112 Don Gaspar Ave., The Plaza* ☎ *505/992–0800* ⊕ *www.monroegallery.com.*

★ New Mexico History Museum

HISTORY MUSEUM | **FAMILY** | This impressive, modern museum anchors a campus that encompasses the Palace of the Governors, the Palace Print Shop & Bindery, the Fray Angélico Chávez History Library, and Photo Archives (an assemblage of more than 1 million images dating from the 1850s). Behind the palace on Lincoln Avenue, the museum thoroughly explores the early history of Indigenous people, Spanish colonization, the Mexican Period, and travel and commerce on the legendary Santa Fe Trail. Inside are changing and permanent exhibits. By appointment, visitors can tour the comprehensive Fray Angélico Chávez History Library and its rare maps, manuscripts, and photographs (more than 120,000 prints and negatives). The Palace Print Shop & Bindery, which prints books, pamphlets, and cards on antique presses, also hosts bookbinding demonstrations, lectures, and slide shows. The Palace of the Governors is a humble one-story neo-Pueblo adobe on the north side of the Plaza, and is the oldest public building in the United States. Its rooms contain period furnishings and exhibits illustrating the building's many functions over the past four centuries. Built at the same time as the Plaza, circa 1610, it was the seat of four regional governments—those of Spain, Mexico, the Confederacy, and the U.S. territory that preceded New Mexico's statehood, which was achieved in 1912. It served as the residence for 100 Spanish, Mexican, and American governors, including Governor Lew Wallace, who wrote his epic *Ben Hur* in its then drafty rooms, all the while complaining of the dust and mud that fell from its earthen ceiling.

Dozens of Native American vendors gather daily under the portal of the Palace of the Governors to sell pottery, jewelry, bread, and other goods. With few exceptions, the more than 500 artists and craftspeople registered to sell here are Pueblo or Navajo Indians. The merchandise for sale is required to meet strict standards. Prices tend to reflect the high quality of the merchandise but are often significantly less than what you'd pay in a shop. Please remember not to take photographs without permission. ⊠ *Palace Ave., north side of Plaza, 113 Lincoln Ave., The Plaza* ☎ *505/476–5200* ⊕ *www.nmhistorymuseum.org* ✉ *$12* ☉ *Summer and winter hours may vary.*

★ New Mexico Museum of Art

ART MUSEUM | Designed by Isaac Hamilton Rapp in 1917, this museum is one of Santa Fe's earliest Pueblo Revival structures, inspired by the adobe structures at Acoma Pueblo. Split-cedar *latillas* (branches set in a crosshatch pattern) and hand-hewn vigas form the ceilings. The 20,000-piece permanent collection, of which only a fraction is exhibited at any given time, emphasizes the work of regional and nationally renowned artists, including Georgia O'Keeffe; realist Robert Henri; the Cinco Pintores (five painters) of Santa Fe (including Fremont Ellis and Will Shuster, the creative mind behind Zozóbra); members of the Taos Society of Artists (Ernest L. Blumenschein, Bert G. Phillips, Joseph H. Sharp, and E. Irving Couse, among others); and the works of noted 20th-century photographers of the Southwest, including Laura Gilpin, Ansel Adams, and Dorothea Lange. Rotating exhibits are staged throughout the year. Many excellent examples of Spanish-colonial-style furniture are on display. Other highlights include an interior *placita* (small plaza) with fountains, WPA murals, and sculpture, and the St. Francis Auditorium, where concerts and lectures are often held. ⊠ *107 W. Palace Ave., The Plaza* ☎ *505/476–5072* ⊕ *www.nmartmuseum.org* ✉ *$12* ☉ *Closed Nov.–Apr. and Mon.*

Sena Plaza

PLAZA/SQUARE | This brick courtyard is an oasis of flowering fruit trees and inviting benches, along with a charming fountain. Surrounding it is a plethora of interesting shops selling clothing, shoes, chocolates, and various other artsy and touristy items. Longtime favorite La Casa Sena has a popular patio that takes up a good chunk of the courtyard, creating a downright magical environment for summer dining. The buildings, erected in the 1700s as a single-family residence, once included quarters for blacksmiths, bakers, farmers, and all manner of help. ⊠ *125 E. Palace Ave., The Plaza.*

🍴 Restaurants

The Anasazi Restaurant, Bar & Lounge

$$$$ | **MODERN AMERICAN** | This romantic restaurant with hardwood floors, soft lighting, and stone walls has a menu that presents upscale versions of classic fare such as steak, fish, and chicken. For a less formal vibe, have dinner and cocktails at the convivial bar or enjoy breakfast on the lively street side patio. **Known for:** pleasant patio in warm weather; delightful cocktails and lively bar scene; extensive wine and tequila lists. ⑤ *Average main:* $52 ✉ *Rosewood Inn of the Anasazi, 113 Washington Ave., The Plaza* ☎ *505/988–3030* ⊕ *www.rosewoodhotels.com/en/ inn-of-the-anasazi-santa-fe/dining/anasazi-restaurant.*

★ Cafe Pasqual's

$$$ | **SOUTHWESTERN** | This cheerful cubbyhole is owned by James Beard Award–winning chef and cookbook author Katharine Kagel, who champions organic, local ingredients, and whose expert kitchen staff produces mouthwatering breakfast and lunch specialties like *huevos motuleños* (eggs in a tangy tomatillo salsa with black beans and fried bananas) and mahi-mahi tostadas. Dinner offerings range from chicken enchiladas to warm Thai noodle salad. **Known for:** smoked trout on potato pancakes; colorful folk art and murals; long waits without reservations (only available for dinner). ⑤ *Average main: $35* ✉ *121 Don Gaspar Ave., The Plaza* ☎ *505/983–9340* ⊕ *www.pasquals.com.*

★ Coyote Cafe

$$$$ | **AMERICAN** | A Santa Fe hot spot since it opened in 1987, this pioneer of contemporary Southwestern cuisine has been renovated and modernized over the last decade under the guidance of owner Quinn Stephenson. Today, the restaurant serves some of the most consistently perfectly executed cuisine in the city, led by a professional and knowledgeable culinary team. **Known for:** consistently excellent food and staff; impressive wine list; creative cocktails. ⑤ *Average main: $52* ✉ *132 W. Water St., The Plaza* ☎ *505/983–1615* ⊕ *www.coyotecafe.com* ⊗ *No lunch.*

Fiesta Oaxaca

$ | **MODERN MEXICAN** | **FAMILY** | The cities of Oaxaca and Santa Fe actually have several things in common (a thriving art scene, a complex history, and fantastic food), and this modern Mexican eatery brings a bite of Oaxacan culture into its dishes based upon Mesoamerican culinary traditions. A tribute to the cuisine of its namesake region, the star of the show here is, of course, mole,

Dozens of restaurants and shops surround the city's historic Plaza.

which you can enjoy with a number of mouthwatering sauces over meats and vegetables. **Known for:** variety of creative mole sauces; festive and colorful interior; fantastic tacos. ⑤ *Average main: $16* ✉ *135 West Palace Ave., The Plaza* ☎ *505/982–9525* ⊕ *www. fiestaoaxacasf.com* ☷ *Closed Wed. No dinner Sun.*

★ Horno
$$ | **FUSION** | Since its 2021 opening, this family-owned and -run restaurant has quickly become one of Santa Fe's favorite dining spots, thanks to chef David Sellers's reputation for great food and his goal of ensuring that Horno remains attainable for locals. Unlike the sticker shock many downtown eateries impose, Horno has a seasonal, rotating menu of delectable street food dishes with global influences at decent prices. **Known for:** interesting and varied wine list; convivial atmosphere; constantly changing menu. ⑤ *Average main: $18* ✉ *95 West Marcy St., The Plaza* ☎ *505/303–3469* ⊕ *www.hornorestaurant.com* ☷ *Closed Sun. No lunch.*

★ La Boca and Taberna
$$$ | **SPANISH** | An eight-time James Beard nominee, chef/owner James Campbell Caruso is known for his authentic yet creatively updated Spanish tapas, which are served at both his intimate dining room called La Boca, and the more lively, bustling Spanish pub located directly behind it and aptly named Taberna. La Boca has a more leisurely and romantic vibe and its big windows look out onto fashionable Marcy Street, while Taberna offers a livelier, communal atmosphere featuring live music and ample seating,

spilling out into a cloistered courtyard. **Known for:** fine Spanish meats and cheeses; extensive selection of authentic Spanish tapas; nice variety of Spanish sherries. $ *Average main: $26* ⌖ *72 W. Marcy St., The Plaza* ☎ *505/982–3433* ⊕ *www.labocasantafe. com* ⊙ *Closed Sun. and Mon.*

La Casa Sena

$$$$ | **CONTEMPORARY** | The Southwestern-accented and Mediterranean fare created by chef Jose Rodriguez here is beautifully presented, and the scenery, especially during the warmer months, is part of the charm. Get a table on the patio surrounded by hollyhocks, flowering shrubs, and centuries-old adobe walls, or for a musical meal (evenings only), sit in the restaurant's adjacent Club Legato, which features live jazz and talented singers. **Known for:** perfect Moroccan lamb tagine; gorgeous patio and live jazz in bar; on-site wine shop. $ *Average main: $46* ⌖ *Sena Plaza, 125 E. Palace Ave., The Plaza* ☎ *505/988–9232* ⊕ *lacasasena.com.*

Plaza Café Downtown

$$ | **SOUTHWESTERN** | **FAMILY** | Run with homespun care by the Razatos family since 1947, this café has been a fixture on the Plaza since 1905. The food runs the gamut of New Mexican fare, including salads, sandwiches, burgers, and tacos (don't miss the delicious crispy avocado tacos). **Known for:** great vegetarian options; retro diner charm; breakfast all day. $ *Average main: $19* ⌖ *54 Lincoln Ave., The Plaza* ☎ *505/982–1664* ⊕ *www.plazacafe-santafe.com.*

★ Sassella

$$$$ | **MODERN ITALIAN** | Chef Cristian Pontiggia's enthusiasm and desire for perfection are both evident via the artfully presented dishes served here. The native of Lombardy, Italy, presents elegant food with some whimsical molecular gastronomy flare, and he has racked up multiple awards from the international Chaine de Rotisseurs Society. **Known for:** wide selection of amari; sous-vide wild boar with asparagus and black truffle demi-glace; special tasting menus and wine dinners. $ *Average main: $39* ⌖ *225 Johnson St., The Plaza* ☎ *505/982–6734* ⊕ *www.sassellasantafe. com* ⊙ *No dinner Sun. No lunch Tues. and Wed.*

Sazón

$$$$ | **MODERN MEXICAN** | James Beard Award–winning, Mexico City–born chef Fernando Olea has been working his culinary magic at different Santa Fe restaurants since 1991 and now offers his upscale take on regional Mexican fare, complete with an exhaustive list of artisan tequilas and mezcals, at Sazón. Within the handsome dining room warmed by a kiva fireplace and filled with

Frida Kahlo and Day of the Dead–inspired artwork, the focus is on one of Mexico's greatest dishes, mole. **Known for:** house-made mole sauces; chef's set degustation menu; encyclopedic selection of artisan mezcals. ⑤ *Average main: $42* ⊠ *221 Shelby St., The Plaza* ☎ *505/983–8604* ⊕ *www.sazonsantafe.com* ⊗ *Closed Sun. No lunch.*

★ The Shed

$ | **SOUTHWESTERN** | **FAMILY** | Expect to wait in line at this downtown eatery that's been family operated since 1953, serving flavorful New Mexican food and popular margaritas. Even if you're a devoted green chile fan, definitely try the locally grown red chile the place is famous for; it is rich and earthy, with a bit of spice. **Known for:** red-chile enchiladas and posole; mocha cake; historic adobe setting dating from 1692. ⑤ *Average main: $16* ⊠ *113½ E. Palace Ave., The Plaza* ☎ *505/982–9030* ⊕ *www.sfshed.com* ⊗ *Closed Sun.*

★ Tia Sophia's

$ | **SOUTHWESTERN** | **FAMILY** | This family-run downtown joint has been in operation since 1974, serving some of the area's best New Mexican breakfasts and lunches. Order anything and expect a true taste of local tradition, including perfectly flaky, light sopaipilla; Tia's delicious burritos stuffed with homemade chorizo disappear fast on Saturday so get there early. **Known for:** huge breakfast burritos; popularity with locals; traditional New Mexican cuisine, down to the fiery chiles. ⑤ *Average main: $10* ⊠ *210 W. San Francisco St., The Plaza* ☎ *505/983–9880* ⊕ *www.facebook. com/tiasophias* ⊗ *No dinner.*

35 North Coffee

$ | **CAFÉ** | There are plenty of spots near the Plaza for grabbing a latte, but this coffeehouse stands out for brewing exceptional house-roasted, single-origin coffees from Guatamala, Kenya, Sumatra, and other java hot spots around the world. You can order a pour-over made with beans of your choosing, or sample the house-made chai, nitro cold brew, and "latitude adjustment" (coffee blended with organic grass-fed butter, MCT oil, and coconut oil). **Known for:** high-grade single-origin coffees; house-made chai; breakfast croissants. ⑤ *Average main: $6* ⊠ *60 E. San Francisco St., The Plaza* ☎ *505/983–6138* ⊕ *www.35northcoffee.com* ⊗ *No dinner.*

The famed Inn at Loretto has a partnership with tour company Heritage Inspirations, offering guided tours around the area.

Hotels

Eldorado Hotel & Spa

$$$$ | HOTEL | FAMILY | This large, yet inviting, hotel comes with individually decorated rooms and stunning mountain views. **Pros:** attractive accommodations three blocks from Plaza; great view from rooftop pool (especially at sunset); lively bar with great late-night food menu. **Cons:** staff's attention to service varies considerably; can be very expensive during busy periods; convention space can make it feel impersonal. *⑤ Rooms from: $449 ✉ 309 W. San Francisco St., The Plaza ☎ 505/988–4455, 800/955–4455 ⊕ www.eldoradohotel.com ⇆ 213 rooms ⏐⊙⏐ No Meals.*

Hotel Chimayó de Santa Fe

$$$ | HOTEL | FAMILY | One of the few slightly more affordable, full-service hotels near the Plaza, this attractive, Territorial-style adobe hotel with a mix of spacious standard rooms and even bigger suites is a solid option, especially given the extensive amenities available in many units—wet bars, kitchenettes, spacious sitting areas. **Pros:** unbeatable location; spacious rooms; nice restaurant on-site. **Cons:** in a crowded part of Downtown; no pool or gym; can have some street noise. *⑤ Rooms from: $271 ✉ 125 Washington Ave., The Plaza ☎ 505/988–4900, 855/752–9273 ⊕ www.hotelchimayo.com ⇆ 54 rooms ⏐⊙⏐ No Meals.*

Hotel St. Francis

$$$ | **HOTEL** | Just south of the Plaza, this stately three-story hotel retains a historic vibe but has been given a modern flair—with expansive stone floors, plaster walls, and spare furnishings lit by massive pillar candles at night, the lobby feels a bit like a monastery. **Pros:** stylish, contemporary vibe in a historic building; two blocks from the Plaza and near many shops; excellent dining and nightlife on-site. **Cons:** breakfast not included; some rooms (and especially bathrooms) are quite small; some rooms can have noise from the street. ⑤ *Rooms from: $389* ⊠ *210 Don Gaspar Ave., The Plaza* ☏ *505/983–5700* ⊕ *www.hotelstfrancis.com* ⤳ *80 rooms* ⑩ *No Meals.*

★ Inn and Spa at Loretto

$$$$ | **HOTEL** | **FAMILY** | This eye-catching, oft-photographed, pueblo-inspired property attracts a loyal clientele, many of whom swear by the friendly staff and high decorating standards. **Pros:** great location; gorgeous grounds and pool; distinctive architecture. **Cons:** expensive parking and resort fees; bathrooms feel a bit ordinary, small, and dated, and they also lack counter space; some rooms can have noise from the road. ⑤ *Rooms from: $499* ⊠ *211 Old Santa Fe Trail, The Plaza* ☏ *505/988–5531* ⊕ *www.hotelloretto. com* ⤳ *134 rooms* ⑩ *No Meals.*

★ Inn of the Governors

$$$ | **HOTEL** | **FAMILY** | This historic, reasonably priced hotel by the Santa Fe River has cheerful rooms with a Mexican theme, bright colors, hand-painted folk art, feather pillows, Southwestern fabrics, and handmade furnishings; deluxe rooms also have balconies and fireplaces. **Pros:** close to Plaza; year-round, heated pool; free parking (unusual for downtown). **Cons:** standard rooms are a bit small; some rooms view parking lot; some traffic noise. ⑤ *Rooms from: $289* ⊠ *101 W. Alameda St., The Plaza* ☏ *505/982–4333, 800/234–4534* ⊕ *www.innofthegovernors.com* ⤳ *100 rooms* ⑩ *Free Breakfast.*

★ La Fonda on the Plaza

$$$ | **HOTEL** | **FAMILY** | This venerable downtown landmark comes with modern amenities but still retains a warm, artful design—including whimsical painted headboards and handcrafted furniture that's faithful to the vision of Mary Elizabeth Jane Colter, the vaunted architect responsible for the hotel's elegant Southwestern aesthetic. **Pros:** iconic building steeped in history and art; Plaza is right outside the door; excellent restaurant, bars, and pool. **Cons:** lobby often packed with tourists and nonguests; fitness facilities are modest for an upscale hotel; busy Downtown location means some noise. ⑤ *Rooms from: $379* ⊠ *100 E. San Francisco St., The*

Plaza ☎ *505/982–5511, 800/523–5002* ⊕ *www.lafondasantafe. com* ⤳ *180 rooms* ⃝ *No Meals.*

★ Rosewood Inn of the Anasazi

$$$$ | **HOTEL** | This intimate and artfully designed boutique hotel steps from the Plaza has superb architectural detail, top-notch service, and a much-celebrated restaurant, bar, and lounge. **Pros:** thoughtful luxurious touches throughout; superb restaurant and charming bar; beautiful, lodgelike public spaces that are ideal for conversation or curling up with a book. **Cons:** standard rooms are a bit small for the price; only a few rooms have balconies; no hot tub or pool. ⑤ *Rooms from: $850* ✉ *113 Washington Ave., The Plaza* ☎ *505/988–3030, 888/767–3966* ⊕ *www.rosewoodhotels. com* ⤳ *58 rooms* ⃝ *No Meals.*

Nightlife

Agave Restaurant & Lounge

BARS | The bar in the Agave restaurant located within the Eldorado Hotel is stylish and contemporary, making it just as much of a hit with locals and nonguests as with those staying on the property. Smart decor and happy hour deals combined with the late-night bar-food menu—from snacks to burgers—are among Agave's key assets. ✉ *Eldorado Hotel, 309 W. San Francisco St., The Plaza* ☎ *505/995–4530* ⊕ *www.eldoradohotel.com/agave-lounge.*

Bell Tower Bar

BARS | The lofty rooftop perch at historic Hotel La Fonda is open only from mid-spring through mid-fall, but during the warmer months it's a lovely spot to sip cocktails while watching the sunset and surrounding mountains. The views make it very popular so try to get there during the off-hours to snag a table. Year-round, you can also enjoy outstanding margaritas and tasty bar food in lively La Fiesta Lounge, just off the hotel lobby, which also features live music. ✉ *La Fonda Hotel, 100 E. San Francisco St., The Plaza* ☎ *505/982–5511* ⊕ *www.lafondasantafe.com.*

★ Del Charro

BARS | The laid-back saloon at the Inn of the Governors serves casual fare even after most of the Downtown restaurants have closed. It also offers a full bar filled with local charm and plenty of characters. It has a laid-back vibe thanks to its old-fashioned Western decor and dark-wood paneling (warmed by the glow of a woodburning fireplace). It is a favorite of locals as well as visitors so it can fill up quickly during peak tourist season. ✉ *Inn of the Governors, 101 W. Alameda St., The Plaza* ☎ *505/954–0320* ⊕ *www.delcharro.com.*

Evangelo's

BARS | A staple in the Downtown social scene for decades, Evangelo's can be loud and pulsing with partiers, which is just how it is meant to be. Adults of all ages enjoy live bands and downstairs pool tables in this shots-and-a-beer kind of place. The staff can be gruff but are beloved by locals. ⊠ *200 W. San Francisco St., The Plaza* ☎ *505/819–1597* ⊕ *www.evangeloscocktaillounge.com.*

Secreto Lounge

BARS | This moody bar inside the historic Hotel St. Francis has long been known for its creative craft cocktails, including a classic Manhattan with a clove tincture spritzed over the top and a popular smoked-sage margarita. Food from the restaurant next door can be enjoyed in the bar, and you can also sample superb New Mexico wines at Gruet Winery's Tasting Room, just across the hotel lobby. ⊠ *Hotel St. Francis, 210 Don Gaspar Ave., The Plaza* ☎ *505/983–5700* ⊕ *www.hotelstfrancis.com.*

Tonic

BARS | At this intimate, high-ceilinged bar with a dapper art deco interior, you can sip deftly crafted cocktails and catch live jazz. It's one of the few spots serving bar food until late. ⊠ *103 E. Water St., The Plaza* ☎ *505/982–1189* ⊕ *www.tonicsantafe.com.*

 Performing Arts

El Flamenco

FOLK/TRADITIONAL DANCE | FAMILY | Several organizations produce flamenco concerts around town, including the prestigious Entreflamenco Company, which offers dinner-and-a-show at El Flamenco just a few blocks from the Plaza. ⊠ *135 W. Palace Ave., The Plaza* ☎ *505/209–1302* ⊕ *www.entreflamenco.com.*

★ Lensic Performing Arts Center

ARTS CENTERS | Santa Fe's vintage Downtown movie house has been fully restored and converted into the 850-seat Lensic Performing Arts Center. The grand 1931 building, with Moorish and Spanish Renaissance influences, hosts the Santa Fe Symphony, theater, classic films, lectures and readings, noted world, pop, and jazz musicians, and many other prominent events. The Lensic 360 program also presents music festivals and large-scale concerts in other locations throughout the city. ⊠ *211 W. San Francisco St., The Plaza* ☎ *505/988–1234* ⊕ *www.lensic.org.*

Performance Santa Fe

ARTS FESTIVALS | FAMILY | From September through May, this non-profit organization (aka the Santa Fe Concert Association) founded in 1937 presents symphony and solo classical concerts, lectures, dance recitals, opera, and family-minded shows at several venues around town, including the Lensic, St. Francis Auditorium, and United Church of Santa Fe. The organization has brought a number of prestigious talents to Santa Fe over the years, including Wynton Marsalis, Patti Lupone, the Russian National Ballet, and the Academy of St. Martin in the Fields Chamber Ensemble. ⊠ *The Plaza* ☎ *505/984–8759* ⊕ *www.performancesantafe.org.*

St. Francis Auditorium

ARTS CENTERS | This historic space with colorful murals inside the Museum of Fine Arts is a top venue for many cultural events such as theatrical productions and concerts. ⊠ *107 W. Palace Ave., The Plaza* ☎ *505/476–5072* ⊕ *www.nmartmuseum.org.*

Shopping

ANTIQUES

Arrediamo

ANTIQUES & COLLECTIBLES | One of the top spots in the Southwest for handmade Turkish, Persian, and Afghan rugs, Arrediamo also carries a fine selection of authentic Navajo rugs and textiles. ⊠ *202 Galisteo St., The Plaza* ☎ *505/820–2231* ⊕ *www.arrediamo. com.*

BOOKS

★ Collected Works Book Store & Coffeehouse

BOOKS | You'll find a great selection of art and travel books here, including a generous selection of titles on Southwestern art, architecture, and general history, as well as the latest in contemporary literature. In a large, inviting space close to the Plaza, you can also enjoy organic lattes, snacks, and sandwiches from the superb Iconik Coffee Roasters. Peruse the local author sections, and don't miss the live readings and music performances. The proprietress and her staff are known for their knowledge and helpfulness. ⊠ *202 Galisteo St., The Plaza* ☎ *505/988–4226* ⊕ *www.collected-worksbookstore.com.*

Travel Bug

BOOKS | Here, you'll find a huge array of guides and books about travel along with maps. You'll also find all sorts of gadgets for hikers and backpackers. There's also a cozy coffeehouse (excellent java) with Wi-Fi. On many Saturday evenings the shop hosts presentations on world travel experiences. ⊠ *839 Paseo de Peralta, The Plaza* ☎ *505/992–0418* ⊕ *www.mapsofnewmexico.com.*

CLOTHING AND ACCESSORIES
Back at the Ranch
SHOES | This cozy space in an old, creaky-floored adobe is stocked with perhaps the finest handmade cowboy boots you will ever see—in every color, style, and embellishment imaginable. If you can't find what you're looking for, they create custom boots too. Other finds, like funky ranch-style furniture, 1950s blanket coats, jewelry, and belt buckles are also sold here. ⊠ *209 E. Marcy St., The Plaza* ☎ *505/989–8110* ⊕ *www.backattheranch.com.*

★ O'Farrell Hat Company
HATS & GLOVES | Scott O'Farrell (son of the shop's late founder, Kevin) and his highly trained staff carry on the tradition of producing carefully designed and constructed classic Western hats. These one-of-a-kind, fur-felt cowboy hats make the ultimate Santa Fe keepsake. Custom work is available and this level of quality comes at a cost, but devoted customers—who have included everyone from cattle ranchers to U.S. presidents—swear by O'Farrell's artful creations. ⊠ *111 E. San Francisco St., The Plaza* ☎ *505/989–9666* ⊕ *www.ofarrellhatco.com.*

Red River Mercantile
MEN'S CLOTHING | This small but well-stocked space is one of the best spots in town for rugged and stylish—but casual—men's wear, along with backpacks, computer bags, watches, wallets, and other accessories. Well-established brands like Filson, Pendleton, Howler Brothers, and Grayer's fill the aisles, and the staff is extremely helpful. ⊠ *235 Don Gaspar Ave., The Plaza* ☎ *505/992–1233.*

FOOD AND DRINK
Artful Tea
OTHER FOOD & DRINK | A paradise for tea lovers, Artful Tea is the city's emporium for loose-leaf or bagged gourmet tea, with global selections from Japan, Nepal, India, and more. Green, matcha, black, rooibos, herbal, and floral of all varieties can be found here along with specialty tea cups and brewing accessories. ⊠ *101 Marcy St., Suite 4, The Plaza* ☎ *505/795–7724* ⊕ *www.artfultea. com.*

Kaune's Neighborhood Market
FOOD | Although Santa Fe has no shortage of gourmet groceries, this neighborhood market near the Capitol building has been stocking its shelves with fine foods since 1896 (its original location was on Washington Street). You'll find specialty and organic goods, many of them local, including fine wines, artisanal cheeses, and chocolates. A short walk from the plaza, it is one

of the few places in the neighborhood to also buy basics such as produce, dairy, and bread. ✉ *511 Old Santa Fe Trail, The Plaza* ☎ *505/982–2629* ⊕ *www.kaunes.com.*

HOME GOODS AND GIFTS

Design Warehouse

HOUSEWARES | A welcome antidote to Santa Fe's preponderance of shops selling Native American and Spanish-colonial antiques, Design Warehouse carries hip, contemporary furniture, kitchenware, home accessories, and other sleek knickknacks, including vaunted brands like Alessi, Knoll, and Normann Copenhagen. Note the select collection of books and magazines focusing on art and design. ✉ *130 Lincoln Ave., The Plaza* ☎ *505/988–1555* ⊕ *www.designwarehousesantafe.com.*

★ Doodlet's

OTHER SPECIALTY STORE | FAMILY | Most locals have fond memories of visiting Doodlet's in childhood because this store has been delighting customers with its whimsical collection of pop-up books, silly postcards, tin art, hooked rugs, and stringed lights for decades. Considered one of Santa Fe's best gift shops, you will find wonderment in every display case, drawing the eye to the unusual. There's something for just about everyone at this delightfully quirky, popular shop, and often it's affordable. ✉ *120 Don Gaspar Ave., The Plaza* ☎ *505/983–3771* ⊕ *doodlets.com.*

Sage Botanical

CRAFTS | This charming lifestyle-centric shop features a carefully curated selection of home goods, clothing, cards, bath and body products, jewelry, vintage finds, and more. The focus here is on hand-crafted, small batch items created primarily by women-owned businesses. ✉ *65 W. Marcy St., The Plaza* ☎ *505/428–9528* ⊕ *www.sabosantafe.com.*

JEWELRY

DeBella Fine Gems & Jewelry

JEWELRY & WATCHES | Owner Joseph DeBella turned his lifelong fascination with rocks and minerals into a decades-long career as a metalsmith and gemologist, traveling the world to learn about and buy precious stones and working for many years making fine jewelry before opening his own Downtown stores; the original shop is on West San Francisco Street while a newer store lives right on the Plaza. Santa Fe is a popular destination for weddings and engagements so many come to DeBella Fine Gems to collaborate on original creations for upcoming nuptials. ✉ *213 W. San Francisco St., The Plaza* ☎ *505/795–7497* ⊕ *www.debellajewelry.com.*

The Plaza is one of the best places in the city to purchase traditional Navajo weavings and blankets, and Shiprock Santa Fe is one of its most popular shops.

LewAllen & LewAllen Jewelry

JEWELRY & WATCHES | Father-and-daughter silversmiths Ross and Laura LewAllen run this fun jewelry shop. Handmade jewelry ranges from whimsical to mystical inside their tiny space just off the Plaza. There's something for everyone here, including delightful charms for your pet's collar. ⊠ *105 E. Palace Ave., The Plaza* ☎ *800/988–5112, 505/983–2657* ⊕ *www.lewallenjewelry.com.*

★ Patina Gallery

JEWELRY & WATCHES | In this slick, museum-like space, you'll find outstanding contemporary jewelry, textiles, and sculptural objects of metal, clay, and wood. With a staff whose courtesy is matched by knowledge of the genre, artists-owners Ivan and Allison Barnett have used their fresh curatorial aesthetic to create a showplace for dozens of American and European artists they represent—many of whom are in permanent collections of museums such as MoMA. ⊠ *131 W. Palace Ave., The Plaza* ☎ *505/986–3432* ⊕ *www.patina-gallery.com.*

NATIVE AMERICAN ARTS AND CRAFTS

★ Andrea Fisher Fine Pottery

CRAFTS | You can browse, and buy, some of the nation's finest examples of both historic and contemporary Native American pottery at this gallery a couple of blocks east of the Plaza. It is especially renowned for its collection of pieces from San Ildefonso Pueblo legend Maria Martinez and her illustrious family. ⊠ *100 W. San Francisco St., The Plaza* ☎ *505/986–1234* ⊕ *www.andreafisherpottery.com.*

Keshi: The Zuni Connection

CRAFTS | Since the early '80s, this gallery specializing in beautiful animal fetishes carved out of turquoise, marble, onyx, and countless other materials has served as a co-op art gallery for western New Mexico's Zuni Pueblo. You'll find fetishes representing an astounding variety of animals, from eagles to mountain lions to turtles, plus fine jewelry and pottery. ⊠ *227 Don Gaspar Ave., The Plaza* 🕿 *505/989–8728* ⊕ *www.keshi.com.*

★ Niman Fine Art

ART GALLERIES | This intimate space focuses on the prolific work of world-renowned, award-winning contemporary Native American artist Dan Namingha whose celebrated paintings and sculptures are part of exclusive collections all around the world. His sons Arlo and Michael are also artists working in bronze, wood, and stone as well as digital imagery. The family founded the Namingha Institute to help instruct and guide new generations of Indigenous artists. ⊠ *125 Lincoln Ave., The Plaza* 🕿 *505/988–5091* ⊕ *www. namingha.com.*

The Rainbow Man

CRAFTS | Established in 1945, this colorful, if touristy, shop does business in an old, rambling adobe complex, part of which dates from before the 1680 Pueblo Revolt and also served as offices for the Manhattan Project. The shop carries early Navajo, Mexican, and Chimayó textiles, along with photographs, a breathtaking collection of vintage pawn and Mexican jewelry, Day of the Dead figures, Oaxacan folk animals, New Mexican folk art, kachinas, and contemporary jewelry from local artists. The friendly staff possesses an encyclopedic knowledge of the art here. ⊠ *107 E. Palace Ave., The Plaza* 🕿 *505/982–8706* ⊕ *www.rainbowman.com.*

★ Shiprock Santa Fe

ANTIQUES & COLLECTIBLES | This rustic and light-filled space showcases a beautifully curated collection of Navajo rugs and blankets, contemporary and vintage Native American jewelry, pottery, sculpture, folk art, fine art, and more. The vision of fifth-generation art dealer Jed Foutz, who was raised in a family of art traders on the Navajo Nation, the gallery is notable for its dedication to showcasing exquisite vintage pieces alongside vanguard contemporary works. ⊠ *53 Old Santa Fe Trail, 2nd fl., The Plaza* 🕿 *505/982–8478* ⊕ *www.shiprocksantafe.com.*

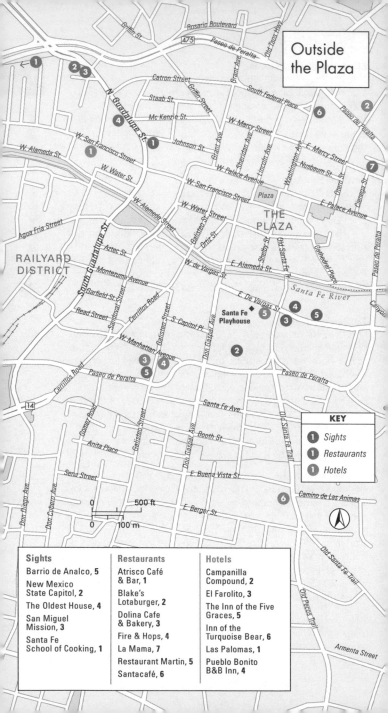

Outside the Plaza

KEY

- **1** *Sights*
- **1** *Restaurants*
- **1** *Hotels*

Sights

Barrio de Analco, **5**

New Mexico
State Capitol, **2**

The Oldest House, **4**

San Miguel
Mission, **3**

Santa Fe
School of Cooking, **1**

Restaurants

Atrisco Café
& Bar, **1**

Blake's
Lotaburger, **2**

Dolina Cafe
& Bakery, **3**

Fire & Hops, **4**

La Mama, **7**

Restaurant Martin, **5**

Santacafé, **6**

Hotels

Campanilla
Compound, **2**

El Farolito, **3**

The Inn of the Five
Graces, **5**

Inn of the
Turquoise Bear, **6**

Las Palomas, **1**

Pueblo Bonito
B&B Inn, **4**

Outside the Plaza

◉ Sights

Barrio de Analco

NEIGHBORHOOD | Along the south bank of the Santa Fe River, the barrio—its name means "District on the Other Side of the Water"—is one of America's oldest neighborhoods, settled in the early 1600s by the Tlaxcalan Indians (who were forbidden to live with the Spanish near the Plaza) and in the 1690s by soldiers who had helped recapture New Mexico after the Pueblo Revolt. The historic district was named a National Historic Landmark in 1968 and is a great place to experience Santa Fe's unique history of Native American, Spanish, Mexican, and American cultural influence. Plaques on houses on East De Vargas Street will help you locate some of the important structures. Check the performance schedule at the Santa Fe Playhouse on De Vargas Street, founded by writer Mary Austin and other Santa Feans in 1922. ⊠ *Old Santa Fe Trail at E. De Vargas St., The Plaza.*

New Mexico State Capitol

GOVERNMENT BUILDING | FAMILY | The symbol of the Zía Pueblo, which represents the Circle of Life, was the inspiration for the state's capitol building, also known as the Roundhouse. Doorways at opposing sides of the 1966 structure symbolize the four times of day, the four directions, the four stages of life, and the four seasons. Take time to walk through the building to see the outstanding 600-work collection of the Capitol Art Foundation, historical and cultural displays, and handcrafted furniture—it's a superb and somewhat overlooked array of fine art. The Governor's Gallery hosts temporary exhibits. Six acres of imaginatively landscaped gardens shelter outstanding sculptures. ⊠ *490 Old Santa Fe Trail, The Plaza* 🕾 *505/986–4589* ⊕ *www.nmlegis.gov/visitors* ⊠ Free ⊗ *Closed Sun.*

The Oldest House

NOTABLE BUILDING | FAMILY | Also called the DeVargas Street House, this adobe dwelling is said to be the oldest in the United States—a sign on the exterior puts the date at 1646. Some say it's much older, but historians currently can verify only that it dates back to the mid-1700s. Inside the tiny museum, a small gift shop features Harvey House jewelry, kachinas, paintings, pottery, and more. ⊠ *215 E. De Vargas St., The Plaza* 🕾 *505/988–2488* ⊕ *www.oldesthousesantafe.com.*

San Miguel Mission

CHURCH | FAMILY | Believed to be the oldest church still in use in the United States, this simple earth-hewn adobe structure was built around 1610 by the Tlaxcalan Indians of Mexico, who came to New Mexico as servants of the Spanish. Badly damaged in the 1680 Pueblo Revolt, the structure was restored and enlarged in 1710. On display in the chapel are priceless statues and paintings and the San José Bell, weighing nearly 800 pounds, which is believed to have been cast in Spain in 1356. In winter the church sometimes closes before its official closing hour. Latin mass is held daily at 2 pm, and new mass is on Sunday at 5 pm. ⊠ *401 Old Santa Fe Trail, The Plaza* ☎ *505/983–3974* ⊕ *www.sanmiguel-chapel.org.*

★ Santa Fe School of Cooking

SCHOOL | If you'd like to bring the flavors of the Southwest to your own kitchen, consider taking one of the wildly popular and fun cooking classes at the Santa Fe School of Cooking. Regular classes are taught during the day, with some evening classes available. There are also the ever-popular walking tours of Santa Fe's most notable restaurants, which usually include special visits with the chefs. Reservations are advised. The school also has a cookery story and operates an online market where you can purchase all sorts of New Mexico culinary goods and gifts. And check the schedule for Dave's Jazz Bistro pop-up dinners which happen a few times each year. ⊠ *125 N. Guadalupe St., The Plaza* ☎ *505/983–4511, 800/982–4688* ⊕ *www.santafeschoolofcooking.com.*

Restaurants

Atrisco Café & Bar

$ | SOUTHWESTERN | FAMILY | Run by the family behind Tia Sophia's and Tomasita's, this casual New Mexican restaurant is where locals go to avoid the crowds at other Downtown eateries. Located inside DeVargas shopping center (just five minutes north of the Plaza), Atrisco offers authentic dishes the way Santa Feans like them—smothered in red or green chile (or both, referred to as "Christmas" style). **Known for:** lamb-stuffed sopaipillas; excellent margaritas; weekend breakfasts. ⑤ *Average main: $16* ⊠ *DeVargas Center, 193 Paseo de Peralta, West of the Plaza* ☎ *505/983–7401* ⊕ *www.atriscocafe.com.*

Blake's Lotaburger

$ | BURGER | FAMILY | This old-school, regional fast-food chain serves tasty breakfast burritos and juicy burgers. Perfect for a quick bite with the kids, don't forget to get a healthy helping of

The interior of San Miguel Mission, the oldest church in America, still reflects its 1610 origins.

green chile on your burger. **Known for:** green chile cheeseburgers; thick milkshakes; local family favorite. ⑤ *Average main: $9* ✉ *404 N. Guadalupe St., West of the Plaza* ☎ *505/983–4915* ⊕ *www. lotaburger.com.*

Dolina Cafe & Bakery

$ | **CAFÉ** | Slovakian transplant Annamaria O'Brien's bustling bakery and brunch spot is as bright and crisp as her food. The menu borrows a bit from the chef's Eastern European roots with favorites such as paprikash, langos, and goulash, but also features regional American dishes like cornmeal waffles with buttermilk fried chicken and a surprising bone broth "morning soup." The quiche of the day is always delicious. **Known for:** Eastern European pastries; eclectic and hearty breakfast-brunch fare; farm-fresh local ingredients. ⑤ *Average main: $16* ✉ *402 N. Guadalupe St., The Plaza* ☎ *505/982–9394* ⊕ *www.dolinasantafe.com* ⊙ *Closed Tues. No dinner.*

Fire & Hops

$$ | **ECLECTIC** | **FAMILY** | Tucked inside a cozy house on busy Guadalupe Street, Fire & Hops turns out flavorful, local, seasonal, and affordable gastropub-style food while also offering a stellar list of craft beers from regional breweries such as Bosque, Bow & Arrow, La Cumbre, Marble, and Ex Novo. Fire & Hops also features an extensive wine and cider list, and reserves a tap for hard kombucha crafted by celebrated local producer HoneyMoon Brewery. **Known for:** upscale pub food; small plates like crispy fried Brussels sprouts; great beer, cider, and hard kombucha.

⑤ *Average main: $18* ⊠ *222 N. Guadalupe St., The Plaza* ☎ *505/954–1635* ⊕ *www.fireandhopsgastropub.com* ◷ *Closed Mon. No lunch.*

La Mama

$ | **AMERICAN** | This modern American café has a strong hipster vibe that's in step with the influx of newcomers to Santa Fe who've brought whispers of Portland, Austin, and Santa Monica. The menu features basics done well, including bagels and granola for breakfast and burgers and grain bowls for lunch. **Known for:** great front porch for dining or chilling with a beverage; gourmet grocery items; tarot card readings available on Sunday. ⑤ *Average main: $16* ⊠ *225 E. Marcy St., The Plaza* ☎ *505/780–5626* ⊕ *www. lamamasantafe.com.*

Restaurant Martin

$$$$ | **MODERN AMERICAN** | Having cooked at some of the best restaurants in town (Geronimo, the Old House, Anasazi), acclaimed James Beard–nominated chef Martín Rios now flexes his culinary muscles in his own simple, elegant restaurant with a gorgeous patio. Rios prepares progressive American cuisine, which is heavily influenced by his French culinary training. **Known for:** daily-changing vegetarian tasting plate; wine and cocktails made with local spirits; attractively landscaped patio. ⑤ *Average main: $49* ⊠ *526 Galisteo St., The Plaza* ☎ *505/820–0919* ⊕ *www.restaurant-martin.com* ◷ *Closed Mon. and Tues. No lunch.*

★ Santacafé

$$$$ | **MODERN AMERICAN** | Owner Quinn Stephenson (who also owns fine dining institution Coyote Cafe) now runs this long-acclaimed member of Santa Fe's culinary vanguard with a lighter menu focused on fresh, fusion cuisine, and it remains one of Santa Fe's must-eat destinations. The minimalist, elegant restaurant is located two blocks north of the Plaza in the historic Padre Gallegos House and offers inventive dishes from chef Dale Kester. **Known for:** one of the city's dining institutions; fantastic patio popular with locals and visitors alike; creative cocktails and impressive wine list. ⑤ *Average main: $42* ⊠ *231 Washington Ave., The Plaza* ☎ *505/984–1788* ⊕ *www.santacafe.com* ◷ *No lunch Sun.*

Hotels

★ Campanilla Compound

$$ | **APARTMENT** | **FAMILY** | This luxurious, secluded, yet centrally located tract of about 15 spacious one- and two-bedroom vacation rentals is located on a hill just north of Downtown. **Pros:** perfect for extended stays; beautiful furnishings and high-end appliances;

close to Plaza but still very private. **Cons:** the walk from Plaza is uphill; there's a two-night minimum stay; can book up well in advance in summer. ⑤ *Rooms from: $250* ✉ *334 Otero St., The Plaza* ☎ *505/988–7585* ⊕ *www.campanillacompound.com* ⌨ *15 units* ⦿ *No Meals.*

El Farolito

$$$ | **B&B/INN** | All the beautiful Southwestern and Mexican furniture in this small, upscale compound is custom-made, and all the art and photography is original. **Pros:** excellent breakfast; half of the casitas have private patios, and half have shared patio areas; ample free off-street parking. **Cons:** no on-site pool or hot tub; about a 10-minute walk to the Plaza; a bit of neighborhood noise. ⑤ *Rooms from: $285* ✉ *514 Galisteo St., The Plaza* ☎ *505/988– 1631, 888/634–8782* ⊕ *www.farolito.com* ⌨ *8 rooms* ⦿ *Free Breakfast.*

★ The Inn of the Five Graces

$$$$ | **B&B/INN** | This sumptuous yet relaxed Relais & Chateaux hotel has an unmistakable East-meets-West feel, fitting right in with the kind of memorable lodgings you hear about in Morocco and Bali. **Pros:** tucked into a quiet, ancient neighborhood; loads of cushy perks and in-room amenities; fantastic staff—attentive but not overbearing. **Cons:** very steep rates; a short walk to downtown; can hear faint city noise from certain rooms. ⑤ *Rooms from: $985* ✉ *150 E. DeVargas St., The Plaza* ☎ *505/992–0957, 866/992–0957* ⊕ *www.fivegraces.com* ⌨ *26 rooms* ⦿ *Free Breakfast.*

Inn of the Turquoise Bear

$$$$ | **B&B/INN** | In the 1920s, poet Witter Bynner played host to an eccentric circle of artists and intellectuals, as well as some wild parties in his mid-19th-century Spanish–Pueblo Revival home, which is now a superb bed-and-breakfast with a great location a few blocks from the capitol; in sum, it's the quintessential Santa Fe inn. **Pros:** gorgeous grounds and a house steeped in local history; knowledgeable staff; tasty gourmet breakfasts. **Cons:** no pool or hot tub on-site; quirky layout of some rooms isn't for everyone; about a 15-minute walk to the Plaza. ⑤ *Rooms from: $450* ✉ *342 E. Buena Vista, The Plaza* ☎ *505/983–0798, 800/396–4104* ⊕ *www.turquoisebear.com* ⌨ *9 rooms* ⦿ *Free Breakfast.*

Las Palomas

$$$ | **B&B/INN** | It's a pleasant 10-minute walk west of the Plaza to reach this group of properties consisting of a few historic, luxurious compounds, one of them Spanish Pueblo–style adobe, another done in the Territorial style, and others ranging from rooms in renovated Victorian houses to contemporary condos

with up to three bedrooms. **Pros:** kid-friendly, with swings and a play yard; free Downtown shuttle service; most units feel very private and self-contained. **Cons:** big variations among the accommodations; no hot tub or pool on-site (guests may use pool at the Hotel Santa Fe); location requires transport to most local sights. ⑤ *Rooms from: $319* ⊠ *460 W. San Francisco St., The Plaza* ☎ *505/982–5560, 855/982–5560* ⊕ *www.laspalomas.com* ⇌ *50 casitas* ⦿ *Free Breakfast.*

Pueblo Bonito B&B Inn

$$ | B&B/INN | Rooms in this reasonably priced 1873 adobe compound have handmade and hand-painted furnishings, Navajo weavings, brick and hardwood floors, sand paintings and pottery, locally carved *santos* (Catholic saints), and Western art. **Pros:** intimate, cozy inn on peaceful grounds; excellent value; hearty breakfasts. **Cons:** bathrooms tend to be small; on a slightly noisy street; short walk to major sights. ⑤ *Rooms from: $200* ⊠ *138 W. Manhattan Ave., The Plaza* ☎ *505/984–8001, 800/461–4599* ⊕ *www.pueblobonitoinn.com* ⇌ *19 rooms* ⦿ *Free Breakfast.*

🎟 Performing Arts

Santa Fe Playhouse

THEATER | The oldest extant theater company west of the Mississippi, the Santa Fe Playhouse occupies a converted 19th-century adobe stable and has been presenting an adventurous mix of avant-garde pieces, classical drama, and musical comedy since 1922—the season runs year-round. The Fiesta Melodrama—a spoof of the Santa Fe scene—pokes sly fun from late August to mid-September. ⊠ *142 E. De Vargas St., The Plaza* ☎ *505/988–4262* ⊕ *www.santafeplayhouse.org.*

THE EAST SIDE WITH CANYON ROAD AND MUSEUM HILL

Updated by
Natalie Bovis

⊙ Sights   🍴 Restaurants   🛏 Hotels   🛍 Shopping   🍸 Nightlife

★★★★★   ★★★☆☆   ★★★★☆   ★★★★★   ★★★★★

NEIGHBORHOOD SNAPSHOT

TOP EXPERIENCES

■ **Stroll down Canyon Road:** Spend the day walking up and down Canyon Road enjoying the street's many art galleries, sculpture gardens, lifestyle shops, and popular restaurants.

■ **Spend an afternoon in a museum (or several):** Family-friendly Museum Hill offers something intriguing for nearly every age and interest, from Native American art and culture to folk art.

■ **Take time to wander:** There are many historic homes and gardens to see in this area. Stop by the Historic Santa Fe Foundation on Canyon Road for suggestions on walking tours.

■ **Appreciate the natural beauty:** Stroll around the Santa Fe Botanical Garden at Museum Hill, which features beautiful and unexpected plant combinations showcasing the vast possibilities of low-water landscaping.

VIEWFINDER

■ At the entrance to Museum Hill, you'll find a life-sized bronze of a covered wagon that is not only a great spot for photos but truly a marvelous piece of art unto itself.

GETTING HERE AND AROUND

The winding roads of this historic area are great for walking, but some sections can be a bit of a hike from Downtown. Parking is limited on Canyon Road itself with only a couple of small lots drivers can use. A better option is to park along Alameda, which is parallel to Canyon and has some access bridges. The attractions on Museum Hill have plenty of free parking and are far enough from Downtown that driving is the best option, though some hotels offer free shuttles. A great alternative for both areas is the city's free "Santa Fe Pick-Up" shuttle, which runs Canyon Road and Museum Hill routes daily from Downtown, approximately every 30 minutes.

The historic neighborhoods of the East Side are infinitely walkable and a slow stroll makes for a great way to experience Santa Fe's famous pueblo revival architecture.

While most buildings in the city are required to adhere to this style, it is in the East Side neighborhoods where you will find true historic adobe homes, made of earthen bricks, versus newer concrete and stucco finishes. Even where facades are crumbling, a peek of adobe just adds to the charm. Topping these East Side neighborhoods, Museum Hill has spectacular vistas and, of course, is a culture haven thanks to its impressive museums; it also serves as a gateway to the many walking and hiking trails that line the foothills of the Sangre de Christos.

The East Side is anchored by Canyon Road. Once a trail used by Indigenous people to access water and the lush forest in the foothills east of town, then a route for Hispanic woodcutters and their burros, and for most of the 20th century a prosaic residential street with only a gas station and a general store, Canyon Road today is lined with nearly 100 mostly upscale art galleries along with a handful of shops and restaurants. The narrow road begins at the eastern curve of Paseo de Peralta and stretches for about 2 miles uphill at a moderate incline. Upper Canyon Road (past East Alameda) is narrow and residential, with access to hiking and biking trails along the way, and the Randall Davey Audubon Center at the far east end.

There are few places as festive as Canyon Road on Christmas Eve, when thousands of *farolitos* illuminate walkways, walls, roofs, and even trees. In May the scent of lilacs wafts over the adobe walls, and in August red hollyhocks enhance the surreal color of the blue sky on a dry summer day.

What used to be the outskirts of town became the site of gracious, neo-Pueblo style homes in the mid-20th century, many of them designed by the famed architect John Gaw Meem. Elsewhere on neighboring streets in the East Side, you'll find a few bed-and-breakfasts as well as the beautifully situated campus of St. John's College, but this part of town is mostly residential. Old Santa Fe Trail, part of the long-traveled commercial route that connected the region to the Midwest and Mexico City (via El Camino

Real), takes you to Camino Lejo, aka Museum Hill, where you'll find four excellent museums, a botanical garden, and a café.

To take advantage of all the East Side has to offer, you might plan for a morning walk around one of its historic neighborhoods and after lunch, you can continue on to visit Canyon Road's eclectic galleries. With four museums and the Santa Fe Botanical Garden, Museum Hill is another spot where you could spend an entire day; if everyone in your party has different interests, you can split up to explore museums of interest and meet back up for lunch or a glass of wine at the conveniently located Museum Hill Cafe.

Sights

Bellas Artes Gallery

ART GALLERY | A sophisticated gallery with a serene sculpture garden, Bellas Artes has a captivating collection of ceramics, paintings, photography, and sculptural work, and represents internationally renowned artists. ⊠ *653 Canyon Rd., East Side and Canyon Road* ☎ *505/983–2745* ⊕ *www.bellasartesgallery.com* ☉ *Closed Sun. and Mon.*

Cristo Rey Church

CHURCH | Built in 1940 and designed by legendary Santa Fe architect John Gaw Meem to commemorate the 400th anniversary of Francisco Vásquez de Coronado's exploration of the Southwest, this church is the largest Spanish adobe structure in the United States and is considered by some to be the finest example of Pueblo-style architecture anywhere. The church was constructed in the old-fashioned way by parishioners, who mixed the more than 200,000 mud-and-straw adobe bricks and hauled them into place. The 225-ton white stone *reredos* (altar screen) is magnificent. ⊠ *1120 Canyon Rd., East Side and Canyon Road* ☎ *505/983–8528* ⊕ *www.cristoreyparish.org* ☑ *Free.*

El Zaguan

GARDEN | Headquarters of the Historic Santa Fe Foundation (HSFF), this 19th-century Territorial-style house has a small exhibit on Santa Fe architecture and preservation, but the real draw is the small but stunning garden abundant with lavender, roses, and mid-19th-century trees. Relax on a wrought-iron bench and take in the fine views of the hills northeast of town. The HSFF is a wealth of information on Santa Fe's historic properties, offering a great brochure for self-guided walking tours. They also sponsor monthly Salon El Zaguán lectures and rotating exhibits. It is free to visit the garden but guided tours cost extra. ⊠ *545 Canyon Rd., East Side and Canyon Road* ☎ *505/983–2567* ⊕ *www.historicsantafe.*

org 🖾 Garden free, tours $50 ⊗ Office closed weekends, garden closed Sun.

Gerald Peters Gallery

ART GALLERY | While under construction, this 32,000-square-foot building was dubbed the "ninth northern pueblo," its scale supposedly rivaling that of the eight northern pueblos around Santa Fe. The Pueblo-style gallery is now a showcase for American and European art from the 19th century to the present. The sister contemporary showroom features more avant-garde pieces. The whole space feels like a museum, but all the works are for sale. 🖾 1005 Paseo de Peralta, East Side and Canyon Road ☎ 505/954–5700 ⊕ www.gpgallery.com 🖾 Free ⊗ Closed Sun.

Giacobbe-Fritz

ART GALLERY | Stop inside this late-1890s adobe building to admire a truly diverse collection of paintings, drawings, and sculpture, much of it with a regional and traditional approach, and some of it downright whimsical. The owners also operate the excellent GF Contemporary, across the street, which focuses more on modern and abstract works. 🖾 702 Canyon Rd., East Side and Canyon Road ☎ 505/986–1156 ⊕ www.giacobbefritz.com.

★ Kyiv International Gallery

ART GALLERY | Founded in Baltimore in 1995, owner Dianna Lennon, an educator and advocate for Ukrainian art, opened this space in Santa Fe in 2003. Originally called the Art of Russia, she has since changed the name to spotlight generations of influential Ukrainian artists. A native of Kyiv herself, her focus is on contemporary artists and old masters from her home country. 🖾 225 Canyon Rd., #5, East Side and Canyon Road ☎ 505/466–1718 ⊕ www.kyivinternationalgallery.com ⊗ Closed Sun.

Meyer Gallery

ART GALLERY | One of the oldest and most prestigious galleries in the Southwest, Meyer's location at the bottom of Canyon Road makes it a good place to begin a stroll up the historic street. The work shown in this expansive gallery gives a good sense of the traditional Santa Fe art scene along with an eclectic selection of modern works focused on contemporary realism. They also offer an array of interesting resale art on consignment. 🖾 225 Canyon Rd., #14, East Side and Canyon Road ☎ 800/779–7387 ⊕ www.meyergalleries.com.

Museum of Indian Arts and Culture

ART MUSEUM | Located in the cluster of museums at Museum Hill, this interactive, multimedia exhibition tells the story of Native American history in the Southwest, merging contemporary Native

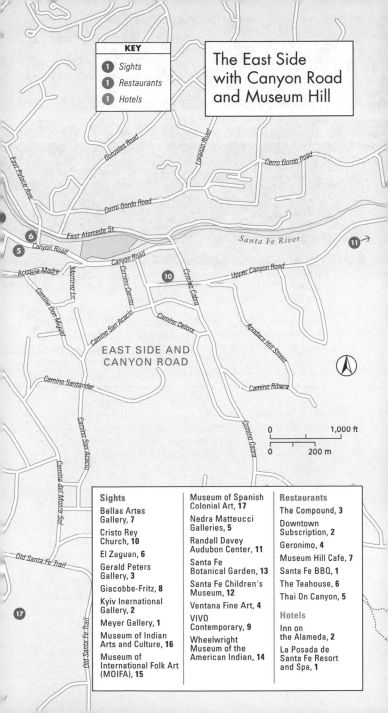

The East Side with Canyon Road and Museum Hill

Gonzales Road

Lorenza Road

Cerro Gordo Road

East Palace Ave.

Cerro Gordo Road

East Alameda St.

Santa Fe River

6

5 Canyon Road

11

Canyon Road

Acequia Madre

Martinez Ln.

Camino Cerro

10

Camino Cabra

Upper Canyon Road

Camino Don Miguel

Camino San Acacio

Camino Detora

Apodaca Hill Street

EAST SIDE AND
CANYON ROAD

Camino Santander

Camino Ribera

Camino San Acacio

Camino Cabra

0   1,000 ft

0   200 m

Camino del Monte Sol

Old Santa Fe Trail

17

Old Santa Fe Trail

Sights		Restaurants
Sights	Museum of Spanish Colonial Art, **17**	**Restaurants**
Bellas Artes Gallery, **7**	Nedra Matteucci Galleries, **5**	The Compound, **3**
Cristo Rey Church, **10**	Randall Davey Audubon Center, **11**	Downtown Subscription, **2**
El Zaguan, **6**	Santa Fe Botanical Garden, **13**	Geronimo, **4**
Gerald Peters Gallery, **3**	Santa Fe Children's Museum, **12**	Museum Hill Cafe, **7**
Giacobbe-Fritz, **8**	Ventana Fine Art, **4**	Santa Fe BBQ, **1**
Kyiv Inernational Gallery, **2**	VIVO Contemporary, **9**	The Teahouse, **6**
Meyer Gallery, **1**	Wheelwright Museum of the American Indian, **14**	Thai On Canyon, **5**
Museum of Indian Arts and Culture, **16**		**Hotels**
Museum of International Folk Art (MOIFA), **15**		Inn on the Alameda, **2**
		La Posada de Santa Fe Resort and Spa, **1**

The Museum of International Folk Art features a wide variety of art, much of it handmade and often reflecting shared cultural traditions.

American experience with historical accounts and artifacts. The collection includes some of New Mexico's oldest works of art: pottery vessels, fine stone and silver jewelry, intricate textiles, and other arts and crafts created by Pueblo, Navajo, and Apache artisans. Changing exhibitions feature arts and traditions of historic and contemporary Native Americans. while the long-standing *Here, Now and Always* exhibition shares glimpses into the lives and culture of area tribes. You can also see art demonstrations and a video about the life and work of Pueblo potter Maria Martinez. ✉ *710 Camino Lejo, East Side and Canyon Road* ☎ *505/476–1269* ⊕ *www.indianartsandculture.org* 🎫 *$12* 🕙 *Closed Mon. in Nov.–May.*

★ Museum of International Folk Art (MOIFA)

ART MUSEUM | FAMILY | Located atop Museum Hill, this museum delights visitors of all ages with its permanent collection of more than 130,000 objects from about 100 countries. In the Girard Wing, you'll find thousands of amazingly inventive handmade objects such as a tin Madonna, a devil made from bread dough, dolls from around the world, and miniature village scenes. The Hispanic Heritage Wing rotates exhibitions of art from throughout Latin America, dating from New Mexico's Spanish-colonial period (1598–1821) to the present. The exhibits in the Neutrogena Wing rotate, showing subjects ranging from outsider art to the magnificent quilts of Gee's Bend. Lloyd's Treasure Chest, the wing's innovative basement section, provides a behind-the-scenes look at the museum's permanent collection and explores the question of what exactly constitutes folk art. The innovative Gallery of Conscience explores topics at the intersection of folk art and social justice. Each exhibition also includes educational activities for both kids and adults. Allow time to visit the outstanding gift shop and bookstore. ⊠ *706 Camino Lejo, East Side and Canyon Road* ☎ *505/476–1200* ⊕ *www.internationalfolkart.org* ⊠ *$12* ⊘ *Closed Mon. in Nov.–Apr.*

Museum of Spanish Colonial Art

ART MUSEUM | Located at the entrance of Museum Hill, this adobe museum occupies a classically Southwestern former home designed in 1930 by acclaimed regional architect John Gaw Meem. The Spanish Colonial Art Society formed in Santa Fe in 1925 to preserve traditional Spanish-colonial art and culture, and the museum, which sits next to the Museum of International Folk Art and the Museum of Indian Arts and Culture complex, displays the fruits of the society's labor: one of the most comprehensive collections of Spanish-colonial art in the world. The objects here, dating from the 16th century to the present, include retablos, elaborate santos, tinwork, straw appliqué, furniture, ceramics, and ironwork. The contemporary collection of works by New Mexico Hispanic artists helps put all this history into regional context. The museum also hosts national traveling shows and its gift shop features artwork from participants in Santa Fe's yearly Spanish Market. ⊠ *750 Camino Lejo, East Side and Canyon Road* ☎ *505/982–2226* ⊕ *www.spanishcolonial.org* ⊠ *$12* ⊘ *Closed Mon. in Sept.–May.*

★ Nedra Matteucci Galleries

ART GALLERY | One of the Southwest's premier galleries, Matteucci Galleries exhibits works by California regionalists, members of the early Taos and Santa Fe schools, and masters of American impressionism and modernism. Spanish-colonial furniture, Indian antiquities, and a fantastic sculpture garden are other draws of this well-respected establishment. Visitors can also find jewelry, pottery, and books. The old adobe building that the gallery is in is a beautifully preserved example of Santa Fe–style architecture. Matteucci also owns Morning Star Gallery around the corner at 513 Canyon Road. ⊠ *1075 Paseo de Peralta, East Side and Canyon Road* ☎ *505/982–4631* ⊕ *www.matteucci.com.*

★ Randall Davey Audubon Center

NATURE PRESERVE | **FAMILY** | At the end of Upper Canyon Road, located at the mouth of the canyon as it wends into the foothills, the 135-acre Randall Davey Audubon Center harbors diverse birds (nearly 200 species have been identified) and other wildlife. Free guided nature walks are given most Saturday mornings at

The exterior of the Wheelwright Museum of the American Indian is shaped like a traditional octagonal Navajo hogan.

8:30; there are also two major hiking trails that you can tackle on your own. The home and studio of Randall Davey, a prolific early Santa Fe artist, can be toured on Friday afternoon. There's also a nature bookstore, and be sure to check out the treehouse and seed library. No pets are allowed other than leashed service dogs. ⊠ *1800 Upper Canyon Rd., East Side and Canyon Road* ☎ *505/983–4609* ⊕ *randalldavey.audubon.org* ✆ *Docent-led tours of the historic Randall Davey House and Studio $5* ☉ *Closed Sun.*

Santa Fe Botanical Garden
GARDEN | FAMILY | This 14-acre garden, located across the road from the Folk Art and Native American museums, provides another great reason for exploring Museum Hill. Situated on a bluff with fantastic views of the surrounding mountains, the facility is divided into four sections that emphasize distinct elements of New Mexico's flora and terrain: the Orchard Gardens, Ojos y Manos: Eyes and Hands, the Courtyard Gardens, and the Arroyo Trails. You can gain a much fuller sense of what's planted and why by embarking on one of the free guided tours, offered daily (call for hours). Also be sure to check the website to see which events might be happening at the outdoor amphitheater. ⊠ *725 Camino Lejo, East Side and Canyon Road* ☎ *505/471–9103* ⊕ *www.santafebotanicalgarden.org* ✆ *$12* ☉ *Closed Mon.–Wed. in Nov.–Mar.*

Santa Fe Children's Museum
CHILDREN'S MUSEUM | FAMILY | Stimulating hands-on exhibits, a solar greenhouse, oversize geometric forms, and an 18-foot indoor rock-climbing wall all contribute to this museum's popularity with

kids. Outdoor gardens with climbing structures, forts, and hands-on activities are great for whiling away the time in the shade of big trees. Puppeteers and storytellers perform often. ⊠ *1050 Old Pecos Trail, East Side and Canyon Road* ☎ *505/989–8359* ⊕ *www. santafechildrensmuseum.org* ⊠ *$8* ⊙ *Closed Mon. and Tues.*

★ Ventana Fine Art

ART GALLERY | Set in a dramatic and expansive Victorian redbrick schoolhouse on Canyon Road, Ventana has been at the forefront of Santa Fe's constantly shifting contemporary art scene since the mid-1980s. The gallery represents notable local talents as well as rising artists; the sculpture offerings, as seen both indoors and throughout the lovely gardens, are particularly noteworthy. The gallery has expanded to an additional location at 403 Canyon Road. ⊠ *400 Canyon Rd., East Side and Canyon Road* ☎ *505/983–8815, 800/746–8815* ⊕ *www.ventanafineart.com.*

VIVO Contemporary

ART GALLERY | Distinct in that it focuses solely on Santa Fe artists who produce contemporary works, VIVO also offers some very interesting programming from its handsome two-level space on Canyon Road, including an annual show featuring paintings and poems together. Works often rotate throughout the space and are available for purchase. ⊠ *725 Canyon Rd., East Side and Canyon Road* ☎ *505/982–1320* ⊕ *www.vivocontemporary.com.*

★ Wheelwright Museum of the American Indian

ART MUSEUM | A private institution in a building shaped like a traditional octagonal Navajo hogan, the Wheelwright opened in 1937. Founded by Boston scholar Mary Cabot Wheelwright and Navajo medicine man Hastiin Klah, the museum originated as a place to house ceremonial materials. Those items were returned to the Navajo in 1977, but what remains is an incredible collection of 19th- and 20th-century baskets, pottery, sculpture, weavings, metalwork, photography, and paintings, including contemporary works by Native American artists, and typically fascinating changing exhibits. The Case Trading Post on the lower level is modeled after the trading posts that dotted the Southwestern frontier more than 100 years ago. It carries an outstanding selection of books and contemporary Native American jewelry, kachina dolls, weaving, and pottery. There are also several interesting educational programs for visitors and locals to enjoy. ⊠ *704 Camino Lejo, East Side and Canyon Road* ☎ *505/982–4636* ⊕ *www.wheelwright.org* ⊠ *$10.*

 Restaurants

The Compound

$$$$ | **MODERN AMERICAN** | This folk-art-filled restaurant, with decor by famed designer Alexander Girard, is one of the most well-known dining spots in town. The oft-changing menu is devoted to seasonal and local ingredients with a variety of meats, fish, and pastas. **Known for:** excellent wine list; small yet lively bar area; cozy dining room and lovely outdoor patio. ⑤ *Average main: $55* ⊠ *653 Canyon Rd., East Side and Canyon Road* ☎ *505/982–4353* ⊕ *www.compoundrestaurant.com* ⊗ *Closed Sun. and Mon.*

Downtown Subscription

$ | **CAFÉ** | **FAMILY** | This neighborhood café-newsstand sells fancy coffees, various snacks, and sumptuous pastries as well as one of the largest assortments of newspapers and magazines in town. The shaded patio is a fun spot to people-watch and a great place to fuel a Canyon Road stroll. **Known for:** rotating art exhibitions; quality lattes; friendly atmosphere. ⑤ *Average main: $8* ⊠ *376 Garcia St., East Side and Canyon Road* ☎ *505/983–3085* ⊕ *www. facebook.com/downtownsubscription* ⊗ *No dinner.*

★ Geronimo

$$$$ | **MODERN AMERICAN** | This bastion of sophisticated contemporary cuisine occupies the historic Borrego House, built in 1756 by Geronimo Lopez, a massive-walled Canyon Road adobe with intimate white dining rooms, beamed ceilings, wood floors, fireplaces, and cushioned *bancos* (banquettes). It's a popular destination for a special meal, perhaps local rack of lamb with roasted leeks and a Merlot–natural jus reduction or mesquite grilled Maine lobster tails with a creamy garlic chile sauce. **Known for:** sophisticated contemporary fare; beautiful 18th-century Canyon Road adobe setting; cozy bar. ⑤ *Average main: $54* ⊠ *724 Canyon Rd., East Side and Canyon Road* ☎ *505/982–1500* ⊕ *www.geroni-morestaurant.com* ⊗ *No lunch.*

Museum Hill Cafè

$ | **CAFÉ** | **FAMILY** | A day filled with museums is bound to work up an appetite, and while there aren't too many places to eat around Museum Hill, luckily this café offers burgers, burritos, salads, and soups to help refuel your body and mind. There is a large shaded patio for warm-weather dining, and it also serves beer and wine. **Known for:** beautiful shaded patio great for people-watching; sumptuous weekend brunch menu; solid lunch options. ⑤ *Average main: $16* ⊠ *746 Camino Lejo, East Side and Canyon Road* ☎ *505/984–8900* ⊕ *www.museumhillcafe.net* ⊗ *Closed Mon. No dinner.*

Santa Fe BBQ

$ | BARBECUE | This big red food truck is a constant along Old Santa Fe Trail, serving up quick and delicious BBQ sandwiches, coleslaw, beans, and all the fixins. It's the perfect break from typical New Mexican food while still experiencing some unique local flavor. **Known for:** casual family dining; "Texas-sized" turkey legs; racks of ribs to-go. *$ Average main: $12 ⊠ 502 Old Santa Fe Trail, East Side and Canyon Road ☎ 505/603–9051 ⊕ www.santafebbq.com �he Closed Sun. and Mon.*

The Teahouse

$$ | CAFÉ | FAMILY | In a historic building toward the end of gallery row at the intersection of Canyon Road and East Palace Avenue, you'll find the Teahouse, with several bright dining rooms throughout the converted adobe home, and a tranquil outdoor seating area. In addition to fine teas from all over the world, you can find delicious breakfast, lunch, and dinner options, including baked polenta with poached eggs and romesco sauce, bagels and lox, and wild-mushroom panini. **Known for:** fine teas and coffees; serene garden seating; excellent breakfasts. *$ Average main: $18 ⊠ 821 Canyon Rd., East Side and Canyon Road ☎ 505/992–0972 ⊕ www.teahousesantafe.com.*

Thai On Canyon

$$ | THAI | Located right on famed Canyon Road, this Thai spot is a refreshing change of pace when you've had all the red and green chile you can handle and don't want to drop a few hundred dollars for a meal at the fancy restaurants down the block. Traditional soups, decadent noodle dishes, and flavorful curries are available both for dine-in and take-out. **Known for:** authentic Thai food; reasonably priced dishes; great lunch menu. *$ Average main: $18 ⊠ 802 Canyon Rd., East Side and Canyon Road ☎ 505/365–9869 ⊕ www.thaioncanyon.com �he Closed Tues.*

Hotels

★ Inn on the Alameda

$$$ | HOTEL | Within an easy walk of both the Plaza and Canyon Road, this mid-priced charmer with spacious Southwest-style rooms is one of the city's best small hotels. **Pros:** the solicitous staff is first-rate; excellent, expansive breakfast buffet and afternoon snacks and wine; free parking. **Cons:** rooms closest to Alameda can be a bit noisy; no pool; grounds can be a challenge for strollers or wheelchairs. *$ Rooms from: $299 ⊠ 303 E. Alameda St., East Side and Canyon Road ☎ 505/984–2121, 888/984–2121 ⊕ www.innonthealameda.com ⇆ 72 rooms ¶○¶ Free Breakfast.*

La Posada de Santa Fe Resort and Spa

$$$$ | **RESORT** | **FAMILY** | Rooms on the beautiful, quiet grounds of this Tribute Portfolio resort and spa vary greatly in size and configuration, but the level of luxury befits the somewhat steep rates, especially given the considerable amenities and appealing East Side location. **Pros:** numerous amenities, including a top-notch spa and restaurant; a few blocks from Plaza and similarly close to Canyon Road; a large pool. **Cons:** resort can sometimes feel crowded; daily resort fee; some rooms have street noise. $ *Rooms from: $425* ✉ *330 E. Palace Ave., East Side and Canyon Road* ☎ *505/986–0000, 855/210–7210* ⊕ *www.laposadadesantafe. com* ⌖ *157 rooms* ⧓ *No Meals.*

Nightlife

★ El Farol

LIVE MUSIC | With its long front portal and expansive back patio, this ancient adobe restaurant is a lovely spot to enjoy the afternoons and evenings of summer. The roomy, rustic lounge has a true Old West atmosphere—there's been a bar on the premises since 1835—and you can order some fine Spanish brandies and sherries in addition to cold beers, sangria, and margaritas, and the kitchen turns out authentic Spanish fare, from hearty paellas to lighter tapas. There's a daily happy hour from 3 to 5 pm, and it's a great place to see a variety of music as the dance floor fills up with a friendly crowd. For a fun night out, book a table to watch one of the fantastic flamenco shows. ✉ *808 Canyon Rd., East Side and Canyon Road* ☎ *505/983–9912* ⊕ *www.elfarolsantafe.com.*

Shopping

ANTIQUES, GIFTS, AND HOME FURNISHINGS

★ Cielo Handcrafted

CRAFTS | This family-run lifestyle gallery specializes in goods produced by local artists and craftspeople including pottery, clothing, art, furniture, and home goods. Of particular interest is the stunning jewelry created by local artist Gloria Olazabal as well as the beautiful wood cutting boards and serving trays featuring inlaid turquoise by Wild Edge Woodworks. ✉ *836 Canyon Rd., East Side and Canyon Road* ☎ *575/551–8390* ⊕ *www.cielohandcrafted.com.*

Hecho a Mano

CRAFTS | Focusing on handmade items from both local craftspeople and artists in Oaxaca, this lifestyle gallery offers beautiful prints, ceramics, jewelry, and more, at all price points. Owner and "Creative Conductor" Frank Rose also sells an impressive collection of prints by Mexican artists including Diego Rivera and Rufino Tamayo. ⊠ *830 Canyon Rd., East Side and Canyon Road* ☎ *505/916–1341* ⊕ *www.hechoamano.org.*

La Mesa

CRAFTS | This shop has become well known for showcasing contemporary handcrafted, mostly functional, works by more than two dozen, mostly local, artists. Collections include 3-D wall art, leather works, glass sculpture, pottery, lighting, fine art, and accessories. ⊠ *225 Canyon Rd., East Side and Canyon Road* ☎ *505/984–1688* ⊕ *www.lamesaofsantafe.com.*

BOOKS

Garcia Street Books

BOOKS | **FAMILY** | This outstanding independent shop is strong on art, architecture, cookbooks, literature, and regional Southwestern works—it's a block from the Canyon Road galleries and hosts frequent talks by authors in person and via interviews posted to the shop's website. ⊠ *376 Garcia St., East Side and Canyon Road* ☎ *505/986–0151* ⊕ *www.garciastreetbooks.com.*

CLOTHING

★ Homefrocks

WOMEN'S CLOTHING | This shop features simple, yet exquisite, women's clothing designed by local artist Nancy Traugott. The natural silk and linen fabrics are colored by hand with botanical dyes, making each classic piece truly one-of-a-kind. Equally appropriate for a farmers' market stroll or a night at the opera, these breezy yet substantial mix-and-match dresses, scarves, pants, and jackets are certainly an investment but are sure to become staples in any wardrobe. ⊠ *550 Canyon Rd., East Side and Canyon Road* ☎ *505/986–5800* ⊕ *www.homefrocks.com.*

FOOD AND DRINK

★ Kakawa

CHOCOLATE | **FAMILY** | You're unlikely to ever have tasted anything like the divine, agave-sweetened, artisanal creations that emerge from this sweet shop. Historically accurate chocolate drinks, like the Aztec Warrior Elixir, divine caramels, and gluten-free chocolate baked goods are served in this cozy, welcoming establishment that's as much an educational experience as a chance to indulge in exceptional sweets. There are three more locations: one is on Rufina Street near Meow Wolf, another sits in midtown on San Mateo Road, and the other is all the way in Salem, Massachusetts. ⊠ *1050 Paseo de Peralta, East Side and Canyon Road* ☎ *505/982–0388* ⊕ *www.kakawachocolates.com.*

NATIVE AMERICAN ARTS AND CRAFTS
Morning Star Gallery

CRAFTS | Owned by the prestigious Nedra Matteucci Galleries, this is a veritable museum of Native American art. An adobe shaded by a huge cottonwood tree houses antique basketry, pre-1940 Navajo silver jewelry, Northwest Coast Native American carvings, Navajo weavings, and art of the Plains Indians. Prices and quality span the spectrum, making this a great stop for both new and experienced collectors. ⊠ *513 Canyon Rd., East Side and Canyon Road* ☎ *505/982–8187* ⊕ *www.morningstargallery.com.*

Activities

HIKING
★ Atalaya Trail

HIKING & WALKING | Spurring off the Dale Ball Trail system, the steep but rewarding (and dog-friendly) Atalaya Trail runs from the visitor parking lot of St. John's College, up a winding, ponderosa pine–studded trail to the peak of Mt. Atalaya, which affords incredible 270-degree views of Santa Fe. The nearly 6-mile round-trip hike climbs almost 2,000 feet (to an elevation of 9,121 feet), so pace yourself. The good news: the return to the parking area is nearly all downhill. ⊠ *1160 Camino de Cruz Blanca, East Side and Canyon Road.*

Dale Ball Foothills Trail Network

HIKING & WALKING | A favorite spot for a ramble, with a vast system of trails, is the Dale Ball Foothills Trail Network, a 24-mile network of paths that winds and wends up through the foothills east of town and can be accessed at a few points, including Hyde Park Road (en route to the ski valley), the upper end of Canyon Road at Cerro Gordo, and from Camino de Cruz Blanca near St. John's College. There are trail maps and signs at these points, and the trails are very well marked. ⊠ *East Side and Canyon Road* ⊕ *www.sfct.org/dale-ball-trails.*

THE RAILYARD DISTRICT

Updated by
Natalie Bovis

👁 **Sights** 🍴 **Restaurants** 🛏 **Hotels** 🛍 **Shopping** 🍸 **Nightlife**
★★★★☆ ★★★★☆ ★★☆☆☆ ★★★★☆ ★★★★☆

NEIGHBORHOOD SNAPSHOT

TOP EXPERIENCES

■ **Search for vintage items:** One-of-a-kind treasures are waiting to be discovered at the many well-curated secondhand shops along Guadalupe Street.

■ **Shop like a local:** Around the Railyard you'll find dozens of specialty boutiques selling everything from colorful cowboy boots to local art.

■ **Plan your next meal:** Try whatever is fresh, local, and delicious at the famous Santa Fe Farmers' Market.

■ **Enjoy the city's nightlife:** Dance the night away to live music at local watering holes or the Railyard's free summer concert series.

■ **Appreciate art:** Art abounds in the Railyard District, whether it's within a big gallery, a local artist's studio, SITE Santa Fe, or the Vladem Museum.

GETTING HERE AND AROUND

The Railyard District is easily accessible by car and within walking distance of Downtown. While most parking is metered street parking, there is a large parking garage, as well as a few small lots, at the Railyard itself. Walk the winding streets around the area to see some of the historic homes and buildings. The free "Santa Fe Pick-Up" shuttle also offers a historic district loop that runs around Downtown and to the Railyard, with pick-ups/drop-offs approximately every 15 minutes.

VIEWFINDER

■ The Railyard's iconic water tower sits alongside the railroad tracks next to the Santa Fe Farmers' Market, making it a popular meeting place and social center of the neighborhood. Locals and visitors find it highly Insta-grammable, busk-ers set up nearby to serenade the masses for mone-tary donations, and families duck into its shade to enjoy a snack from the market.

The most significant development in Santa Fe in recent years has taken place in the Railyard District, a neighborhood just south of the Plaza that was for years called the Guadalupe District (and is occasionally still known by that name).

Comprising a few easily walked blocks along Guadalupe Street between Agua Fria and Paseo de Peralta, the district has been revitalized with a snazzy park and outdoor performance space, a permanent indoor–outdoor home for the farmers' market, and quite a few notable restaurants, shops, and galleries.

This historic warehouse and rail district endured several decades of neglect after the demise of the train route through town. But rather than tearing the buildings down (this is a city where 200-year-old mud-brick buildings sell at a premium, after all), the city, with extensive input from residents, worked with developers to gradually convert the low-lying warehouses into artists' studios, antiques shops, bookstores, indie shops, and restaurants. The Rail Runner commuter train to Albuquerque has put the rail tracks as well as the vintage mission-style depot back into use.

A central feature of the district's redevelopment is Railyard Park, at the corner of Cerrillos Road and Guadalupe Street, which was designed to highlight native plants and provide citizens with a lush, urban space. The buildings just north, in the direction of the Plaza, contain the vibrant Santa Fe Farmers' Market, the stunning SITE Santa Fe museum, art galleries, shops, restaurants, and live-work spaces for artists. This dramatic development reveals the fascinating way Santa Feans have worked to meet the needs of an expanding city while paying strict attention to the city's historic relevance.

On weekends, the Railyard District is a lively spot thanks to the ever-popular Santa Fe Farmers' Market and the Sunday Artisan Market. One could easily spend an entire day perusing the many contemporary galleries, vintage shops, and quirky boutiques that surround the Railyard. In the evenings, you can often dance the night away at free community concerts or to a live band at local nightlife staple, the Cowgirl BBQ.

Sights

★ Container

ART GALLERY | This 5,000-square-foot art space in the ever-transforming Baca Street neighborhood presents itself as both museum and art gallery. It is owned by the duo behind Turner Carroll Gallery, who aim to present eclectic and significant artwork from around the world. Their global relationships facilitate and attract influential stars in the art world to exhibit, speak, and share with like-minded aficionados in Santa Fe. ⊠ *1226 Flagman Way, Railyard District* ☎ *505/995–0012* ⊕ *www.containertc.org* ⊗ *Closed Mon.*

Charlotte Jackson Fine Art

ART GALLERY | This industrial and airy space set in a renovated warehouse focuses primarily on monochromatic "radical" painting and sculpture. Many of the pieces here are large-scale, with "drama" as the guiding force. Exhibitions rotate every few months so check the website for current and upcoming showings. ⊠ *554 S. Guadalupe St., Railyard District* ☎ *505/989–8688* ⊕ *www.charlottejackson.com* ⊗ *Closed Sun. and Mon.*

El Museo Cultural de Santa Fe

ARTS CENTER | FAMILY | Also operating as a community gathering space with lectures and classes, the 31,000-square-foot El Museo celebrates New Mexico's rich Hispanic heritage with a wide range of events, from children's theater to musical concerts. It also hosts the Antique American Indian Art Show, during which dozens of craftspersons and artists exhibit their work in early August along with the Mercado, held on weekends from late September through late May and featuring a varied array of vendors selling folk, tribal, and Western art and memorabilia. A small gallery shows contemporary art by Hispanic artists. ⊠ *555 Camino de la Familia, Railyard District* ☎ *505/992–0591* ⊕ *www.elmuseocultural.org* ▨ *Free; prices vary for events and shows* ⊗ *Closed Mon.*

★ EVOKE Contemporary

ART GALLERY | In a striking, high-ceilinged space, EVOKE ranks among the more diverse contemporary galleries in town. It veers away from the standard Southwestern focus seen in many Santa Fe galleries and more toward modern pieces that evoke (wink, wink) conversation and personal reflection. Single artist and group exhibitions rotate through the schedule, featuring creatives from around the globe. Intriguing lectures on varied topics also draw crowds. ⊠ *550 S. Guadalupe St., Railyard District* ☎ *505/995–9902* ⊕ *www.evokecontemporary.com* ⊗ *Closed Sun.*

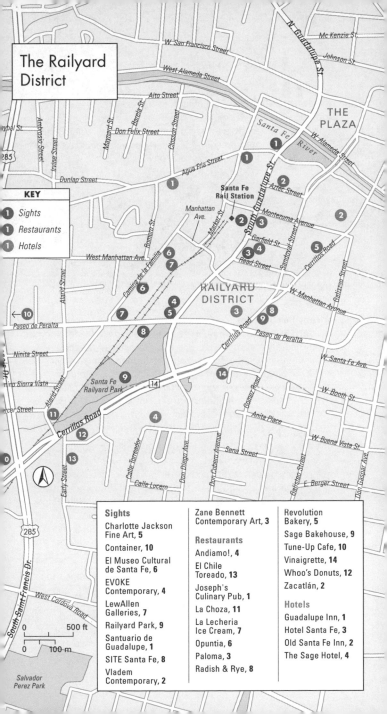

The Railyard District

KEY

- ① Sights
- ① Restaurants
- ① Hotels

Sights

Charlotte Jackson Fine Art, **5**

Container, **10**

El Museo Cultural de Santa Fe, **6**

EVOKE Contemporary, **4**

LewAllen Galleries, **7**

Railyard Park, **9**

Santuario de Guadalupe, **1**

SITE Santa Fe, **8**

Vladem Contemporary, **2**

Zane Bennett Contemporary Art, **3**

Restaurants

Andiamo!, **4**

El Chile Toreado, **13**

Joseph's Culinary Pub, **1**

La Choza, **11**

La Lecheria Ice Cream, **7**

Opuntia, **6**

Paloma, **3**

Radish & Rye, **8**

Revolution Bakery, **5**

Sage Bakehouse, **9**

Tune-Up Cafe, **10**

Vinaigrette, **14**

Whoo's Donuts, **12**

Zacatlán, **2**

Hotels

Guadalupe Inn, **1**

Hotel Santa Fe, **3**

Old Santa Fe Inn, **2**

The Sage Hotel, **4**

The Santuario de Guadalupe honors the patron saint of Mexico, Our Lady of Guadalupe.

★ LewAllen Galleries

ART GALLERY | This longtime Santa Fe art dealer is a leader in both contemporary and modern art, with a dramatic 14,000-square-foot neo-industrial building across from the farmers' market. You'll also find a dazzling collection of abstract sculptures, photography, and paintings by up-and-coming regional and international talents. ⊠ *1613 Paseo de Peralta, Railyard District* ☎ *505/988–3250* ⊕ *lewallengalleries.com* ⊗ *Closed Sun.*

★ Railyard Park

CITY PARK | **FAMILY** | A 12-acre expanse that helped redefine the neighborhood, Railyard Park is an urban park with orchards, a community garden, a bird and butterfly garden, children's play areas, picnic areas, and some fantastic public art. In summer, there are free outdoor evening movies. The park runs past SITE Santa Fe to the Railyard Plaza via the walkable and bikeable "Rail Trail." ⊠ *740 Cerrillos Rd., Railyard District* ☎ *505/316–3596* ⊕ *www. railyardpark.org.*

Santuario de Guadalupe

CHURCH | A massive-walled adobe structure built by Franciscan missionaries between 1776 and 1795, this is the oldest shrine in the United States to Our Lady of Guadalupe, Mexico's patron saint. The church's adobe walls are nearly 3 feet thick, and among the sanctuary's religious art and artifacts is a beloved image of Nuestra Virgen de Guadalupe, painted by Mexican master Jose de Alcibar in 1783. Highlights are the traditional New Mexican carved and painted altar screen called a reredos, an authentic 19th-century sacristy, a pictorial-history archive, a library devoted to Archbishop Jean Baptiste Lamy that is furnished with many of his belongings, and a garden with plants from the Holy Land. ⊠ *100 Guadalupe St., Railyard District* ☎ *505/988–2027* ⊕ *www. santuariodeguadalupesantafe.com* ⊠ *Donations accepted.*

★ SITE Santa Fe

ARTS CENTER | FAMILY | The events at this 18,000 square foot nexus of international contemporary art include lectures, concerts, author readings, films, performance art, and gallery shows. The facility also hosts a biennial exhibition, SITElines, staged every even-numbered year. Exhibitions are often provocative, and the immense, open space provides an ideal setting for the many larger-than-life installations. The on-site museum store, Curated, offers a tasteful selection of unique, artist-made items. ⊠ *1606 Paseo de Peralta, Railyard District* ☎ *505/989–1199* ⊕ *sitesantafe.org* ⊠ *Free* ۞ *Closed Tues. and Wed.*

★ Vladem Contemporary

ART MUSEUM | FAMILY | The newest outpost of the New Mexico Museum of Art, Vladem boasts a more modern approach to the artistic experience than the city's historic buildings provide. The striking structure was purposefully designed to accommodate large-scale installations, multimedia exhibitions, performances, educational programs, and much-needed art storage, including a photography vault for fragile historic photos. With nearly 10,000 square feet of gallery space and over 2,500 square feet of outdoor space, plan to spend at least a couple of hours exploring the artwork and grounds. The $12 admission also gets visitors into its sister museum at 107 West Palace Avenue in the Plaza. ⊠ *404 Montezuma Ave., Railyard District* ☎ *505/476–5063* ⊕ *www. nmartmuseum.org* ⊠ *$12* ۞ *Closed Mon. in Nov.–Apr.*

Zane Bennett Contemporary Art

ART GALLERY | The sleek design of this airy, two-story gallery with a skylighted atrium is a fitting venue for the cutting-edge photography, paintings, sculptures, and mixed-media works within. Next door, its sister venue Form & Concept is focused on crafts and design. The space sits on a parcel of Native land within the town which the gallery owners consciously acknowledge with respectful reverence. ⊠ *435 S. Guadalupe St., Railyard District* ☎ *505/982–8111* ⊕ *www.zanebennettgallery.com* ۞ *Closed Sun. and Mon.*

🍴 Restaurants

Andiamo!

$$ | **ITALIAN** | A longtime locals' favorite, Andiamo! scores high marks for its friendly staff, consistently good northern Italian food, and comfortable dining room. Produce from the farmers' market down the street adds to the seasonal surprises of this intimate restaurant set inside a sweet cottage in the Railyard District. **Known for:** crispy duck leg confit with polenta; great pizzas; charming cottage setting. ⑤ *Average main: $17* ✉ *322 Garfield St., Railyard District* ☎ *505/995–9595* ⊕ *www.andiamosantafe.com* ⊘ *No lunch.*

El Chile Toreado

$ | **MEXICAN** | **FAMILY** | Considered one of Santa Fe's best food trucks, El Chile Toreado offers hearty, delicious, and affordable New Mexican breakfast and lunch. Although it has made it onto many "must-eat" lists, it has retained both quality and convenience, cementing itself as a perennial local favorite. **Known for:** tasty hot dogs; mix-and-match tacos; good vegetarian options. ⑤ *Average main: $12* ✉ *807 Early St., Railyard District* ☎ *505/500–0033* ⊕ *elchiletoreado.com* ⊘ *Closed Sun. No dinner.*

Joseph's Culinary Pub

$$$ | **MODERN AMERICAN** | Chef-restauranteur Joseph Wrede has garnered countless accolades since the 1990s at various restaurants in Taos and then Santa Fe, and his current eatery—a stylish gastropub set in a vintage adobe with low beamed ceilings, slate floors, and a cozy patio—continues to showcase his considerable talents, featuring a menu of deliciously updated comfort fare. Dishes you're already familiar with receive novel twists, including caviar-topped duck fat-fried potato chips with crème fraîche, pickled onion, and cured egg yolk; and posole verde with chicken, a farm egg, tomatillos, and avocado. **Known for:** duck fat fries; excellent steak au poivre; stellar beer and wine selection. ⑤ *Average main: $30* ✉ *428 Agua Fria St., Railyard District* ☎ *505/982–1272* ⊕ *www.josephsofsantafe.com* ⊘ *Closed Mon. and Tues. No lunch.*

La Choza

$ | **SOUTHWESTERN** | **FAMILY** | Sister to the Shed restaurant located downtown, La Choza (which means "the shed" in Spanish), serves tasty, traditional New Mexican fare. It's hard to go wrong here: chicken or pork *carne adovada* (marinated in red chile and slow-cooked until tender) burritos, white clam chowder spiced with green chiles, green chile stew, and the classic huevos rancheros are exceptional. **Known for:** stuffed sopaipilla; outstanding and extensive margarita and premium-tequila list; long waits unless you make a reservation. $ *Average main: $14* ⊠ *905 Alarid St., Railyard District* ☎ *505/982–0909* ⊕ *www.lachozasf.com* ⊗ *Closed Sun.*

La Lecheria Ice Cream

$ | ICE CREAM | FAMILY | Take a break from wandering the markets, stores, and galleries of the Railyard with an adventurous dive into seasonal ice cream flavors like red chile honey, butterscotch miso, citrus basil, and sweet corn (traditionalists can still enjoy a scoop of vanilla bean, mint chip, or chocolate sea salt). Santa Fe native Joel Coleman brings years of experience to this old-fashioned creamery that sources organic dairy and eggs, forgoing preservatives and stabilizers. **Known for:** family-friendly atmosphere; organic ingredients; unusual ice cream flavors. $ *Average main: $4* ⊠ *500 Market St., #110, Railyard District* ☎ *505/428–0077* ⊕ *www. lalecherianm.com.*

Opuntia

$ | CAFÉ | FAMILY | This modern café sits above the hustle and bustle of the Railyard, offering sweeping views of downtown Santa Fe and the surrounding landscape. With a focus on house-made, locally sourced, and seasonal ingredients, the dishes aren't tied to any specific cuisine but are crafted more to complement Opuntia's carefully curated selection of fine teas. **Known for:** impressive selection of tea, Belgian beers, sake, wine, ciders, and cocktails; creative design aesthetic that blurs indoors and outdoors; fun on-site cactus and succulent shop. $ *Average main: $16* ⊠ *1607 Alcadesa St., 2nd fl., Railyard District* ☎ *505/780–5796* ⊕ *www. opuntia.cafe* ⊗ *No dinner Mon. and Tues.*

★ Paloma

$$ | MODERN MEXICAN | A fun go-to for happy hour or an intimate dinner, this bright and bustling modern take on a Mexican cantina offers an impressive mezcal-focused cocktail program, plenty of shareable small plates, and seasonal entrées such as squash blossom enmoladas and a perfectly roasted half chicken with grilled chard, charro beans, and a classic mole poblano sauce. Street tacos—crispy Baja-style sea bass, cauliflower with marcona almonds, or lamb barbacoa with smoky adobo sauce—are another specialty, as is the remolacha salad of hibiscus beets, citrus, seasonal fruits, and frisee. **Known for:** street-food-style tacos; craft cocktails; Mexican and Tex-Mex classics. $ *Average main: $21* ⊠ *401 S. Guadalupe St., Railyard District* ☎ *505/467–8624* ⊕ *www. palomasantafe.com* ⊗ *Closed Mon. No lunch.*

Radish & Rye

$$$$ | **MODERN AMERICAN** | Set in a rustic yet modern space, Radish & Rye stands out both for its deftly crafted American food and one of the best small-batch bourbon selections in the Southwest. The kitchen focuses on "farm-inspired" victuals—seasonally rotating dishes like roasted beets and labneh cheese with piñon vinaigrette, and grilled local pork chops with bacon, polenta, and wild mushrooms. **Known for:** local and seasonal ingredients; bourbon pecan pie; encyclopedic list of small-batch bourbons. $ *Average main: $58* ⊠ *505 Cerrillos Rd., Railyard District* 🕾 *505/930–5325* ⊕ *www.radishandrye.com* ⊙ *No lunch.*

Revolution Bakery

$ | **BAKERY** | **FAMILY** | This gluten-free bakery serves baked goods, soups, sandwiches, and other goodies (with lots of vegan options) that are so delicious you won't miss the gluten. And good news for visitors who fall in love with the treats here: they ship nationwide. **Known for:** non-GMO ingredients whenever possible; gluten-free bread; casual atmosphere. $ *Average main: $5* ⊠ *The Design Center, 418 Cerrillos Rd., Railyard District* 🕾 *505/346–2669* ⊕ *www.revolutionbakery.com* ⊙ *Closed Sun. and Mon. No dinner.*

★ Sage Bakehouse

$ | **BAKERY** | **FAMILY** | This artisanal bakery produces some of the best bread you'll ever taste along with delectable pastries, panini, tartines, quiches, soups, and salads. While many items are made to grab n' go, taking the time to enjoy a fresh-made meal in the small café is a nice break from a busy day. **Known for:** artisanal bread and baked goods; seasonal soups, panini, and tartines; charming ambience. $ *Average main: $9* ⊠ *535 Cerrillos Rd., Railyard District* 🕾 *505/820–7243* ⊕ *www.sagebakehouse.com* ⊙ *Closed Sun. No dinner.*

Tune-Up Cafe

$ | **SOUTHWESTERN** | **FAMILY** | This funky spot has colorful walls and wood details, booths, a few individual tables, and a community table. The shaded patio out front is a great summertime spot to enjoy the toothsome Southwest-inspired cooking, from breakfast through dinner. **Known for:** breakfast rellenos; vegetarian, vegan, and gluten-free options; homemade cakes and pies. $ *Average main: $15* ⊠ *1115 Hickox St., Railyard District* 🕾 *505/983–7060* ⊕ *www.tuneupsantafe.com.*

Vinaigrette

$$ | **AMERICAN** | **FAMILY** | A refreshing alternative to the many Santa Fe restaurants that favor filling (and often fattening) dishes, Vinaigrette is all about the greens. This isn't mere rabbit food, however—the hearty salads make a satisfying meal, especially

when you add toppings like grilled flank steak, lemon-herb chicken breast, or griddled tofu. **Known for:** hearty (and expensive) salads; daily house-made fruit pies; baked panko-crusted goat cheese (which can be added to any salad). ⑤ *Average main: $24* ⊠ *709 Don Cubero Alley, Railyard District* ☎ *505/820–9205* ⊕ *www. vinaigretteonline.com* ⊗ *Closed Sun.*

★ Whoo's Donuts

$ | **BAKERY** | **FAMILY** | With a near-fanatical following for its traditional and creative doughnuts, Whoo's offers mouth-watering flavors that incorporate outside-of-the-box combinations and local flare. For those preferring savory over sweet, try the delicious hand-held breakfast burritos. **Known for:** green chile apple fritters; blue corn blueberry doughnuts with lavender icing; organic coffee and tea. ⑤ *Average main: $2* ⊠ *851 Cerrillos Rd., Railyard District* ☎ *505/629–1678* ⊕ *www.whoosdonuts.com* ⊗ *No dinner.*

★ Zacatlán

$$$$ | **MEXICAN FUSION** | Chef Eduardo Rodriguez led some of Santa Fe's most famous kitchens for nearly 25 years before opening his own eatery, naming it after the north-central Mexican region of his birth. The culinary marriage between the southwestern United States and Mexico shows up in dishes like mole negro chilaquiles (eggs, Chihuahuan cheese, black beans, chicken, and mole sauce) for brunch and whole fried snapper with crab saffron risotto, *calabacitas* (sautéed zucchini), and salsa Veracruz for dinner. **Known for:** Southwest meets Mexico flavors; intimate atmosphere; fresh, creative cuisine. ⑤ *Average main: $40* ⊠ *317 Aztec St., Railyard District* ☎ *505/780–5174* ⊕ *www.zacatlanrestaurant.com* ⊗ *No lunch Mon.–Wed.*

Hotels

★ Guadalupe Inn

$$ | **B&B/INN** | This locally owned, intimate bed-and-breakfast sits only seven blocks from the Plaza on a piece of land that has been in the Quintana family since long before New Mexico became part of the United States. **Pros:** cool historic vibe; reasonable prices; free parking. **Cons:** breakfast is a bit lackluster; no bar or restaurant on-site; no elevator. ⑤ *Rooms from: $200* ⊠ *604 Agua Frida, Railyard District* ☎ *505/989–7422* ⊕ *www.guadalupeinn.com* ⇌ *12 rooms* ⑩ *Free Breakfast.*

Hotel Santa Fe

$$$$ | **HOTEL** | Picurís Pueblo has controlling interest in this handsome Pueblo-style three-story hotel on the Railyard District's edge and a 15-minute walk from the Plaza. **Pros:** lots of amenities,

including spa and pool; easy access to Railyard District's trendy shopping and dining; interesting focus on Native American history and culture. **Cons:** standard rooms are a bit small; room rates vary greatly; a bit far from Downtown. ⑤ *Rooms from: $400* ✉ *1501 Paseo de Peralta, Railyard District* ☎ *855/825–9876* ⊕ *www.hotelsantafe.com* ⇌ *158 rooms* ⦿ *No Meals.*

★ Old Santa Fe Inn

$$ | HOTEL | This contemporary motor court–style inn looks from the outside like an attractive, if fairly ordinary, adobe motel, but it has stunning and spotless rooms with elegant Southwestern decor. **Pros:** rooms are more inviting than several more-expensive Downtown hotels; short walk to the Plaza; free parking. **Cons:** rooms set around parking lot; noise from other rooms; decor can be a bit drab in places. ⑤ *Rooms from: $200* ✉ *201 Montezuma Ave., Railyard District* ☎ *505/995–0800* ⊕ *www.oldsantafeinn.com* ⇌ *58 rooms* ⦿ *Free Breakfast.*

The Sage Hotel

$$ | HOTEL | FAMILY | On the southern edge of the Railyard District, this smart motel offers affordable comfort, modern bohemian Southwestern decor, and a location that's just about a five-minute walk to the Railyard and a 15-minute walk from the Plaza. **Pros:** comfortable and affordable; small but nice pool; close to Railyard District attractions and galleries. **Cons:** rooms nearest the street can be noisy; parking lot views; extra $15 fee to use all amenities. ⑤ *Rooms from: $199* ✉ *725 Cerrillos Rd., Railyard District* ☎ *505/982–5952* ⊕ *www.thesagesf.com* ⇌ *145 rooms* ⦿ *Free Breakfast.*

Nightlife

★ As Above So Below Distillery

BARS | More female distillers are gaining recognition in the spirits industry, and Caley Shoemaker is one of today's most intriguing women in the business. After honing her craft at several big-name beverage companies, the Colorado native and her husband moved to Santa Fe to open their own spot just across the railroad tracks from the Santa Fe Farmers' Market. Guests are treated to a view of Lilleth, their impressive pot still, just behind a glass wall beyond the tasting room's cocktail bar. Best known for Sigil gin and tantalizing Aradia aperitivo, the seasonal drink menu spotlights homegrown spirits, and the bottle shop sells limited-run tippling treats. ✉ *545 Camino de la Familia, Railyard District* ☎ *505/916–8596* ⊕ *www.aasbdistillery.com.*

★ Bosque Brewing Co.

BARS | One of the state's most celebrated craft brewing companies, Bosque Brewing Co.'s Santa Fe taproom offers rotating taps including favorites such as the Jetty Jack Amber and Elephants on Parade wheat ale. The kitchen serves up beer-friendly foods ranging from nachos and deep-fried cheese curds to street tacos, burgers, and fish-and-chips. It's a great spot to relax and people-watch. ⊠ *500 Market St., Railyard District* ☎ *505/433-3889* ⊕ *www.bosquebrewing.com.*

★ Cowgirl BBQ

GATHERING PLACES | **FAMILY** | This rollicking barbecue, burger, and Southwestern soul food joint is one of the most popular places in town for live blues, country, rock, folk, and even karaoke. The bar is friendly and reasonable drink prices provide bang for your buck. The kids' patio out back keeps little ones entertained, and the fun pool hall and central outdoor patio can get wild as the night gets late. ⊠ *319 S. Guadalupe St., Railyard District* ☎ *505/982-2505* ⊕ *www.cowgirlsantafe.com.*

Santa Fe Spirits Downtown Tasting Room

BARS | Microdistillery Santa Fe Spirits operates this convivial tasting room from a small adobe home tucked on a side street. Known for its award-winning Colkegan Single Malt Whiskey, Wheeler's Gin, and Apple Brandy, among several other robust elixirs, it's a great place to sip drinks on the cute little patio on warm evenings. Distillery tours, by reservation, are available at the main production facility out near the Santa Fe airport. ⊠ *308 Read St., Railyard District* ☎ *505/780-5906* ⊕ *www.santafespirits.com.*

Second Street Brewery

BREWPUBS | **FAMILY** | The Railyard location of this local brewpub is especially popular thanks to the easy walking distance from Downtown hotels. There's great live music (usually rock or folk) or DJs most nights along with a rotating selection of terrific beers. A substantial food menu includes good burgers and pub favorites. ⊠ *1607 Paseo de Peralta, Suite 10, Railyard District* ☎ *505/989-3278* ⊕ *www.secondstreetbrewery.com.*

 Performing Arts

★ Jean Cocteau Cinema

FILM | Author and Santa Fe resident George R. R. Martin, of *Game of Thrones* fame, restored this intimate, funky Railyard District art-movie house into a busy neighborhood favorite. The single-screen theater is a great place to catch first-run films, indie flicks, cult classics, and traveling selections from international film festivals. The lobby has a small bar and coffee shop to complete the indie vibe. Next door, Martin also operates Beastly Books which focuses, of course, on science fiction and fantasy. ✉ *418 Montezuma Ave., Railyard District* ☎ *505/466–5528* ⊕ *www. jeancocteaucinema.com.*

Violet Crown Cinema

FILM | FAMILY | This state-of-the-art multiscreen cinema shows everything from blockbusters to indie and vintage movies and offers a restaurant and bar featuring craft brews and ciders, fine wine, and sophisticated food options, which you can eat in the theaters. The food and drink selection is actually so good that many people choose the Violet Crown simply to hang out—you'll frequently see locals meeting in the bar for a weekly game of cards. Reserved seating means never having to settle for a bad row and each screening room has air-conditioning, making it a great hot weather escape. ✉ *1606 Alcaldesa St., Railyard District* ☎ *505/216–5678* ⊕ *santafe.violetcrown.com.*

Shopping

BOOKS

★ The Ark

BOOKS | FAMILY | Santa Fe is well-known for its mystical side and the Ark is where locals go to feed their spiritual souls. Mainly a metaphysical bookstore, the Ark also offers a diverse selection of cards, gemstones, candles, and crystals as well as gifts of all kinds, from Tibetan prayer flags and wind chimes to yoga mats and clothing. ✉ *133 Romero St., Railyard District* ☎ *505/988–3709* ⊕ *www.arkbooks.com.*

★ Beastly Books

BOOKS | FAMILY | Famed Santa Fe resident George R. R. Martin owns this fantasy-and-science-fiction-focused bookstore as well as Jean Cocteau Cinema next-door. Named after Cocteau's 1946 classic *Beauty and the Beast* (which was also a television show the *Game of Thrones* author worked on in the 1980s), the shop features books of all genres, each signed by its writer. This, of course, includes Martin's many offerings, but also books by Diana Gabaldon, Leonard Maltin, Erica Jong, and Walter Jon Williams. ✉ *418 Montezuma Ave., Railyard District* ☎ *505/395–2628* ⊕ *www.beastlybooks.com.*

The weekly Santa Fe Farmers' Market is one of the Railyard District's biggest draws.

CLOTHING AND ACCESSORIES
Double Take
MIXED CLOTHING | This rambling 25,000-square-foot shop ranks among the best consignment stores in the West, carrying elaborately embroidered vintage cowboy shirts, hundreds of pairs of boots, funky old prints, antique Southwestern-style furniture, and amazing vintage Indian pawn and Mexican jewelry. The store comprises several sections that also include contemporary clothing and accessories for men and women and a pottery showroom. ✉ *320 Aztec St., Railyard District* ☎ *505/989–8886* ⊕ *www.santafedoubletake.com.*

FOOD AND DRINK
Modern General Feed & Seed
GENERAL STORE | With a clean, orderly aesthetic that seems right out of the pages of *Kinfolk,* this upscale take on a general store carries gorgeous kitchenware and table linens, from salvaged-olive-wood cutting boards to handwoven dish towels. Fine hardware, garden tools, and books related to kitchen and home are also on offer. It's adjacent to and run by the team at Vinaigrette restaurant, and you can dine here, too—there's a juice bar and a small café proffering delicious breakfast fare, sandwiches, pies, and more. Owner Erin Wade is well-known in the restaurant community for her creative sustainability solutions, such as reusable take-out containers, to-go cups, and composting initiatives. ✉ *637 Cerrillos Rd., Railyard District* ☎ *505/930–5462* ⊕ *www.moderngeneralfeedandseed.com.*

HOME FURNISHINGS
Array
HOUSEWARES | In this cozy Railyard District shop you'll find a well-curated selection of home goods—tableware, candles and folk art from Mexico, tote bags, toys, and even a few antiques. Note the very nice selection of lotions and body-care products made in New Mexico. ⊠ *322 S. Guadalupe St., Railyard District* ☎ *505/699–2760* ⊕ *www.arrayhome.com.*

Casa Nova
HOUSEWARES | A spacious shop that sells functional and decorative art from around the world, Casa Nova deftly mixes colors, textures, and cultural icons—old and new—from stylish pewter tableware from South Africa to vintage hand-carved ex-votos (votive offerings) from Brazil. There is a major emphasis here on goods produced by artists and cooperatives focused on sustainable economic development. ⊠ *530 S. Guadalupe St., Railyard District* ☎ *505/983–8558* ⊕ *www.casanovagallery.com* ۞ *Closed Sun. and Mon.*

JEWELRY
Eidos
JEWELRY & WATCHES | Check out "concept-led" minimalist contemporary jewelry from European designers and Deborah Alexander and Gordon Lawrie, who own the store. The contemporary space has a fascinating array of materials, good range of prices, and helpful staff. ⊠ *508A Camino de la Familia, Railyard District* ☎ *505/992–0020* ⊕ *www.eidosjewelry.com.*

MARKETS
★ Santa Fe Farmers' Market
MARKET | **FAMILY** | Browse through the vast selection of local produce, meat, flowers, honey, wine, jams, and cheese—much of it organic—at the thriving Santa Fe Farmers' Market. Dozens of stalls are arranged inside a snazzy, modern building in the Railyard and adjacent to it; it's open year-round on Saturday morning (7 am to 1 pm in summer, 8 am to 1 pm in winter) and additionally on Tuesday morning May through mid-December. The lively space also hosts an artisan market on Sunday from 10 to 3. It's a great people-watching venue, with entertainment for kids as well as food vendors selling terrific breakfast burritos, green chile bread, Taos Cow ice cream, and other goodies. For those staying on the Southside of town, be sure to check out the satellite Del Sur Market, Tuesday from 3 to 6, July through September, at the Presbyterian Medical Center (⊠ *4801 Buckner Road*). ⊠ *1607 Paseo de Peralta, Railyard District* ☎ *505/983–4098* ⊕ *www.santafefarmersmarket.com.*

GREATER SANTA FE

Updated by
Natalie Bovis

◉ Sights ❶ Restaurants 🛏 Hotels ● Shopping ☻ Nightlife
★★★★☆ ★★★★☆ ★★★☆☆ ★★★☆☆ ★★★☆☆

NEIGHBORHOOD SNAPSHOT

TOP EXPERIENCES

■ **Take a ski and spa day:** In winter, work up a sweat on the slopes of Ski Santa Fe then soak it out at one of the area's luxurious spas such as Ten Thousand Waves or Ojo Santa Fe.

■ **Embrace the mystery and magic of Meow Wolf:** The House of Eternal Return puts your mind to work solving an expansive mystery while inviting you to explore tactile nooks and crannies with surprises at every turn.

■ **Take a hike:** Make the journey up Aspen Vista to experience the city's most incredible mountain views.

■ **Experience open-air opera:** The famous Santa Fe opera performs regularly in a gorgeous indoor-outdoor amphitheater carved into a hillside.

GETTING HERE AND AROUND

The north, west, and south sides of Santa Fe are easily reachable by car. Areas in the north are more rural so parking is rarely an issue. The same goes for the south side as it is highly developed, therefore parking lots abound. The area to the west of town, save for DeVargas Center, can pose a bit more of a parking problem as the historic streets are narrow and most parking is reserved for residents. Your best bet is to park in one of the nearby city parking garages and walk while exploring the area.

PLANNING YOUR TIME

■ If you have a car, exploring Santa Fe's surrounding neighborhoods is worth a full day on your itinerary. Head north to Tesuque and admire the vistas of the famous Santa Fe Opera before winding down at a popular eatery like El Nido. If you time it right, the hills surrounding Santa Fe are prime spots to enjoy one of Santa Fe's spectacular sunsets. Most people will make Meow Wolf the focal point of an excursion out of the city center, and it deserves at least two hours of your time; tickets are good for a whole day and it closes at 8 pm most evenings and 10 pm on Friday and Saturday, so you can fit it in either as your first stop of the day or your last (or even both).

Beyond Santa Fe's commercial core, you'll find a bevy of other notable attractions, restaurants, shops, and inns around the easy-to-access north, west, and south sides of town.

The north claims some of the area's most stunning scenery including the winding drive up to the Santa Fe ski area. Among the area's rolling hills and sagebrush-dotted mesas sits the famed Santa Fe Opera, the distinctive Four Seasons Rancho Encantado, and the remodeled Bishop's Lodge Resort. A trip northeast through the verdant foothills of the Sangre de Christos is the way to go if you're looking for day hikes, beautiful vistas, enchanting spa experiences, or an adrenaline rush down the slopes of Ski Santa Fe.

West of Downtown, the area along Guadalupe Street between Alameda Street and Paseo de Peralta (and the historic blocks just west) nurtures many independent businesses, from hip record stores and cozy inns to breweries and gastropubs. At the intersection of Paseo de Peralta and Guadalupe, you'll find the expansive DeVargas Center shopping mall, which has a few notable shops and eateries, a bustling bowling alley/bar, and some larger grocery and big-box stores that can come in handy if you just need basic supplies (and are still within walking distance of the Plaza).

The majority of Santa Feans live on the Southside, which encompasses a vast stretch of relatively level mesa land. What this somewhat sprawling part of town lacks in scenic beauty—especially along traffic-choked and strip-mall-lined Cerrillos Road (a stretch of the original Route 66)—it makes up for in convenient services, good food, and creative experiences. This is where you're going to find most of the area's midrange and budget chain accommodations and fast-food restaurants, along with an increasing number of genuinely notable eateries, from down-home neighborhood favorites like Horseman's Haven and El Parasol to inspired contemporary spots like Rowley Farmhouse Ales. One sub-neighborhood on the Southside, the Midtown Innovation District, stretches along Siler Road—just off Cerrillos Road—and is anchored by experiential art collective Meow Wolf as well as a growing number of hip breweries, eateries, galleries, and art studios.

Sights

El Rancho de las Golondrinas

MUSEUM VILLAGE | FAMILY | Sometimes dubbed the "Colonial Williamsburg of the Southwest," El Rancho de las Golondrinas ("Ranch of the Swallows") is a reconstruction of a small agricultural village with buildings from the 17th to 19th centuries. Travelers on El Camino Real would stop at the ranch before making the final leg of the journey north, a half-day ride from Santa Fe in horse-and-wagon time. By car, the ranch is only a 25-minute drive from the Plaza. It's also a 10-minute drive from where the Turquoise Trail (NM 14) intersects with Interstate 25, making it a fun stop—especially for kids—on your way to or from Albuquerque. Self-guided tours interpret the lives of locals in those bygone eras while farm animals roam through the barnyards on the 200-acre complex. During the ranch's many festivals—Spring & Fiber Fest, the Herb & Lavender Festival, Viva México, La Panza Llena New Mexico Food Fest, Santa Fe Wine Festival, the Renaissance Faire, and others—music, dance, food, and crafts are offered. In April, May, and October, the museum is open weekdays, by advance reservation only. ✉ *334 Los Pinos Rd., South Side* ☎ *505/471–2261* ⊕ *www. golondrinas.org* 💲 *$6* ⊘ *Closed Nov.–Mar. and Mon. and Tues in Apr.–Oct.*

★ Meow Wolf

OTHER ATTRACTION | FAMILY | Once an ambitious visual and musical arts collective, Meow Wolf is now a dazzling multimillion-dollar arts complex located inside the shell of a former bowling alley (with much of the funding coming from Santa Fe–based *Game of Thrones* author George R. R. Martin). Visitors flock to the arts complex's first permanent exhibition: a self-billed "immersive art installation" *House of Eternal Return,* an interactive phenomenon that has become one of the city's leading attractions. Give yourself at least a couple of hours to tour this sci-fi-inspired, 20,000-square-foot interactive exhibit in which you'll encounter hidden doorways, mysterious corridors, ambient music, and clever, surrealistic, and often slyly humorous artistic renderings. It's a strange and enchanting experience, wildly imaginative, occasionally eerie, and absolutely family-friendly. Tickets are good throughout the day—you can leave and reenter the installation, and perhaps break up the experience by enjoying a light bite and craft beer at the lobby bar/café. Be aware that the experience is highly sensory and can be a little overstimulating for those who are sensitive to noise, changing lighting, and crowds. Meow Wolf is open until 8 most evenings and 10 on Friday and Saturday. It's also a frequent venue for sold-out music concerts.

At El Rancho de las Golondrinas, you'll see what life was like in the area from the 17th to 19th centuries, including the use of traditional kiva stoves.

✉ *1352 Rufina Cir., South Side* ☎ *505/395–6369* ⊕ *www.meow-wolf.com* 🎟 *From $39* ⊘ *Closed days vary; check online ticketing calendar for exact dates.*

★ Santa Fe Opera

PERFORMANCE VENUE | To watch opera in this strikingly modern structure—a 2,128-seat, indoor–outdoor amphitheater with excellent acoustics and sight lines—is a memorable visual and auditory experience. Carved into the natural curves of a hillside 7 miles north of the Plaza, the opera overlooks mountains, mesas, and sky. Add some of the most acclaimed operatic talents from Europe and the United States, and you begin to understand the excitement that builds every summer. This world-renowned company presents five works in repertory each year—a blend of seasoned classics, neglected masterpieces, and world premieres. Many evenings sell out far in advance, but less expensive stand-ing-room tickets are often available on the day of the performance. A favorite pre-opera pastime is tailgating in the parking lot before the evening performance—many guests set up elaborate picnics of their own, but you can also preorder picnic meals at the opera website by calling 24 hours in advance or ordering a take-out meal from one of the many local restaurants that offer opera meals. In the off-season, the opera house hosts shows by contemporary artists. ✉ *301 Opera Dr., North Side* ☎ *505/986–5900, 800/280–4654* ⊕ *www.santafeopera.org* 🎟 *Tours $10, performances from $200* ⊘ *Closed Sept.–May. No tours Sun.*

At Meow Wolf, you can experience the immersive, psychedelic art installation known as *House of Eternal Return*.

🍴 Restaurants

★ Arroyo Vino

$$$$ | MODERN AMERICAN | It's worth making the trek out to Santa Fe's western mesa to dine at this outstanding bistro/wineshop with a following among locals. At the store, stock up on often hard-to-find vintages from all over the world (for a $30 corkage fee, you can enjoy your Bordeaux or Albariño in the airy dining room or, when the weather allows, the charming outdoor patio) and enjoy the menu of contemporary American fare that changes regularly and is based on the incredible variety of seasonal produce grown on Arroyo Vino's on-site farm. **Known for:** garden-fresh seasonal produce; excellent chicken liver pâté; stellar wine shop and selection. $ *Average main: $49* ✉ *218 Camino la Tierra, off NM 599, 4 miles west of U.S. 285/84, West of the Plaza* ☎ *505/983–2100* ⊕ *www.arroyovino.com* ⊘ *Closed Sun. and Mon.*

★ Back Road Pizza

$$$ | PIZZA | FAMILY | Voted Santa Fe's best pizza for over a decade and featured in several national magazines and TV shows, this midtown spot is clearly a local favorite for dine-in or take-out. The unique flour crust is rolled in cornmeal (there's also a gluten-free version), and the meat is sourced from local farms known to treat the cows and pigs humanely and raise cage-free chickens. **Known for:** quality local ingredients; gluten-free options; some of the best pizza in the city. $ *Average main: $28* ✉ *1807 Second St., South*

Side ☎ 505/955–9055 ⊕ www.backroadpizza.com ⊘ Closed Mon.
No lunch Tues.

Chocolate Maven

$ | **BAKERY** | **FAMILY** | Although the name of this cheery bakery
suggests sweets, and it does sweets especially well, Chocolate
Maven also produces impressive savory breakfast and lunch
fare. Meals are "farmers' market–inspired" and feature seasonal dishes, including wild-mushroom-and-goat-cheese focaccia
sandwiches, eggs ménage à trois (one each of eggs Benedict,
Florentine, and Madison—the latter consisting of smoked salmon
and poached egg), and Caprese salad of fresh mozzarella, basil,
and tomatoes. **Known for:** excellent breakfast burritos; delicious
baked goods and desserts; local, seasonal ingredients. ⑤ *Average
main: $16* ⊠ *821 W. San Mateo St., South Side* ☎ *505/984–1980*
⊕ *www.chocolatemaven.com* ⊘ *No dinner.*

Clafoutis

$ | **CAFÉ** | **FAMILY** | Undeniably French, this bustling café serves
authentic, delicious food. Walk through the door of this bright,
open space and you'll almost certainly be greeted with a cheery
"bonjour" from Anne-Laure, who owns it with her husband,
Philippe. **Known for:** bounteous salads and French omelets;
famous clafoutis for dessert; French-style cafe au lait. ⑤ *Average
main: $13* ⊠ *333 W. Cordova Rd., South Side* ☎ *505/988–1809*
⊕ *www.clafoutis.biz* ⊘ *Closed Sun. No dinner.*

Counter Culture

$ | **CAFÉ** | **FAMILY** | This low-key, slightly off-the-beaten-path café is
worth finding for its delicious breakfasts, lunches, and dinners,
or even just for an afternoon coffee break. Inside the industrial
space, tuck into plates of huevos rancheros and other eggy fare
in the morning, and a mix of Southwestern and Asian dishes later
in the day. **Known for:** smothered breakfast burritos; well-prepared
espresso drinks; cash-only policy. ⑤ *Average main: $14* ⊠ *930
Baca St., South Side* ☎ *505/995–1105* ⊕ *www.counterculturesan-
tafe.com* ▭ *No credit cards* ⊘ *No dinner.*

El Nido

$$$$ | **ECLECTIC** | This stylish restaurant located in the heart of
Tesuque village has a rustic American à la carte menu specializing
in items cooked over an open-flame grill as well as a separate
Omakase sushi set menu option. Grilled favorites include cast-iron
tenderloin, Wagyu burgers, and whole grilled branzino. **Known for:**
pre-Santa Fe Opera dinners; wood-fire grilled favorites; omakase
sushi option. ⑤ *Average main: $55* ⊠ *1577 Bishop's Lodge Rd.,
Tesuque* ☎ *505/954–1272* ⊕ *www.elnidosantafe.com* ⊘ *Closed
Mon. No lunch.*

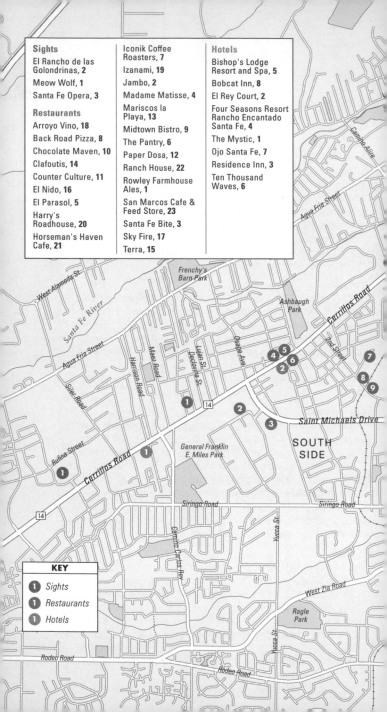

Sights
El Rancho de las Golondrinas, **2**
Meow Wolf, **1**
Santa Fe Opera, **3**

Restaurants
Arroyo Vino, **18**
Back Road Pizza, **8**
Chocolate Maven, **10**
Clafoutis, **14**
Counter Culture, **11**
El Nido, **16**
El Parasol, **5**
Harry's Roadhouse, **20**
Horseman's Haven Cafe, **21**
Iconik Coffee Roasters, **7**
Izanami, **19**
Jambo, **2**
Madame Matisse, **4**
Mariscos la Playa, **13**
Midtown Bistro, **9**
The Pantry, **6**
Paper Dosa, **12**
Ranch House, **22**
Rowley Farmhouse Ales, **1**
San Marcos Cafe & Feed Store, **23**
Santa Fe Bite, **3**
Sky Fire, **17**
Terra, **15**

Hotels
Bishop's Lodge Resort and Spa, **5**
Bobcat Inn, **8**
El Rey Court, **2**
Four Seasons Resort Rancho Encantado Santa Fe, **4**
The Mystic, **1**
Ojo Santa Fe, **7**
Residence Inn, **3**
Ten Thousand Waves, **6**

KEY
1 Sights
1 Restaurants
1 Hotels

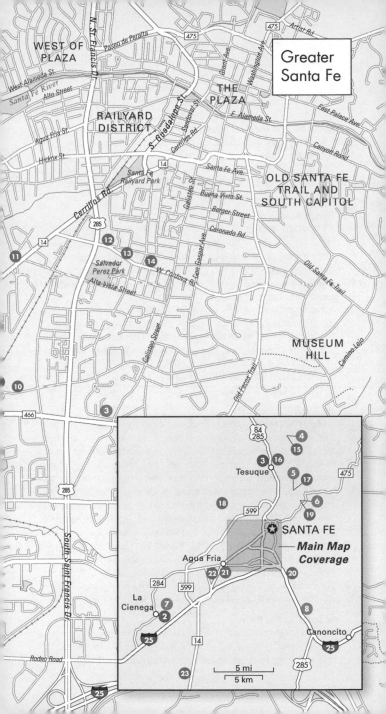

Greater Santa Fe

WEST OF PLAZA

THE PLAZA

RAILYARD DISTRICT

OLD SANTA FE TRAIL AND SOUTH CAPITOL

MUSEUM HILL

N. St. Francis Dr.

Paseo de Peralta

West Alameda St.
Santa Fe River
Alta Street

Agua Fria St.

Hickox St.

S. Guadalupe St.

Sandoval St.

Cerrillos Rd.

Santa Fe Ave.

Galisteo St.

Buena Vista St.

Berger Street

Coronado Rd.

Con Gabriel Ave.

W. Cordova Rd.

Salvador Perez Park

Alta Vista Street

Galisteo Street

Old Pecos Trail

Old Santa Fe Trail

East Palace Ave.

Canyon Rd.

Camino Lejo

Artist Rd.

Grant Ave.

Washington Ave.

E. Alameda St.

Santa Fe Railyard Park

475

14

285

14

11

(10)

(3)

466

285

South Saint Francis Dr.

Rodeo Road

25

12

13

14

Main Map Coverage

84 285

Tesuque

599

Agua Fria

284

599

La Cienega

25

14

23

25

SANTA FE

4

15

3 16

5 17

18

6

19

22 21

20

8

Canoncito

285

25

5 mi
5 km

El Parasol

$ | SOUTHWESTERN | FAMILY | This no-frills, family-owned local chain might not look like much from the outside, but its fast, fresh New Mexican cuisine is a standard favorite among northern New Mexicans. Consistently praised for its superior chile, tacos, carne adovada, and breakfast burritos by locals and national media alike, it's worth a stop for those looking for a true New Mexican food experience. **Known for:** excellent breakfast burritos and tacos; casual, family-friendly atmosphere; quick lunch spot. $ *Average main: $10* ⊠ *1833 Cerrillos Rd., South Side* ☎ *505/995–8015* ⊕ *www.elparasol.com* ⊘ *No dinner Sun.*

Harry's Roadhouse

$ | ECLECTIC | FAMILY | This busy, friendly, art-filled compound 6 miles southeast of Downtown consists of several inviting rooms, from a diner-style space with counter seating to a cozier nook with a fireplace, and an enchanting courtyard out back with juniper trees and flower gardens. The varied menu of contemporary diner favorites, pizzas, New Mexican fare, and bountiful salads is supplemented by a long list of daily specials, which often include delicious international dishes and an array of scrumptious home-made desserts. **Known for:** friendly neighborhood hangout; stellar margaritas; house-made desserts. $ *Average main: $13* ⊠ *96-B Old Las Vegas Hwy., 1 mile east of Old Pecos Trail exit off I–25, South Side* ☎ *505/989–4629* ⊕ *www.harrysroadhousesantafe.com* ⊘ *Closed Mon. and Tues.*

Horseman's Haven Cafe

$ | SOUTHWESTERN | FAMILY | Tucked behind the Giant gas station, this no-frills diner-style restaurant close to the many chain hotels along lower Cerrillos Road has long been a standout for some of the spiciest and tastiest northern New Mexican fare in town, including superb green chile-bacon-cheeseburgers, blue-corn tacos packed with beef or chicken, huevos rancheros, and the hearty *plato sabroso* (a 12-ounce rib steak with rolled enchilada, beans, posole, rice, and hot sopaipilla with honey). Grab one of the comfy red-leatherette corner booths or a stool at the counter, and enjoy the people-watching. **Known for:** blue corn tacos with beef or chicken; green-chile bacon cheeseburgers; hearty New Mexican breakfasts. $ *Average main: $10* ⊠ *4354 Cerrillos Rd., South Side* ☎ *505/471–5420* ⊕ *restaurantwebexperts.com/Horse-mansHaven* ⊘ *Closed Mon. No dinner Sun. and Tues.*

★ Iconik Coffee Roasters

$ | CAFÉ | FAMILY | First and foremost a lively coffeehouse that turns out expertly prepared pour-overs, lattes, cold brews, and other delicious espresso drinks using house-roasted beans, this funky, inviting space also serves tasty and eclectic salads, sandwiches, and tapas. The menu spans the globe, featuring breakfast tacos, Korean steak bowls, Ponzu salmon, and birria quesadillas. **Known for:** pour-over single-origin coffees; horchata lattes; unique crunch burger. $ *Average main: $12* ✉ *1600 Lena St., Suite A2, South Side* ☎ *505/428–0996* ⊕ *www.iconikcoffee.com* ⊗ *No dinner.*

Izanami

$$$ | JAPANESE | Set in the pine-scented foothills northeast of town, the ethereal boutique resort and spa Ten Thousand Waves has always cultivated a tranquil Japanese aesthetic, and its on-site restaurant is no exception. The menu is izakaya-style and features an extensive list of sakes and shareable small plates—two or three per person is typically sufficient; highlights include roasted mushrooms in a rich tamari butter sauce, grilled avocado with nori sea salt and fresh wasabi, and pork belly tacos. **Known for:** omakase chef's choice tasting menu; beautiful forest views; an outstanding selection of first-rate sakes. $ *Average main: $30* ✉ *Ten Thousand Waves, 21 Ten Thousand Waves Way, North Side* ☎ *505/982–9304* ⊕ *www.tenthousandwaves.com/food* ⊗ *No lunch Tues.*

Jambo

$$ | AFRICAN | FAMILY | Ahmed Obo, the Kenyan-born owner who regularly tops the local paper's "best chef" list, applies great skill and enthusiasm to the Afro-Caribbean food at this casual, homey eatery in a shopping center a couple of miles south of the Plaza. Flavors of coconut, peanuts, and curry influence everything from shrimp to goat stew. **Known for:** Caribbean goat stew; East African coconut lentil stew; African music and art. $ *Average main: $19* ✉ *2010 Cerrillos Rd., South Side* ☎ *505/473–1269* ⊕ *www.jambo-cafe.net* ⊗ *Closed Sun.*

Madame Matisse

$ | FRENCH | FAMILY | This bright, modern bakery and café is tucked away just off the hustle and bustle of busy Cerrillos Road. The interior is crisp and clean with Matisse-inspired pops of color, and the food is French-inspired casual fare that includes crepes, salads, and sandwiches. **Known for:** delicious baked goods; casual French cuisine; tasty omelets. $ *Average main: $13* ✉ *1291 San Felipe Ave., South Side* ☎ *505/772–0949* ⊕ *www.madamematisse.com* ⊗ *Closed Sun. and Mon. No dinner.*

Mariscos la Playa

$$ | MEXICAN | FAMILY | Yes, even in landlocked Santa Fe it's possible to find incredibly fresh and well-prepared seafood served in big portions. This cheery, colorful Mexican restaurant surrounded by strip malls is just a short hop south of Downtown, and favorite dishes include the absolutely delicious shrimp wrapped in bacon

with Mexican cheese and *caldo vuelve a la vida* ("come back to life"), a hearty soup of shrimp, octopus, scallops, clams, crab, and calamari. **Known for:** delightfully friendly staff; ceviche tostadas; trout grilled with butter and paprika. $ *Average main: $17* ⊠ *537 W. Cordova Rd., South Side* ☎ *505/982–2790* ⊕ *www.facebook. com/mariscoslaplayanm.*

Midtown Bistro

$$ | **MODERN AMERICAN** | A couple of miles south of Downtown in a spacious adobe building with pitched ceilings and a charming patio, Midtown Bistro offers modern American cuisine, such as pork chops with truffle oil, crab cakes with lemon aioli, or vegan quinoa and black bean pilaf. It's a spot that delights visitors wishing to avoid the downtown Plaza crowds in high season. **Known for:** grilled rib eye steak with blue corn enchiladas; leafy patio in summer months; casual lunches. $ *Average main: $24* ⊠ *901 W. San Mateo St., South Side* ☎ *505/820–3121* ⊙ *Closed Sun. No lunch Sat.*

The Pantry

$ | **DINER** | **FAMILY** | Since 1948, this beloved, family-owned greasy spoon has been pleasing locals and visitors with consistently tasty, New Mexican–style diner fare. Popular choices here include buckwheat pancakes, *huevos consuelo* (a corn tortilla topped with two eggs, spicy chile, and cheese, with the Pantry's famous home fries), green-chile stew, tortilla burgers, and chicken-fried steak. **Known for:** excellent huevos consuelo; good value prices; down-home atmosphere. $ *Average main: $14* ⊠ *1820 Cerrillos Rd., South Side* ☎ *505/986–0022* ⊕ *www.pantrysantafe.com.*

★ Paper Dosa

$$ | **MODERN INDIAN** | **FAMILY** | Begun as a catering business that threw occasional pop-up dinners, Paper Dosa became so beloved for its boldly flavored southern Indian cuisine that the owners opened what has become a popular brick-and-mortar restaurant. Dosas (large, thin crepes made with fermented rice and lentils and stuffed with different fillings) are the specialty here and come in about 10 varieties, from paneer and peas to a locally inspired version with green chile and three cheeses. **Known for:** dosas with interesting fillings; variety of chutneys and curries; a thoughtful, diverse wine list. $ *Average main: $19* ⊠ *551 W. Cordova Rd., South Side* ☎ *505/930–5521* ⊕ *www.paper-dosa.com* ⊙ *Closed Mon. No lunch.*

Ranch House

$$ | **BARBECUE** | **FAMILY** | Given New Mexico's deep ties to its easterly neighbor, the Lone Star State, it's hardly surprising that the region has some top-notch barbecue joints, including this spacious, contemporary adobe building with two large patios. It turns out superb, fall-off-the-bone barbecue brisket, baby-back ribs, pulled pork, and smoked half-chicken. **Known for:** barbecue brisket; steaks and fish tacos; daily happy hour from 4 to 6. $ *Average main: $18* ⊠ *2571 Cristo's Rd., South Side* ☎ *505/424–8900* ⊕ *www.theranchhousesantafe.com.*

Rowley Farmhouse Ales

$$ | **AMERICAN** | **FAMILY** | Tiny Rowley Farmhouse Ales has won several awards at the Great American Beer Festival, including three medals for its sour-style ales, so if you like beer (any kind of beer) a stop at Rowley is a must. In addition to offering its own brews, Rowley also has an extensive list of local and imported beers and ciders that it finds inspiring, along with comfort foods like shrimp po'boys, cast-iron skillet green chile mac 'n' cheese, and chicken and waffles. **Known for:** award-winning small-batch sour ales; creative pub food; extensive international beer list. $ *Average main: $18* ⊠ *1405 Maclovia St., South Side* ☎ *505/428–0719* ⊕ *www. rowleyfarmhouse.com.*

San Marcos Cafe & Feed Store

$ | **CAFÉ** | **FAMILY** | In Lone Butte, about 20 miles south of Downtown Santa Fe along the northern end of the scenic Turquoise Trail, this funky spot is known for its creative fare and nontraditional setting: an actual feed store selling propane, hardware, tools, and farm animal feed, with roosters, turkeys, and peacocks running about outside. In one of the two bric-a-brac–filled dining rooms, sample rich cinnamon rolls and such delectables as burritos stuffed with roast beef and potatoes and topped with green chile. **Known for:** the Feed Store burrito (with hash browns, bacon, cheese, chile, and egg); offbeat farmyard setting; long waits on weekend mornings. $ *Average main: $11* ⊠ *3877 NM 14, South Side* ☎ *505/471–9298* ☉ *Closed Sun. No dinner.*

Santa Fe Bite

$ | **BURGER** | **FAMILY** | This descendant of the legendary Bobcat Bite burger joint is now an employee-owned spot where guests come for the juicy green-chile cheeseburgers and humongous 15-ounce "Big Bite" burgers—along with hefty steaks, enchiladas, and tacos—in a kitsch-filled strip mall space south of town. There's breakfast, too; morning highlights include huevos rancheros, gluten-free buttermilk waffles, and traditional steak-and-eggs. **Known for:** green-chile cheeseburgers; hearty breakfast fare; malted milkshakes. $ *Average main: $16* ⊠ *1616 St. Michaels Dr., South Side* ☎ *505/428–0328* ⊕ *www.santafebite.com* ☉ *Closed Sun. and Mon.*

SkyFire

$$$$ | **SOUTHWESTERN** | Aptly named after the brilliant and colorful sunsets enjoyed from its outdoor patio, SkyFire, part of Bishop's Lodge Resort, is both elegant and comfortable. The menu melds Mexican and Southwestern fare with lighter offerings such as Hamachi ceviche, Wapiti tamal, and duck enchiladas as well as heftier options like elk short ribs, whole fried fish, and a 31-ounce bison tomahawk steak. **Known for:** unique pan de elote for dessert, served with horchata ice cream; gorgeous views; many ingredients sourced from local purveyors. $ *Average main: $58* ⌂ *Bishop's Lodge Resort, 1297 Bishops Lodge Rd., Tesuque* ☎ *505/390–7682* ⊕ *www.aubergeresorts.com/bishopslodge.*

★ Terra

$$$$ | **MODERN AMERICAN** | Among the many reasons guests of the Four Seasons Rancho Encantado often find it difficult to ever leave the gloriously situated property is this handsome yet down-to-earth restaurant that serves tantalizingly delicious and creative contemporary American and Southwestern cuisine. Favorites include seafood paella, green chile and bison meatballs, and an Australian Wagyu rib eye. **Known for:** creatively prepared seafood; romantic atmosphere; stunning mountain views. $ *Average main: $48* ⌂ *Four Seasons Rancho Encantado, 198 NM 592, North Side* ☎ *505/946–5700* ⊕ *www.fourseasons.com/santafe.*

Hotels

★ Bishop's Lodge Resort and Spa

$$$$ | **RESORT** | **FAMILY** | Although this historic resort is just a 10-minute drive from the Plaza, its setting in a bucolic valley at the foot of the Sangre de Cristo Mountains makes it feel worlds apart. **Pros:** staff is friendly and well-trained; stunning bucolic setting; luxurious amenities. **Cons:** resort is spread out over 700 acres and some rooms seem rather far-flung; hefty resort fee; recent renovations may cause hiccups with availability of some amenities (such as trail rides). $ *Rooms from: $899* ⌂ *1297 Bishop's Lodge Rd., 2½ miles north of Downtown, North Side* ☎ *505/819–0095* ⊕ *www.aubergeresorts.com/bishopslodge* ⇌ *110 bedrooms* �☐ *No Meals.*

Bobcat Inn

$$ | **B&B/INN** | A delightful, affordable, country hacienda that's a 15-minute drive southeast of the Plaza, this adobe bed-and-breakfast sits amid 10 secluded acres of piñon and ponderosa pine, with grand views of the Ortiz Mountains and the area's high-desert mesas. **Pros:** gracious inn and secluded location; wonderful hosts; spectacular views. **Cons:** located outside of town; small bathrooms in some rooms; breakfast not served until 8:30 am. ⑤ *Rooms from: $165* ✉ *442 Old Las Vegas Hwy., South Side* ☎ *505/988–9239* ⊕ *www.bobcatinn.com* ⮐ *8 rooms* ❍❘ *Free Breakfast.*

El Rey Court

$$ | **HOTEL** | Once a run-down motor court dating to 1936, El Rey Court was redesigned and now attracts design aficionados and Instagram influencers with its hip take on modern, 1950s-inspired Southwest decor. **Pros:** Instagrammable modern Southwestern design; fun on-site bar; friendly and laid-back vibe. **Cons:** some noise from the bar; rates vary widely; no restaurant on-site. ⑤ *Rooms from: $200* ✉ *1862 Cerrillos Rd., South Side* ☎ *505/982–1931* ⊕ *www.elreycourt.com* ⮐ *86 rooms* ❍❘ *No Meals.*

★ Four Seasons Resort Rancho Encantado Santa Fe

$$$$ | **RESORT** | This secluded and stunning luxury compound on a dramatic, sunset-facing bluff in the Sangre de Cristo foothills exemplifies the Four Seasons brand's famously flawless sense of gracious hospitality and efficiency. **Pros:** freestanding couples spa suites; complimentary minibar (nonalcoholic beverages only); stunning rooms and views. **Cons:** several of the private terraces overlook parking lots; remote location; large property requires walking but on-site transport is readily available. ⑤ *Rooms from: $900* ✉ *198 NM 592, North Side* ☎ *505/946–5700, 855/674–5401* ⊕ *www.fourseasons.com/santafe* ⮐ *65 rooms* ❍❘ *No Meals.*

The Mystic

$$ | **MOTEL** | **FAMILY** | Once an old motel on the original Route 66 in need of a major facelift, the Mystic is now a hip hang-out with a funky Joshua Tree vibe that is heavy on the pastel colors and folky artwork. **Pros:** very affordable; decent bar on-site; interesting art and murals throughout the property. **Cons:** Cerrillos Road can be a bit noisy; not many restaurants or sights within walking distance; aesthetic is more Marfa than Santa Fe. ⑤ *Rooms from: $150* ✉ *2810 Cerrillos Rd., South Side* ☎ *505/471–7663* ⊕ *www. themysticsantafe.com* ⮐ *23 rooms* ❍❘ *No Meals.*

★ Ojo Santa Fe

$$$ | **RESORT** | This tranquil 70-acre resort offers 32 rooms overlooking verdant gardens and 20 casitas with gas fireplaces and secluded patios, plus a first-rate spa focused on energy healing and integrative medicine, a variety of open-air soaking tubs, a large outdoor pool, yoga and fitness studios, a sweat lodge, and an outstanding restaurant—Blue Heron—serving healthy, locally sourced contemporary fare. **Pros:** great restaurant using organic vegetables and herbs grown on-site; soothing cottonwood-shaded soaking tubs; superb spa with an extensive list of treatments (including playing with puppies!). **Cons:** 20-minute drive away from downtown; located in very rural setting; property size requires a lot of walking. ⑤ *Rooms from: $350* ⊠ *242 Los Pinos Rd., South Side* ☎ *877/977–8212* ⊕ *ojosantafe.ojospa.com* ⤳ *52 rooms* ⚭ *No Meals.*

Residence Inn Santa Fe
$$ | HOTEL | This compound consists of clusters of three-story town houses with pitched roofs and tall chimneys. **Pros:** complimentary full breakfast; evening socials; grocery-shopping service. **Cons:** not many restaurants or attractions within easy walking distance; near hospital so there can be siren noise; very busy business area. ⑤ *Rooms from: $179* ⊠ *1698 Galisteo St., South Side* ☎ *505/988–7300, 800/331–3131* ⊕ *www.marriott.com/safnm* ⤳ *120 suites* ⚭ *Free Breakfast.*

★ Ten Thousand Waves
$$$ | RESORT | Devotees appreciate the authentic *onsen* (Japanese-style baths) atmosphere of this award-winning 20-acre Japanese-inspired spa and boutique resort in the picturesque foothills a few miles northeast of town. **Pros:** sleek, stylish decor; outstanding restaurant; a soothing, spiritual vibe. **Cons:** a bit remote; spa and communal baths can get crowded with day visitors; some areas can be difficult to access. ⑤ *Rooms from: $400* ⊠ *3451 Hyde Park Rd., 4 miles northeast of the Plaza, North Side* ☎ *505/982–9304* ⊕ *www.tenthousandwaves.com* ⤳ *14 cottages* ⚭ *Free Breakfast.*

Nightlife

The Alley
GATHERING PLACES | FAMILY | This hybrid family fun center/date night/ sports bar/bowling alley in DeVargas Center truly has something for everyone. Both food and bar service are available throughout the facility, whether you're knocking down pins on the 12-lane bowling alley, cracking some bocce balls on one of two indoor courts, or chalking up your cue stick at one of the various pool tables. A couple of shuffleboard tables and some arcade games round out the experience. It's a great option for families taking a break from sightseeing or a little indoor fun on a rainy day, but it's also a lot of fun at night when things really get hopping. ⊠ *DeVargas Center, 153 Paseo de Peralta, Santa Fe* ☎ *505/557–6789* ⊕ *www.thealleysantafe.com.*

★ HoneyMoon Brewery
BARS | FAMILY | The Southwest's first producer of artisanal alcoholic kombucha is impressive not just for the quality of its fermented

brews, but also for its upstart business plan, garnering seed capital from both Los Alamos National Laboratory's Venture Acceleration Fund and Miller Lite's "Tap the Future" Business Plan Competition. The laid-back tasting room, located in a convenient shopping center, welcomes visitors to bring their own food from neighboring restaurants or the co-op grocery store and is both family-friendly and good for a date night. If you haven't tried "hard" kombucha, this is your chance. Kombuchas are available in tasting flights, as well as by glass or to-go. For those with differing tastes, beer and wine are also available. Live music and a chill atmosphere make this a great spot to try something new and relax with a creative group of locals. ⊠ *Solana Shopping Center, 907 W. Alameda St., Suite B, South Side* ☎ *505/303–3139* ⊕ *www.honeymoonbrewery.com.*

Santa Fe Brewing Company

BARS | FAMILY | A bit off the beaten path, about a 20-minute drive south of the Plaza right where the Turquoise Trail intersects with Interstate 25, the state's oldest brewery serves fine ales at its two-story flagship location, the Beer Hall at HQ. Food is sometimes available via an outdoor shipping container kitchen. Across the parking lot, the outdoor music venue, the Bridge, hosts live bands. Santa Fe Brewing Company also has a small downtown tasting room called the Brakeroom tucked into a historic building on Galisteo Street. ⊠ *35 Fire Pl., off NM 14, South Side* ☎ *505/424–3333* ⊕ *www.santafebrewing.com.*

Second Street Brewery Rufina Taproom

BARS | FAMILY | The lively taproom of local favorite Second Street Brewery is located in a 20,000-square-foot building that houses a production brewery and canning line. Popular for its live music line-up, it offers an extensive pub food menu (including everything from tater tots to ramen), and has a large, dog-friendly deck. Located near Meow Wolf and other arts-focused start-ups and nonprofits, it's one of the best places to rub elbows with Santa Fe's hippest locals. ⊠ *2920 Rufina St., Santa Fe* ☎ *505/954–1068* ⊕ *www.secondstreetbrewery.com.*

Tumbleroot Brewery and Distillery

BARS | FAMILY | Within this large industrial building in a quiet neighborhood south of town, you'll find a lively gathering place that hosts regular live music acts, DJs, and more. Families can take advantage of the large outdoor area for kids to play and there is plenty of space for large groups inside the building. Also inside you'll find some of the region's best scratch-made beers and spirits, from Juicy IPA and Honey Hibiscus Wheat to gin and whiskey crafted with local ingredients. Pub fare is available from the on-site kitchen as well as several food trucks that rotate regularly. On busy weekends, it can get pretty crowded and the line for a drink can have you waiting a while so arrive early to enjoy a cocktail before the place starts jumping. ⊠ *2791 Agua Fria St., South Side* ☎ *505/780–5730* ⊕ *www.tumblerootbreweryand-distillery.com.*

Shopping

BOOKS

★ photo-eye Bookstore and Gallery

BOOKS | The place to go for an almost unbelievable collection of new, rare, and out-of-print photography books; the staff is made up of photographers who are excellent sources of information and advice on great spots to shoot in and around Santa Fe. The store has an impressive gallery in the Railyard District (⊠ *541 S. Guadalupe St.*) that presents fine photography. ⊠ *1300 Rufina Circle, Suite A3, South Side* ☎ *505/988–5152* ⊕ *www.photoeye.com.*

FOOD AND DRINK

Barrio Brinery

FOOD | Along tree-lined Alameda Street, away from the Plaza about a mile or so, you will find locally owned Barrio Brinery. This fermentation fantasy shop is known for its salt-brined pickles, sauerkraut, and escabeche. They're perfect if you're packing for a picnic or looking for a unique souvenir to take back home. You'll also notice their products mentioned by name on some of Santa Fe's finest restaurant menus. ⊠ *1413-B W. Alameda St., West of the Plaza* ☎ *505/699–9812* ⊕ *www.barriobrinery.com.*

Las Cosas Kitchen Shoppe & Cooking School

HOUSEWARES | FAMILY | In DeVargas shopping center, Las Cosas Kitchen Shoppe stocks a fantastic selection of cookery, tableware, and kitchen gadgetry and gifts. The shop is also renowned for its cooking classes taught by local personality chef Johnny Vee, which touch on everything from high-altitude baking and northern New Mexican specialties to gnocchi workshops and Vietnamese street food. For those looking to really up their culinary game, Johnny Vee also offers regular classes on techniques such as braising, grilling, and fundamentals including knife skills and pressure cooking. Classes are Tuesday and Friday night, as well as Saturday morning. If you've got a tight schedule or a big group, Las Cosas and chef Johnny are happy to schedule something just for you. ⊠ *De Vargas Center, 181 Paseo de Peralta, at N. Guadalupe St., West of the Plaza* ☎ *505/988–3394* ⊕ *www.lascosas-cooking.com.*

While New Mexico is often thought of as a desert locale, there are still some stunning ski slopes, including the ones at Ski Santa Fe.

GIFTS AND HOME FURNISHINGS
★ Jackalope

HOUSEWARES | FAMILY | You could easily spend a couple of hours wandering through this legendary indoor–outdoor bazaar, which sprawls over 7 acres, incorporating pottery barns, a furniture store, endless aisles of knickknacks from Latin America and Asia, and a glassblowing studio. There's also an area where crafts-people, artisans, and others sell their wares—sort of a mini–flea market feel (but with retail prices). ✉ *2820 Cerrillos Rd., South Side* ☎ *505/471–8539* ⊕ *www.jackalope.com.*

Activities

HIKING
★ Aspen Vista

HIKING & WALKING | FAMILY | When autumn's golden aspens shimmer on the mountainside, this trail up near Santa Fe's ski area makes for a memorable hike. After walking a few miles through thick aspen groves, panoramic views open above Santa Fe. The path, which is well marked and gradually inclines toward Tesuque Peak, becomes steeper with elevation—also note that snow has been reported on the upper portions of the trail as late as May. In winter, after heavy snows, the trail is great for intermediate-advanced cross-country skiing. The full hike to the peak makes for a long, rigorous day—it's 12 miles round-trip and sees an elevation gain of 2,000 feet, but it's just 3½ miles to the spectacular overlook. Note that the Aspen Vista Picnic Site is also the trailhead for the Alamo Vista Trail, which leads to the summit of the ski area. Dogs are welcome on the trail as long as they are leashed. ⊠ *Hyde Park Rd. (NM 475), 2 miles before ski area, North Side* ⊹ *Parking lot at Aspen Vista Picnic Site.*

HORSEBACK RIDING

New Mexico's rugged countryside has been the setting for many Hollywood Westerns. Whether you want to ride the range that Gregory Peck and Kevin Costner tamed or just head out feeling tall in the saddle, you can do so year-round.

SKIING

Ski Santa Fe

SKIING & SNOWBOARDING | FAMILY | Open roughly from late November through early April, this midsize ski and snowboard operation receives an average of 225 inches of snow a year and plenty of sunshine. It's one of America's highest ski areas—the 12,075-foot summit has unbelievable views and a varied terrain which make its 1,725 feet of vertical rise and 660 acres seem even bigger. There are some great powder stashes, tough bump runs, and many wide, gentle cruising runs. The 87 trails are ranked 20% beginner, 40% intermediate, and 40% advanced; there are seven lifts: one quad, two triples, two doubles, and two surface lifts. Chipmunk Corner provides day care and supervised kids' skiing. The ski school is excellent. Rentals, a ski shop, and a good restaurant round out the amenities at bright and modern La Casa Lodge base-camp, and Totemoff's Bar and Grill is a welcome mid-mountain option with frequent live music during the season. While Ski Santa Fe doesn't offer cross-country skiing, there are many Nordic trails available off of Hyde Park Road just before the downhill ski area. Ski Santa Fe is also fun for hiking during the summer months and the Super Chief Quad Chair operates from late August through mid-October, catering to hikers and shutterbugs eager to view the high-mountain fall foliage, including acres of shimmering golden aspens. ⊠ *End of NM 475, 18 miles northeast of Downtown, North Side* ☎ *505/982–4429 general info, 505/983–9155 snow report* ⊕ *www.skisantafe.com.*

SIDE TRIPS FROM SANTA FE

Updated by
Andrew Collins

⊙ Sights   🍴 Restaurants   🛏 Hotels   ⬤ Shopping   🍸 Nightlife

★★★★★   ★★★☆☆   ★★★☆☆   ★★★☆☆   ★★★☆☆

WELCOME TO SIDE TRIPS FROM SANTA FE

1 Madrid. The most vibrant community on the Turquoise Trail.

2 Sandia Park. A scenic base for exploring the Sandia Mountains.

3 Kasha-Katuwe Tent Rocks National Monument. A national monument where you can wander amid tent-shaped hoodoos.

4 Pecos. A village home to Pecos National Historical Park.

5 Las Vegas. A well-preserved town that's a great place to learn about the Old Santa Fe Trail.

6 Bandelier National Monument. Home to the ancient cliff dwellings of Frijoles Canyon.

7 Los Alamos. A town filled the historic sights where the atomic bomb was developed.

8 Valles Caldera National Preserve. One of the world's largest calderas.

9 Abiquiú. Where the home and studio of Georgia O'Keeffe can be toured.

10 Ghost Ranch. A former dude and cattle ranch once home to Georgia O'Keeffe.

11 Pojoaque and Nambé Pueblos. The closest High Road villages to Santa Fe.

12 Chimayó. A village famed for its art studios.

13 Truchas. Arguably the most beautiful village on the High Road to Taos.

14 Peñasco. A friendly, scenic village.

15 Dixon. A low-key hub of art and winemaking.

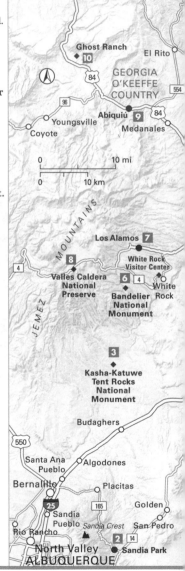

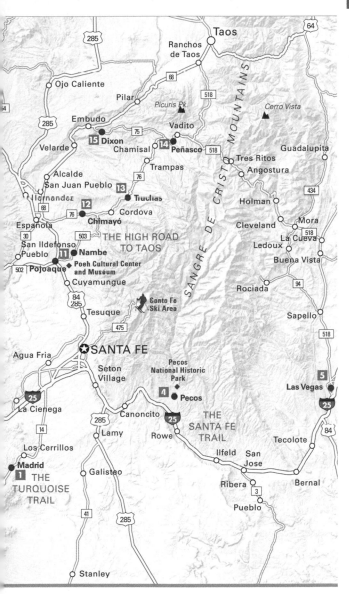

Santa Fe makes a great base for exploring the entire north-central Rio Grande Valley, a region rich in Spanish-colonial and Native American heritage and abounding with scenic drives, dazzling geographical formations, colorful villages, and important historic sites. Every community and attraction covered here could be visited as a full-day road trip, following state and local roads and passing verdant scenery, rushing rivers, and expansive blue skies that nourish the soul.

But each of these regions also have least one or two distinctive lodgings (not to mention plenty of Airbnbs), so to gain a fuller sense of each place—or for the chance to enjoy some time away from the bustle and sometimes steep hotel rates of Santa Fe—consider spending a night or two in any of these inviting destinations.

The entire valley is rich with history. Tucked in the pockets of New Mexico's mountains and high desert plateaus, you'll discover the 1717 mission church ruins in Pecos National Historical Park; the ancestral Pueblo petroglyphs and dwellings at Bandelier National Monument; the dazzling artistry of Georgia O'Keeffe; and the world-changing history of the atomic bomb at Manhattan Project National Historical Park in Los Alamos.

Keep in mind that in this high-elevation region, winters are snowy and summer days are hot. Before hitting the road, stock up on water and snacks as gas stations and convenience stores are few and far between. It's also practical to embark on some of these trips en route to Albuquerque or Taos. For example, you could drive the Turquoise Trail or visit Kasha-Katuwe Tent Rocks on the way to Albuquerque. The side trips to points north—such as the High Road, Bandelier and Los Alamos, and Abiquiú and Georgia O'Keeffe Country—are worth investigating on your way to Taos.

Top Reasons to Go

Hiking stunning landscapes: From the sandstone rock formations of Kasha-Katuwe Tent Rocks National Monument to one of the world's largest calderas in Valles Caldera National Preserve, this area is filled with opportunities for gorgeous hikes.

Georgia O'Keeffe's homestead: Perhaps the most famous artist of the American Southwest, Georgia O'Keeffe spent the final decades of her life at her house in Abiquiú, painting the scenery seen from her cabin in nearby Ghost Ranch.

Native American culture and history: Pecos National Historical Park is filled with the fascinating ruins of a Pueblo village while Bandelier National Monument holds the remnants of a community of Ancestoral Puebloan peoples.

Scenic road trips: Take your time driving down famed road trip routes like the Turquoise Trail and the High Road to Taos, appreciating the beautiful scenery and interesting small towns along the way.

The Turquoise Trail

The most engaging side trip south of Santa Fe is along the fabled Turquoise Trail, an excellent—and leisurely—alternative route to Albuquerque that's far more interesting than Interstate 25. Officially created in the early 1970s by connecting parts of much older roads, the scenic Turquoise Trail (or more prosaically, NM 14) is a National Scenic Byway that's dotted with ghost towns now popular with writers, artists, and other urban refugees. This 70 miles of piñon-studded mountain back road along the eastern flank of the sacred Sandia Mountains is a gentle roller coaster that also affords panoramic views of the Ortiz, Jémez, and Sangre de Cristo mountains. It's believed that 2,000 years ago Native Americans mined turquoise in these hills. The Spanish took up turquoise mining in the 16th century, and the practice continued into the early 20th century, with Tiffany & Co. removing a fair share of the semiprecious stone. Today, turquoise is the official state gem of New Mexico, and its allure to the region has remained. In addition, gold, silver, tin, lead, and coal have been mined in the area.

The town of Madrid along the Turquoise Trail has lots of shops selling local goods.

Madrid

27 miles south of Santa Fe.

Abandoned when its coal mine closed in the 1950s, Madrid (locals put the emphasis on the first syllable: *mah*-drid) has gradually been rebuilt and is now—to the dismay of some longtimers— actually a bit trendy. The entire town was offered for sale for $250,000 back in the 1950s, but there were no takers. Finally, in the early 1970s, a few artists fleeing big cities settled in and began restoration. Weathered houses and old company stores have been repaired and turned into boutiques and galleries, some of them selling high-quality furniture, paintings, and crafts. Big events here include the CrawDaddy Blues Fest in mid-May, the Turquoise Trail Studio Tour over two weekends in late September and early October, and Madrid Christmas Open House, held weekends in December, when galleries and studios are open and the famous Madrid Christmas lights twinkle brightly.

Sights

Cerrillos Hills State Park
STATE/PROVINCIAL PARK | Established as a state park in 2009, this patch of undulating hills dotted with piñon and juniper contains 5 miles of hiking trails, some of them leading to historic mines, as well as interpretative signs related to the 1,100 years of mining

history along the Turquoise Trail. The park itself is just north of the historic village center of Cerrillos, where you'll find a small visitor center (✉ *37 Main Street*) that's typically open weekends or by appointment and contains further exhibits and information on the park. ✉ *CR 59, ½ mile north of Downtown (follow signs), Cerrillos* ☎ *505/474–0196* ⊕ *www.emnrd.state.nm.us/spd/cerrilloshillsstatepark.html* 🎫 *$5 per vehicle.*

Old Coal Town Museum

HISTORY MUSEUM | FAMILY | Part of the rambling 1890s complex that houses the beloved Mine Shaft Tavern, this fascinating trove of local history recounts Madrid's legacy as a booming mining town and then a ghost town. Memorabilia from the mine operations, old photos, and the historic Engine 769 make this a fun diversion, especially with kids. ✉ *2846 NM 14, Madrid* ☎ *505/473–0743* ⊕ *www.themineshafttavern.com/madrid-old-coal-town-museum* 🎫 *$5.*

🍴 Restaurants

★ Black Bird Saloon

$ | MODERN AMERICAN | Sure, it looks like a dusty old cowboy bar and it is set right in the heart of a village that's appeared in several Western movies, but the extensive menu of creative breakfast plates, sandwiches, and grills reveals a locavore-minded approach to food that you might not expect from the setting. You might start the day with the Saloon Scramble, a hefty plate of feathery eggs served with green onions, venison-blueberry sausage, and jalapeño hot sauce; or later in the day, consider the thinly roasted lamb with vegetables, Manchego cheese, and a refreshing yogurt sauce atop naan flatbread. **Known for:** funky Old West vibe; several dishes featuring elk, venison, rabbit, and other wild game; menu of New Mexico spirits and beers. ⑤ *Average main: $16* ✉ *28 Main St., Cerrillos* ☎ *505/438–1821* ⊕ *www.blackbirdsaloon.com* ⊘ *Closed Mon.–Wed. No dinner Sun.*

★ Mineshaft Tavern

$ | AMERICAN | A rollicking old bar and restaurant adjacent to the Old Coal Mine Museum, this boisterous place—there's live music many nights—was a miners' commissary back in the day. Today it serves impressive burgers (available with Angus beef, Wagyu beef, buffalo, or mushroom-veggie), along pizzas, tacos, and other comfort fare. **Known for:** the Mad Chile Burger topped with aged cheddar and chopped green chiles; lively dining room filled with vintage Western murals; Mexican fare in the neighboring Mine Shaft Cantina. ⑤ *Average main: $16* ✉ *2846 NM 14, Madrid* ☎ *505/473–0743* ⊕ *www.themineshafttavern.com.*

Coffee and Quick Bites

Java Junction

$ | CAFÉ | Seasoned hippies, youthful hipsters, and everyone in between congregate at Java Junction for lattes, chai, sandwiches, breakfast burritos, bagels, pastries, and other treats. You can also pick up a number of house-made gourmet goods, from hot sauces to jalapeño-raspberry preserves. **Known for:** eventful people-watching; short walk from many galleries; first-rate coffee drinks. *$ Average main: $7 ⊠ 2855 NM 14, Madrid ☎ 505/438–2772 ⊕ www.java-junction.com ☾ No dinner.*

Shopping

Johnsons of Madrid

ART GALLERIES | Among the most prestigious galleries in a town with quite a few good ones, Johnsons carries paintings, photography, sculpture, and textiles created by some of the region's leading artists. *⊠ 2843 NM 14, Madrid ☎ 505/471–1054 ⊕ www.johnsonsofmadrid.wordpress.com.*

★ Seppanen & Daughters Fine Textiles

HOUSEWARES | You could spend hours browsing the fine rugs and furnishings at this well-established shop. They stock custom Zapotec textiles from Oaxaca, Navajo weavings, Congolese kuba cloths, and carpets from Tibet, Morocco, and Afghanistan as well as fine arts and crafts tables, sofas, and chairs from around the world. *⊠ 2879 NM 14, Madrid ☎ 505/982–1662 ⊕ www.finetextiles.com.*

Shugarman's Little Shop

CANDY | In a region known for artisanal sweets, this cozy candy shop set amid Madrid's string of galleries has earned a cult following for its imaginative edible works of art. Some of the more unusual creations include dark chocolate studded with hibiscus flowers, lemon, and ginger, and creamy white chocolate with lavender sugar and flecks of actual lavender. *⊠ 2842 NM 14, Madrid ☎ 505/474–9041 ⊕ www.shugarmanschocolate.com.*

Activities

★ Broken Saddle Riding Co.

HORSEBACK RIDING | Rides with this popular, well-established outfitter take you around the old turquoise and silver mines for which Cerrillos—just a few miles from Madrid—is famous. On a Tennessee Walker or a Missouri Fox Trotter, rides of all experience levels can explore the majestic Cerrillos hills and canyons, taking in spectacular views of the mountains between Albuquerque and Santa Fe. This is not the usual nose-to-tail trail ride. ✉ *26 Vicksville Rd., Cerrillos* ☎ *505/424–7774* ⊕ *www.brokensaddle.com* 💲 *From $70.*

Sandia Park

24 miles southwest of Madrid, 22 miles northeast of Albuquerque.

The southern stretch of the Turquoise Trail, as you continue from Golden and pass the upscale housing developments around PaaKo Ridge Golf Club, is more developed than the northern section—the scenic towns of Sandia Park (population 260) and Cedar Crest (population 940) are really part of metro Albuquerque. But the route is still stunning as it meanders along the eastern flanks of the Sandia Mountains, past a handful of good places to stop for a bite to eat, before intersecting with Interstate 40, which leads east 10 miles into Albuquerque.

 Sights

Sandia Crest

VIEWPOINT | For awesome views of Albuquerque and half of New Mexico, take NM 536 up the back side of the Sandia Mountains through Cibola National Forest to Sandia Crest. At the 10,378-foot summit, explore the dramatic but relatively level and easy trails along the rim. Always bring an extra layer of clothing, even in summer—the temperature at the crest can be anywhere from 15 to 25 degrees cooler than down in Albuquerque. This is also the route to the popular Sandia Peak Ski Area. ✉ *End of NM 536, Sandia Park* ⊹ *15 miles west of NM 14* ☎ *505/281–3304* ⊕ *www.fs.usda.gov/recarea/cibola/recarea/?recid=64328* 💲 *$3 parking.*

Tinkertown Museum

ART MUSEUM | FAMILY | This quirky and utterly fascinating homage to folk art, found art, and kitsch contains a world of miniature carved-wood characters. Its late founder, Ross Ward, spent more than 40 years carving and collecting the hundreds of figures that populate this cheerfully bizarre museum, including an animated miniature Western village, a Boot Hill cemetery, and a 1940s circus exhibit. Ragtime piano music, a 40-foot sailboat, and a life-size general store are other highlights. The walls surrounding this 22-room museum have been fashioned out of more than 50,000 glass bottles pressed into cement. As you might expect, the gift shop offers plenty of fun oddities. ⌧ *121 Sandia Crest Rd. (NM 536), Sandia Park* ☎ *505/281–5233* ⊕ *www.tinkertown.com* ✉ *$6* ⊙ *Closed Nov.–Mar. and Tues.–Thurs.*

 Restaurants

Rumor Brewing

$ | **PIZZA** | **FAMILY** | Located near the southern end of the Turquoise Trail, just a 15-minute drive from Albuquerque, this friendly brew-pub and brick-oven pizzeria has a lush, pet- and family-friendly beer garden outside and a pool table and tabletop shuffleboard inside. The blistered-crust pizzas are delicious, and there's a nice selection of salads and sandwiches on house-baked focaccia. **Known for:** frequent live music and themed events; old-world (especially Belgian-style) beers; barbecue chicken–and–bacon pizzas. **⑤** *Average main: $13* ⌧ *28 Arroyo Seco Rd., Cedar Crest* ☎ *505/281–2828* ⊕ *www.rumorbrewing.com.*

Hotels

Elaine's, a Bed and Breakfast

$$ | **B&B/INN** | This antiques-filled three-story log-and-stone home is set in the evergreen folds of the Sandia Mountain foothills, with 4 acres of wooded grounds beckoning outside the back door. **Pros:** peaceful setting away from the main road; exceptional views of the mountains; delicious breakfasts. **Cons:** somewhat remote location; decor may be a bit frilly for some; no restaurants within walking distance. **⑤** *Rooms from: $169* ⌧ *72 Snowline Rd., Sandia Park* ☎ *505/281–2467* ⊕ *www.elainesbnb.com* ➵ *5 rooms* ⚭*I Free Breakfast.*

Kasha–Katuwe Tent Rocks National Monument

36 miles west of Santa Fe.

Volcanic tent-shaped hoodoos and narrow slot canyons are the hallmarks of this enchanted landscape accessed from Interstate 25 between Albuquerque and Santa Fe. This is a must whether you're an avid hiker or just seeking a relatively short scramble with big rewards. The national monument was established in 2001 and is managed in cooperation with Cochiti Pueblo, whose residents have called the area Kasha-Katuwe for centuries.

👁 Sights

★ Kasha-Katuwe Tent Rocks National Monument

NATIONAL PARK | FAMILY | The sandstone rock formations here are a visual marvel, resembling stacked tents in a stark, water- and wind-eroded box canyon. Tent Rocks offers superb hiking year-round, although it can get hot in summer, when you should bring extra water. The drive to this magical landscape offers its own delights, as the road from Interstate 25 heads west toward Cochiti Dam and through the cottonwood groves around the pueblo. It's a good hike for kids. Just 2 miles round-trip, hiking Tent Rock takes only about 1½ leisurely hours, but it's the kind of place where you'll want to hang out for a while. Take a camera, but leave your pets at home—no dogs are allowed. There are no facilities here, just a small parking area with a posted trail map and a self-pay admission box; you can get gas and pick up picnic supplies and bottled water (along with some locally made Pueblo items) at Pueblo de Cochiti Convenience Store, a few miles up the road. Note that as of fall 2023, the national monument remained closed to visitors following the COVID-19 pandemic, but plans are under way to reopen the property through a day-use reservation system (to discourage over-crowding); check the website for the latest updates. ⊠ *Cochiti Pueblo, Indian Service Rte. 92, Cochiti Lake* ✛ *Follow signs from NM 22* ☎ *505/331–6259* ⊕ *www.blm. gov/visit/kktr* ⊠ *$5 per vehicle.*

The Santa Fe Trail

Starting in the 1820s, this vast tract of grasslands and prairies, along with the eastern foothills of the Sangre de Cristo range, became the gateway to New Mexico for American settlers headed here from the Midwest via the 900-mile Santa Fe Trail. Towns along the route, which in New Mexico is now largely traced by its modern offspring, Interstate 25, remain popular with road-tripping fans of Old West history. Ancestral Pecos Pueblo Indians, the Spaniards in the 1600s, and the Santa Fe Trail wagon travelers in the 1800s have all lived in or passed through the region.

Pecos

27 miles east of Santa Fe.

This quiet little village just off Interstate 25 is anchored by the remarkable Pecos National Historical Park. There are a few casual eateries and shops in town, but most visitors come to explore the park or continue up NM 63 to access the hiking, fishing, and camping in the Pecos Wilderness of Santa Fe National Forest.

Sights

Pecos National Historical Park

HISTORIC SIGHT | The centerpiece of this national park is the ruins of Pecos, once a major Pueblo village with more than 1,100 rooms. About 2,500 people are thought to have lived in this structure, as high as five stories in places. Pecos, in a fertile valley between the Great Plains and the Rio Grande Valley, was a trading center centuries before the Spanish conquistadors visited in about 1540. The Spanish later returned to build two missions. The pueblo was abandoned in 1838, and its 17 surviving occupants moved to the Jémez Pueblo. Anglo travelers on the Santa Fe Trail observed the mission ruins with a great sense of fascination. You can view the mission ruins and the excavated pueblo on a 1¼-mile self-guided tour, a Civil War battlefield on a 2½-mile trail, and the small but outstanding visitor center museum containing photos, pottery, and artifacts from the pueblo. A half-mile south of the visitor center, the recently restored Kozlowski Trading Post is part of the park and contains exhibits on the Santa Fe Trail and other aspects of the park's rich history. ✉ *1 Peach Dr., Pecos* ✛ *Off NM 63* ☎ *505/757–7241* ⊕ *www.nps.gov/peco* ⊠ *Free.*

Las Vegas

67 miles east of Santa Fe; 42 miles east of Pecos.

The antithesis of its Nevada namesake, Las Vegas—elevation 6,470 feet—is a town of about 13,000 that in many respects looks preserved in time. For decades, Las Vegas was actually two towns divided by Rio Gallinas: West Las Vegas, the Hispanic community anchored by the Spanish-style plaza, and East Las Vegas, where German Jews and Midwesterners established themselves around its own town square. Once an oasis for stagecoach passengers en route to Santa Fe, it became—for a brief period after the railroad arrived in the late 19th century—New Mexico's major center of commerce and its largest town, where more than a million dollars in goods and services were traded annually.

The seat of San Miguel County, Las Vegas lies where the Sangre de Cristo Mountains meet the high plains of New Mexico, and its name, meaning "the meadows," reflects its scenic setting. Several inviting antiques shops, galleries, and eateries occupy the historic buildings around the Old Town Plaza and its main thoroughfare, Bridge Street. Across town, the Victorian-era city center and railroad district, which are bisected by Grand Avenue, also have several notable dining and shopping spots. More than 900 structures in Las Vegas are listed on the National Register of Historic Places, and the town has nine historic districts, many with homes and commercial buildings of ornate Italianate design. Strolling around this very walkable town gives a sense of the area's rough-and-tumble history—Butch Cassidy is rumored to have tended bar here, and miscreants with names like Dirty-Face Mike, Rattlesnake Sam, and Web-Fingered Billy (not to mention Billy the Kid) once roamed the streets. You may also recognize some of the streets and facades from movies; Las Vegas is where scenes from *Wyatt Earp, No Country for Old Men,* and *All the Pretty Horses* were filmed and where Tom Mix shot his vintage Westerns.

Sights

★ Fort Union National Monument

HISTORIC SIGHT | **FAMILY** | The ruins of New Mexico's largest American frontier-era fort sit on an empty windswept plain about a half-hour drive north of Las Vegas. It still echoes with the isolation surely felt by the soldiers stationed here between 1851 and 1890, when the fort was established to protect travelers and settlers along the Santa Fe Trail. It eventually became a military supply depot for the Southwest, but was eventually abandoned. The visitor center provides historical background about the fort and you can walk among the extensive ruins on your own or explore different parts of the grounds on a ranger tour (they're given throughout the year, but more often in the busier spring and fall seasons). ⊠ *NM 161, Watrous* ✛ *Follow signs from exit 366 of I–25* ☎ *505/425–8025* ⊕ *www.nps.gov/foun.*

🍴 Restaurants

★ The Skillet

$ | **MEXICAN FUSION** | On the ground floor of an imposing 1920s stone warehouse on the border between Las Vegas's older and newer downtowns, this bustling gastropub filled with colorful artwork draws a diverse and friendly crowd of creative spirits, students, tourists, and foodies. The reasonably priced menu is a fun fusion of Latin and Asian flavors, including orange-chicken burritos, spicy brisket tacos, and red chile pepper fried chicken sandwiches. **Known for:** pleasant tree-shaded side patio; creative craft cocktails using New Mexico–distilled spirits; cool art murals, sculptures, and pop art installations throughout the dining room. ⑤ *Average main: $12* ⊠ *619 12th St., Las Vegas* ☎ *505/563–0477* ⊕ *www.giant-skillet.com* ⊗ *Closed Sun.*

 # Hotels

★ Castaneda Hotel
$ | HOTEL | After sitting vacant for more than 70 years and undergoing a painstaking restoration, this remarkable 1898 hotel—the first of the famed Fred Harvey company's railroad properties—reopened with 16 individually decorated rooms, a large and bustling high-ceilinged lobby, a convivial bar with a terrace, and a dapper dining room. **Pros:** handy location beside the Amtrak station; beautifully restored common spaces and veranda; excellent bar and restaurant. **Cons:** lobby noise sometimes carries into the rooms; a 20-minute walk from Old Town; no air-conditioning. ⑤ *Rooms from: $149* ⊠ *524 Railroad Ave., Las Vegas* ☎ *505/425–3591* ⊕ *www.castanedahotel.org* ⇴ *16 rooms* ⦶ *No Meals.*

★ Plaza Hotel
$ | HOTEL | Accommodations in this three-story Italianate hotel, which has hosted the likes of Doc Holliday and Jesse James, balance the old and the new—they're not overly fancy, but they and the hotel's common areas, restaurant, and bar exude historic charm and personality, and the central location can't be beat. **Pros:** good value with lots of personality; excellent restaurant and bar; many shops and eateries within walking distance. **Cons:** a bit of street noise; no parking lot (although street parking is free and fairly easy to find); an older property with plenty of quirks. ⑤ *Rooms from: $119* ⊠ *230 Plaza St., Las Vegas* ☎ *505/425–3591* ⊕ *www.plazahotellvnm.com* ⇴ *70 rooms* ⦶ *No Meals.*

 # Shopping

★ Plaza Antiques
ANTIQUES & COLLECTIBLES | This eclectic shop set in a stunningly restored adobe 1870s Victorian with bright blue trim is packed with vintage furniture, Indigenous pottery and jewelry, Navajo rugs, and fine art. ⊠ *1805 Plaza St., Las Vegas* ☎ *505/454–9447* ⊕ *www.plazaantiqueslasvegasnm.com.*

Roughrider Antiques
ANTIQUES & COLLECTIBLES | This hulking old showroom across the street from the historic train station and Hotel Castaneda overflows with the kinds of goods you might expect to have been transported here by wagon and then railroad during the Santa Fe Trail's heyday. Light fixtures, old books, Depression-era

kitchenware, turquoise jewelry, and vintage signs are among the specialties, along with tables, hutches, and larger items. ✉ *501 Railroad Ave., Las Vegas* ☎ *505/454–8063* ⊕ *www.roughrideran-tiqueslasvegasnewmexico.com.*

Bandelier National Monument

40 miles west of Santa Fe.

Seven centuries before the Declaration of Independence was signed, compact city-states existed in the Southwest. Remnants of one of the most impressive examples can be seen at Frijoles Canyon in Bandelier National Monument. At the canyon's base, near a gurgling stream, the remains of cave dwellings, ancient ceremonial kivas, and other stone structures stretch out for more than a mile beneath the sheer walls of the canyon's tree-fringed rim. For hundreds of years the Ancestral Puebloan people, relatives of today's Rio Grande Pueblo Indians, thrived on wild game, corn, and beans. Suddenly, for reasons still undetermined, the settlements were abandoned.

 Sights

★ Bandelier National Monument

INDIGENOUS SIGHT | FAMILY | This 33,677-acre wilderness is home to a fascinating collection of preserved petroglyphs and cave dwellings of the Ancestral Puebloan people. Along a paved, self-guided trail, steep wooden ladders and narrow doorways lead to a series of cave dwellings, one that contains a kiva large and tall enough to stand in. Named after author and ethnologist Adolph Bandelier (his novel *The Delight Makers* is set in Frijoles Canyon), it also contains backcountry wilderness, waterfalls, and wildlife. Some 70 miles of trails traverse the park; the short Pueblo Loop Trail is an easy, self-guided walk. Pick up the $2 trail guide at the visitor center to read about the numbered sites along this trek. A small museum in the visitor center interprets the area's prehistoric and contemporary Native American cultures, with displays of artifacts dating back to the 13th century.

Note that from mid-June to mid-October, visitors arriving by car between 9 am and 3 pm must park at the White Rock Visitor Center 10 miles east on NM 4 and take a free shuttle bus into the park. This sleek, eco-friendly visitor center also serves as a terrific resource for learning about local attractions. The modern, comfortable Hampton Inn & Suites Los Alamos is next door.

One section of the park, an Ancestral Puebloan ruin called Tsankawi (pronounced sank-ah-*wee*) lies 12 miles from the main section, on NM 4 just south of NM 502 (because it is part of Bandelier, you must pay the park admission to enter it). On the 1½-mile loop trail, you can see petroglyphs and south-facing cave dwellings, and there's a large, unexcavated pueblo ruin on top of the mesa. ⊠ *Off NM 4, Los Alamos* ✛ *12 miles southwest of NM 502* ☎ *505/672–3861* ⊕ *www.nps.gov/band* ⌘ *$15 on foot or bicycle; $25 per car.*

🍽 Restaurants

Pig + Fig

$ | **AMERICAN** | Your best bet before or after visiting Bandelier for anything from a light snack to a substantial lunch or early dinner, this cheerful bakery and café features farm-to-table fare and tempting desserts (be sure to try a macaron or two). Share a couple of small plates, dig into a hearty platter of pork schnitzel, or savor one of the outstanding sandwiches, such as the signature "hot pig + fig" with honey-cured ham, spinach, Brie, and fig jam. **Known for:** daily-changing box lunches that are perfect for picnicking at Bandelier; delicous lemon tarts; reasonably priced and well-curated list of wines by the glass. ⑤ *Average main: $15* ⊠ *11 Sherwood Blvd., White Rock* ☎ *505/672–2742* ⊕ *www.pigandfig-cafe.com* ⊗ *Closed Sun.*

Los Alamos

35 miles north of Santa Fe.

Leaf through any pre-1930s books about New Mexico, and you won't find a mention of Los Alamos, a busy town of about 13,000 that has the highest per capita income in the state. Los Alamos was created expressly as a company town, its workers at first secretly toiling away in America's foremost nuclear research facility, Los Alamos National Laboratory (LANL). The facility still employs nearly 13,000 full-time workers, some who reside here and many others who commute from Santa Fe or communities in between.

A few miles from ancient cave dwellings, scientists led by J. Robert Oppenheimer built Fat Man and Little Boy, the atom bombs that in August 1945 decimated Hiroshima and Nagasaki, respectively. LANL had been developed in 1943 under the auspices of the intensely covert Manhattan Project, whose express purpose was to expedite an Allied victory during World War II. Indeed, Japan surrendered—but a full-blown Cold War between Russia and the United States ensued for another four and a half decades.

With its mostly mid-to-late-20th century homes and buildings and an industrious personality, Los Alamos feels sharply different— and unquestionably less charming—than the far more historic and touristy north-central Rio Grande Valley that surrounds it. It does, however, contain some fascinating museums about its compli- cated and compelling legacy, and it's easy to combine a visit here with one to nearby Bandelier National Monument.

Sights

Bradbury Science Museum

SCIENCE MUSEUM | FAMILY | Los Alamos National Laboratory's public showcase, the Bradbury provides a balanced and provoc- ative examination of such topics as atomic weapons and nuclear power. You can experiment with lasers; witness research in solar, geothermal, fission, and fusion energy; learn about DNA finger- printing; and view fascinating exhibits about World War II's Project Y (the Manhattan Project, whose participants developed the atomic bomb). ⊠ *1450 Central Ave., Los Alamos* ☎ *505/667–4444* ⊕ *www.lanl.gov/museum* ☉ *Closed Mon.*

Los Alamos History Museum

HISTORY MUSEUM | Across the street from Ashley Pond and the Manhattan Project National Historical Park Visitor Center, this engaging museum has indoor and outdoor exhibits about the region's Ancestral Puebloan history dating back to the 14th cen- tury, the Boy Scout–influenced prep school for young men from prominent families (including Gore Vidal and William S. Burroughs) that operated here before World War II, the Manhattan Project, and more recent times. A few doors away, the mid-century modern Hans Bethe House depicts home life for the top-level scientists working on the atomic bomb, and next door you can view the exterior of J. Robert Oppenheimer's home (which remains a private residence). Be sure to visit the neighboring Fuller Lodge Art Center (free), a massive log building designed in 1928 by famed New Mexican architect John Gaw Meem as part of the prep school, before it was purchased and converted into the base of operations for the Manhattan Project. Inside there's an art gallery and shop that presents rotating exhibits throughout the year. ⊠ *1050 Bathtub Row, Los Alamos* ☎ *505/709–7794* ⊕ *www. losalamoshistory.org* 🖾 *$5* ☉ *Closed Sun.*

Manhattan Project National Historical Park Visitor Center

VISITOR CENTER | In the heart of this community that's a must for anyone interested in the history of the atomic age, this small visitor center can help you learn what to see and do around town. Start with an orientation film on the people and events that led to the creation of the atomic bomb, then pick up a self-guided tour of the town's notable historic sites. It's beside the Los Alamos Visitor Center, which also has free and excellent brochures on local hiking trails as well as both the town's and the surrounding area's attractions. ⊠ 475 20th St., Los Alamos ☎ 505/661–6277 ⊕ www.nps.gov/mapr ۞ Closed Tues.–Thurs.

★ **Pajarito Environmental Education Center**

SCIENCE MUSEUM | FAMILY | This angular, contemporary nature center stands out as much for its dramatic design as for the engaging exhibits within. Families appreciate the interactive Children's Discovery Area and the giant scale model of the Pajarito Plateau that kids are encouraged to play on. There's also a high-tech planetarium with astronomy shows or films most weekends, nature trails, wildlife and conservation exhibits, and gardens with local flora and plenty of visiting birdlife. ⊠ 2600 Canyon Rd., Los Alamos ☎ 505/662–0460 ⊕ www.peecnature.org ⊠ Free ۞ Closed Sun. and Tues.

★ **Puye Cliff Dwellings**

INDIGENOUS SIGHT | Members of the Santa Clara Pueblo lead guests on one- to two-hour tours of the dramatic cliffs and ancient volcanic-rock dwellings that were inhabited by the tribe's ancestors from the late 900s to 1580. Start by viewing historic photos and cultural displays in the Exhibit Hall, which occupies a restored 1930s guesthouse that was the only lodging ever built by the famed Fred Harvey Company on Native-owned land. Visiting the dwellings—which include a 140-room kiva—and the cliff top with its eye-popping 360-degree vistas are by guided tour only (these last one to two hours, depending on which one you book). The entrance to the dwellings is about 15 miles northeast of Los Alamos. ⊠ 300 NM 30, Española ✛ At junction within NM 5 ☎ 505/917–6650 ⊕ www.puyecliffdwellings.com ⊠ Exhibit Hall free; tours $20–$40 ۞ Closed Tues. and Wed.

🍴 Restaurants

Blue Window Bistro

$$$ | AMERICAN | This brightly colored and elegant restaurant is a welcoming spot for a delicious lunch or dinner that's within walking distance of the city's several downtown museums and historic sites. The kitchen turns out a mix of New Mexican, American,

 You can reach Valles Caldera National Preserve in just over an hour driving from Santa Fe.

and Continental dishes, including grilled jumbo shrimp wrapped in applewood-smoked bacon, Greek salads prepared with locally made feta, and tender steaks. **Known for:** casual menu of creative sandwiches at lunch; outstanding cocktail, wine, and beer menu; stylish dining room and leafy outdoor patio. $ *Average main: $28* ⊠ *1789 Central Ave., Los Alamos* ☎ *505/662–6305* ⊕ *labluewindowbistro.com* ☉ *Closed weekends.*

Valles Caldera National Preserve

17 miles west of Los Alamos.

A high-forest drive brings you to the awe-inspiring Valles Grande, which at 14 miles in diameter is one of the world's largest calderas. This nearly 90,000 acre tract of land became Valles (*vah*-yes) Caldera National Preserve in 2000.

⊙ Sights

★ Valles Caldera National Preserve
NATURE PRESERVE | This famed caldera resulted from the eruption and collapse of a 14,000-foot peak more than 1¼ million years ago; the flow out the bottom created the Pajarito Plateau and the ash from the eruption spread as far east as Kansas. You can't imagine the volcanic crater's immensity until you spot what look like specks of dust on the lush meadow floor and realize they're

elk. The National Park Service manages this 89,000-acre multiuse preserve, which is especially popular for its variety of gorgeous hiking trails as well as for wildlife watching, fly-fishing, mountain biking and e-biking, cross-country skiing, snowshoeing, and horseback riding. From June through September, rangers offer free guided hikes around Cerro la Jara (with a focus on volcanos) and through the Cabin District and History Grove, where you'll learn about the caldera's 11,000-year human history. Stargazing programs and moonlit walks are also offered occasionally, as are fly-fishing clinics. For the foreseeable future, while the park service continues to improve the preserve's infrastructure, there's no fee to enter; check the website for updates. ⊠ *NM 4, mile marker 39.2, 10 miles west of junction with NM 501, Jemez Springs* ☎ *575/829–4100* ⊕ *www.nps.gov/vall.*

Georgia O'Keeffe Country

It's a 20-minute drive north of Santa Fe to reach the Española Valley, from which you can head northwest to behold the striking mesas, cliffs, and valleys that so inspired Georgia O'Keeffe—she lived in this area for the final 50 years of her life. Passing through the small, workaday city of Española, U.S. 84 continues to the sleepy but picturesque village of Abiquiú and eventually up to Ghost Ranch, areas where O'Keeffe both lived and worked. An interesting detour in this region is to tiny Ojo Caliente, famous for its hot-springs spa retreat.

Abiquiú

50 miles northwest of Santa Fe.

This tiny, very traditional Hispanic village was originally home to freed *genizaros,* Indigenous and mixed-blood slaves who served as house servants, shepherds, and other key roles in Spanish, Mexican, and American households well into the 1880s. Many descendants of original families still live here, although since the late 1980s, Abiquiú and its surrounding countryside have become a nesting ground for those fleeing big-city life (actresses Marsha Mason and Shirley MacLaine each lived here at one time). Abiquiú and the Española Valley are also a hotbed of organic farming, with many of the operations selling their goods at the Santa Fe Farmers' Market. A number of artists live in Abiquiú, and several studios showing both traditional Spanish Colonial and contemporary art are open to the public; many others open each year over

Columbus Day/Indigenous Peoples' Day weekend (the second weekend of October) for the annual Abiquiú Studio Tour (⊕ *www. abiquiustudiotour.org*).

⊙ Sights

★ Georgia O'Keeffe Home & Studio

HISTORIC HOME | In 1945 Georgia O'Keeffe bought a large, dilapidated late-18th-century Spanish-colonial adobe compound just off the plaza in Abiquiú. Upon the 1946 death of her husband, photographer Alfred Stieglitz, she left New York City and began dividing her time permanently between this home, which figured prominently in many of her works, and one in nearby Ghost Ranch. The patio is featured in *Black Patio Door* (1955) and *Patio with Cloud* (1956). O'Keeffe died in 1986 at the age of 98 and left provisions in her will to ensure that the property's houses would never be public monuments.

Highly engaging 75- to 90-minute tours are available by advance reservation through Santa Fe's Georgia O'Keeffe Museum, which owns the house and operates the tours from early March through late November. Costs range from $60 for a standard tour to $200 for "Pita's Tour," which is led by Pita Lopez, who served as O'Keeffe's former secretary and companion and shares fascinating first-hand anecdotes about the artist. All of the tours focus on O'Keeffe's distinctly modern decorating style, which drew on Indigenous and Spanish influences. Tours depart by shuttle bus from the welcome center beside the Abiquiu Inn. Book well ahead in summer, as these tours fill up quickly. ⊠ *Welcome Center, 21120 U.S. 84, Abiquiú* ☎ *505/946–1098* ⊕ *www.okeeffemuseum. org* ⊠ *$60* ☽ *Closed Sun., Mon., and late Nov.–early Mar.*

⑪ Restaurants

★ Cafe Sierra Negra

$ | ECLECTIC | Reasonably priced, cheerfully decorated, and offering some of the tastiest food in the Rio Chama Valley, this adobe café-bakery run by the former tour manager of the nearby Georgia O'Keeffe Home & Studio. The eclectic made-from-scratch cooking here runs the gamut from New Mexican (green chile cheeseburgers, roasted and stuffed poblanos) to international (red lentil dal, roasted-turkey crepes with cheddar and cranberry sauce). **Known for:** loaves of savory artisan breads baked daily (perfect to take with you on a picnic or back to your hotel); shrimp tacos with cilantro-jalapeño-feta pesto; occasional themed prix-fixe dinners.

$ Average main: $16 ⊠ 20968 U.S. 84, Abiquiú ☏ 505/685–0086
⊕ www.cafesierranegra-nm.com ⊘ Closed Sun. and Mon.

El Farolito

$ | **MEXICAN** | This endearingly modest hole-in-the-wall on the
tree-shaded main drag of tiny El Rito doesn't look like much from
the outside, but devotees drive for miles to taste the stick-to-
your-ribs classic New Mexican specialties, including a rich, smoky
green chile stew that's garnered numerous awards and accolades.
The drive here—it's about 20 minutes from both Abiquiú and Ojo
Caliente—offers stunning views back east toward the Sangre
de Cristo mountains. **Known for:** inexpensive, unpretentious, and
authentic New Mexican fare; tiny dining room (there can be a wait
for a table); BYOB and cash-only policies. $ Average main: $8
⊠ 1212 NM 554, El Rito ☏ 505/581–9509 ⊕ www.facebook.com/
marisoltrujilloperry ▭ No credit cards ⊘ Closed Mon. and Tues.

★ NOSA

$$$$ | **MODERN AMERICAN** | The name of this refined, romantic
prix-fixe restaurant and inn nestled against towering ramparts in
the Ojo Caliente River Valley stands for NOrth of SAnta Fe, and
indeed this very special culinary retreat is close enough to the city
(a 45-minute drive) to draw foodies for one of the rarefied five-
course, farm-to-table dinners. But NOSA also has four elegantly
furnished suites, in case you'd prefer to spend the night—not a
bad idea, given the restaurant's enticing wine list. **Known for:** artful-
ly plated modern American fare; breathtaking sunset views from
the patio; gluten-free and vegetarian menus with advance notice.
$ Average main: $95 ⊠ 49 Rancho de San Juan, Ojo Caliente
☏ 505/753–0881 ⊕ www.nosanm.com ⊘ Closed Mon.–Thurs. No
dinner Sun. and no lunch Fri. and Sat.

 # Hotels

Abiquiu Inn

$$ | **HOTEL** | In the serene Chama Valley amid the red-rock scenery
that inspired Georgia O'Keeffe, this inn, located beside the Wel-
come Center for tours of the artist's home and studio, contains
casitas, suites, and rooms brightly decorated with Southwestern
accents that may include woodstoves, kiva-style fireplaces, wood-
beam ceilings, verandas, and screen-in porches. **Pros:** good base
for exploring O'Keeffe Country; breathtaking high-desert setting;
sophisticated contemporary restaurant serving three meals a day.
Cons: service is friendly but pretty hands-off; rooms at the front
of the inn get noise from the road; sometimes booked up for
meetings and weddings. $ Rooms from: $189 ⊠ 21120 U.S. 84,

Abiquiú ☎ *505/685–4378* ⊕ *www.abiquiuinn.com* ⇄ *32 rooms* ⑽ *No Meals.*

★ Ojo Caliente Mineral Springs Resort & Spa

$$ | RESORT | Set in the rugged red rock hills of a secluded village between Taos and Abiquiú, this fabled hot springs resort appeals to a wide range of tastes and budgets, from spiritually minded adventurers seeking a moderate-priced wellness retreat to couples wanting an upscale yet secluded spa getaway (it's a favorite of celebs filming movies in New Mexico). **Pros:** reasonably priced (for the simplest rooms); relaxing and serene setting; unpretentious and friendly vibe. **Cons:** a little funky and New Age-y for some tastes; remote location; soaking pools can get crowded and even a little noisy at busy times. ⑤ *Rooms from: $209* ⊠ *50 Los Baños Dr., Ojo Caliente* ☎ *505/583–2233, 877/977–8212* ⊕ *www. ojosparesorts.com* ⇄ *49 units* ⑽ *No Meals.*

 Shopping

Bode's

GENERAL STORE | This funky general store and gas station, pronounced *boh*-dees, has been serving the region since 1919. It offers a thoughtfully curated array of quirky gifts, locally made arts and crafts, local beer and wine, household supplies, and fishing gear (including licenses), along with delicious breakfast burritos, green-chile stew, deli sandwiches, and other light fare. ⊠ *21196 U.S. 84, Abiquiú* ☎ *505/685–4422* ⊕ *www.bodes.com.*

★ Bosshard Gallery

ART GALLERIES | You'll find an incredible collection of fine Spanish Colonial, Mexican, and Indigenous paintings, textiles, carvings, ceramics, sculptures, and furnishings in this rambling gallery, but part of the fun of visiting is just walking through this grand, rambling historic compound in Abiquiú's unpaved village center. It consists of a large old home, a 5,000-square-foot former mercantile, and lush gardens enclosed within massive adobe walls. ⊠ *10 County Rd. 187, Abiquiú* ☎ *505/685–0061.*

Ghost Ranch

15 miles north of Abiquiú.

For art historians, the name Ghost Ranch brings to mind Georgia O'Keeffe, who lived on a small parcel of this 22,000-acre dude and cattle ranch. The ranch's owner in the 1930s—conservationist and publisher of *Nature Magazine,* Arthur Pack—invited O'Keeffe for a

Georgia O'Keeffe was inspired by the stunning landscapes surrounding Ghost Ranch, her longtime summer home.

visit in 1934 and soon sold her the 7-acre plot on which she lived summer through fall for most of the rest of her life. In 1955, Pack donated the rest of the ranch to the Presbyterian Church, which continues to use the original structures and part of the land as a conference center, but Ghost Ranch is also open to visitors for tours, hikes, workshops, and all sorts of other activities.

If you have the time, continue north another 30 miles along gorgeous U.S. 84 to the tiny weaving village of Los Ojos and 12 more miles to Chama, famed for its scenic Cumbres & Toltec Railroad.

Sights

★ Ghost Ranch

FARM/RANCH | FAMILY | Open to the public year-round, this sprawling, stunningly situated ranch is busiest in summer, when the majority of workshops take place, and when visitors drive up after having toured the O'Keeffe home in nearby Abiquiú. Now a retreat center, the ranch also offers a wealth of interesting activities for day visitors, including a few different guided Georgia O'Keeffe tours across the landscape she painted during the five decades she summered here (the house she lived in is not part of the tour and is closed to the public). Other guided (and self-guided) hikes amid the property's dramatic rock formations touch on archaeology and paleontology, history, and the several movies that have been filmed here (*Cowboys and Aliens, City Slickers, Wyatt Earp,* and a few others). Visitors can also tour the Florence Hawley Ellis Museum of Anthropology, which contains Native American tools, pottery, and other artifacts excavated from the Ghost Ranch Gallina digs, and the adjacent Ruth Hall Museum of Paleontology. Workshops, which touch on everything from photography and poetry to yoga and wellness, are offered throughout the year—guests can camp or stay in semi-rustic cottages or casitas. If you're not attending a workshop or retreat, Ghost Ranch opens its accommodations to the general public from November through April (there's a two-night minimum stay, but rates are quite reasonable). Other experiences on the property include art exhibits, trail rides, massage treatments, and kayaking and canoeing in nearby Abiquiú. When you arrive, drop by the welcome center, which also houses a trading post stocked with books, art, O'Keeffe ephemera, and a basic coffee station (there's also a dining hall serving cafeteria-style meals throughout the day). ⊠ *U.S. 84, between mile markers 224 and 225, Abiquiú* ☎ *505/685–1000, 877/804–4678* ⊕ *www.ghostranch.org* ☞ *$10 day pass.*

The High Road to Taos

The fastest drive between Santa Fe and Taos is via NM 68 (sometimes called the Low Road), and it offers plenty of visual drama, especially the stretch that flanks the Rio Grande as you approach Taos. But by far the most spectacular route is the High Road. Towering peaks, lush hillsides, colorful orchards, and rolling meadows frame this drive's tiny, ancient Hispanic villages, which are as picturesque as they are historically fascinating. A smart strategy is to drive *to* Taos via the Low Road, and then to return *from* Taos via the High Road, as the scenery is far prettier on each road driving in these directions.

Pojoaque and Nambé Pueblos

17 miles north of Santa Fe.

The first points of interest you'll encounter as you head up the High Road from Santa Fe, the Pojoaque and Nambé pueblos are sovereign Indigenous nations within the United States. Each has its own government and traditions, and you'll find some engaging things to see and do in each community.

Sights

Nambé Falls and Nambé Lake

BODY OF WATER | There's a shady picnic area and a large fishing lake that's open April through October at this scenic and popular hiking area along the High Road, just east of Pojoaque. It's $15 per carload for a day pass, and an additional $3 to go fishing on the lake; additionally, kayaks are available to rent from $30 per hour. The waterfalls are about a 15-minute hike from the parking and picnic area along a rocky, clearly marked path. The water pours over a rock precipice—a loud and dramatic sight given the river's modest size. ⊠ *Poechunu Poe Rd., Off NM 503, Nambe* 🕾 *505/455–2304* ⊕ *www.nambepueblo.org* 🖅 *$15* 🕙 *Closed Tues. and Wed.*

Poeh Cultural Center and Museum

INDIGENOUS SIGHT | Situated just off U.S. 285/84 at Pojoaque Pueblo, this impressive complex of traditional adobe buildings, including the three-story Sun Tower, makes an engaging first stop as you begin a drive north of Santa Fe toward Taos. The facility comprises a museum, a cultural center, and artists' studios, all with the mission of preserving the arts and culture of Pueblo communities. The museum holds some 10,000 photographs, including many by esteemed early-20th-century photographer Edward S. Curtis, as well as more than 600 works of both traditional and contemporary pottery, jewelry, textiles, and sculpture. There's also a lovely gift shop of locally made Native American arts and crafts. ⊠ *78 Cities of Gold Rd., North Side* 🕾 *505/455–5041* ⊕ *www.poehcenter.org* 🖅 *$10* 🕙 *Closed weekends.*

Hotels

Buffalo Thunder Resort & Casino

$$ | **RESORT** | **FAMILY** | Managed by Hilton, this expansive, upscale gaming and golfing resort is 15 miles north of downtown Santa Fe, just off a freeway but with spectacular views of the mountains and Rio Grande Valley—it's a great option to be close to the start of the High Road or if you'd prefer to stay close to but still a bit outside of the City Different. **Pros:** snazzy rooms with plenty of amenities; convenient to downtown Santa Fe and Low and High roads to Taos; panoramic mountain and mesa views. **Cons:** rates can be a bit steep, especially when there are events on property; lobby is noisy and crowded with gamers on many evenings; a 15-minute drive from the Plaza. ⑤ *Rooms from: $249* ⊠ *20 Buffalo Thunder Trail, North Side* 🕾 *505/455–5555, 877/848–6337* ⊕ *www. hiltonbuffalothunder.com* 🛏 *375 rooms* ⑩ *No Meals.*

The most famous church found on the High Road to Taos is El Santuario de Chimayó.

Chimayó

28 miles north of Santa Fe; 12 miles northeast of Pojoaque and Nambé.

From U.S. 205/84 north of Pojoaque, scenic NM 503 winds past horse paddocks and orchards in the narrow Nambé Valley, then ascends into the red-sandstone canyons with a view of Truchas Peaks to the northeast before dropping into the bucolic village of Chimayó. Nestled into hillsides where gnarled piñons seem to grow from bare bedrock, Chimayó is famed for its weaving, its red chiles, and its two chapels, particularly El Santuario de Chimayó.

Sights

★ El Santuario de Chimayó
CHURCH | This small, frontier, adobe church has a fantastically carved and painted *reredos* (altar screen) and is built on the site where, believers say, a mysterious light came from the ground on Good Friday in 1810 leading to the discovery of a large wooden crucifix beneath the earth. The chapel sits above a sacred *pozito* (a small hole), the dirt from which is believed to have miraculous healing properties. Dozens of abandoned crutches and braces placed in the anteroom—along with many notes, letters, and photos—testify to this. The Santuario draws a steady stream of worshippers year-round—Chimayó is considered the Lourdes of

the Southwest. During Holy Week as many as 30,000 pilgrims come here. The shrine is is surrounded by small adobe shops selling every kind of religious curio imaginable and some very fine traditional Hispanic work from local artists. A smaller chapel, Santo Niño de Atocha, was built in 1857 and lies 200 yards away. As at the more famous Santuario, the dirt in this place of worship is said to have healing properties. ⊠ *15 Santuario Dr., Chimayo* ☎ *505/351–4360* ⊕ *www.holychimayo.us* 🎫 *Free.*

★ High Road Art Tour

SCENIC DRIVE | From Chimayó to Peñasco, the High Road is home to a number of mostly low-key but generally high-quality art galleries, many of them run out of the owners' homes. During the final two weekends in September each year, more than 30 artists show their work in the High Road Art Tour; for a studio map, or plenty of useful information on galleries open not just during the tour but year-round, visit the website. ⊠ *Chimayo* ⊕ *www.highroad-newmexico.com.*

Restaurants

Rancho de Chimayó

$$ | **MEXICAN** | In a century-old adobe hacienda tucked into the mountains, with whitewashed walls, hand-stripped *vigas,* and cozy dining rooms, the Rancho de Chimayó is still owned and operated by the family that first occupied the house. Consistently good, reasonably priced New Mexican fare is served (the carne adovada with posole is especially good), and it's hard to deny the enchanting ambience of the place. **Known for:** beautiful rancho decor and ambience; great gift shop with restaurant items and local artists; gorgeous terraced back patio. ⑤ *Average main: $20* ⊠ *300 Juan Medina Rd., Chimayo* ☎ *505/351–4444* ⊕ *www.ranchodechimayo.com* ۞ *Closed Mon.*

Hotels

Casa Escondida

$$ | **B&B/INN** | Intimate and peaceful, this classic adobe inn offers sweeping views of the Sangre de Cristo range and contains nine charming rooms decorated with antiques and Native American and other regional arts and crafts. **Pros:** gracious, knowledgeable hosts; serene grounds with patios and gardens; convenient to exploring the High Road. **Cons:** you need a car to get around; no TVs in rooms; not a great fit for young kids. ⑤ *Rooms from: $169* ⊠ *64 CR 100, Chimayo* ☎ *505/351–4805* ⊕ *www.casaescondida.com* 🛏 *9 rooms* ۞| *Free Breakfast.*

Shopping

★ Centinela Traditional Arts

ART GALLERIES | The Trujillo family weaving tradition, which started in northern New Mexico more than seven generations ago, is carried out in this colorful, inviting gallery. Irvin Trujillo and his wife, Lisa, are both gifted, renowned master weavers, creating Rio Grande–style tapestry blankets and rugs, many of them with natural dyes that authentically replicate early weavings. Most designs are historically based, but the Trujillos are never shy about innovating and their original works are as breathtaking as the traditional ones. ⊠ *946 NM 76, Chimayo* ☎ *505/351–2180* ⊕ *www. chimayoweavers.com.*

Ortega's Weaving Shop

HOUSEWARES | This shop in the center of town sells Rio Grande- and Chimayó-style textiles made by the family whose Spanish ancestors brought the craft to New Mexico in the 1600s. The Galeria Ortega, next door, sells traditional and contemporary arts and crafts in New Mexican and Native American styles. ⊠ *53 Plaza del Cerro, Chimayo* ☎ *505/351–4215* ⊕ *www.ortegasweaving.com.*

Truchas

9 miles northeast of Chimayó.

The pastoral village of Truchas (Spanish for "trout") is perched dramatically on the rim of a deep canyon beneath the towering Truchas Peaks, mountains high enough to be almost perpetually capped with snow. The tallest of the Truchas Peaks is 13,102 feet, the second-highest point in New Mexico. Robert Redford shot the movie *The Milagro Beanfield War* (based on the novel written by Taos author John Nichols) in this small village that's now home to a number of artists and creative spirits—there are several excellent galleries in town to show for it.

Shopping

★ Eight Million Gods

ART GALLERIES | Owned by renowned Santa Fe chocolatier Hayward Simoneaux, this bright and colorful shop specializes in folk art and carries wonderfully offbeat and eye-catching items from all over the world and at a wide range of price points. Think Spanish-colonial-style leather messenger bags, hand-painted wild boar ceramic piggy banks, Mexican paper-mâché eggs painted to look like *lucha* *libre* masks, and hand-embroidered reversible jackets from India. And yes, you'll also find some carefully curated chocolates for sale. ⊠ *1642 NM 76, Truchas* ☎ *505/992–3855* ⊕ *www.instagram. com/eightmilliongods.*

Hand Artes Gallery

ART GALLERIES | For more than a half-century, this gallery attached to a rambling adobe home with sweeping mountain views has carried works by some of northern New Mexico's leading artists, including painter Alvaro Cardona-Hine, furniture-makers Larry and Nancy Buechley, and sculptor and painter Sheila Mahoney Keefe. Visitors are asked to call first to make an appointment. ⊠ *137 County Rd. 75, Truchas* ☎ *505/689–2443* ⊕ *www.handartesgallery. com.*

Peñasco

15 miles north of Truchas.

Home to around 1,200 residents, Peñasco is one of the "larger" villages along the High Road and a good bet if you need to fill your tank with gas or pick up a snack at a convenience store. The village is also home to a handful of interesting galleries as well as one of the most celebrated small-town restaurants in northern New Mexico, Sugar Nymphs Bistro.

Restaurants

★ Sugar Nymphs Bistro

$ | **AMERICAN** | You can't miss the vivid murals on the building in sleepy Peñasco that houses both a vintage theater and an intimate restaurant where acclaimed chef-owners Kai Harper Leah and Ki Holste serve up tantalizing farm-to-table fare, from bountiful salads and juicy burgers to triple-layer chocolate cake. This is the best restaurant on the High Road, hands down. **Known for:** creatively topped pizzas on weekend evenings; fluffy scones with house-made jam at Sunday brunch; decadent desserts. ⑤ *Average main: $16* ⊠ *15046 NM 75, Peñasco* ☎ *575/587–0311* ⊕ *www.sugarnymphs.com* ⊙ *Closed Mon. and Tues. No dinner Sun., Wed., and Thurs.*

Shopping

Gaucho Blue Gallery

ART GALLERIES | This eclectic gallery carries a great mix of paintings and other pieces by local artists—notably Nick Beason's edgy monotypes and copper etchings and Lise Poulsen's felted kimonos and striking fiberworks. You'll find both contemporary and traditional works here. ⊠ *14148 NM 75, Peñasco* ☎ *575/587–1076* ⊕ *www.gauchoblue.com.*

Dixon

13 miles west of Peñasco.

The small village of Dixon is home to several talented artists as well as a couple of the wineries that have helped put the northern Rio Grande Valley on the map among oenophiles. Artistic sensitivity, as well as generations of dedicated farmers, account for the community's well-tended fields, pretty gardens, and fruit trees. During the first full weekend in November, area artists open up their home studios to the public for the Dixon Studio Tour (⊕ *www.dixonarts.org).*

Sights

★ La Chiripada Winery

WINERY | Nestled under mature shade trees down a dirt lane near Dixon's quaint village center, this producer of first-rate wines is the oldest vintner in the northern part of the state. La Chiripada's Viognier, Special Reserve Riesling, and Dolcetto have all earned considerable acclaim. Also consider a tasting of the nicely crafted New Mexico Port, which pairs well with dessert. There's a small art gallery, and tastings are also offered a few miles away at Blue Heron Brewery. ⊠ *NM 75, Road 1119, Dixon* ☎ *505/579–4437* ⊕ *lachiripada.com.*

★ Los Luceros Historic Site

MUSEUM VILLAGE | **FAMILY** | Set amid cottonwood trees, fertile fields, and lush gardens that back up to the Rio Grande, this beautifully preserved 148-acre ranch just off the Low Road between Española and Dixon is one of the region's underrated gems. After getting oriented and talking with the knowledgeable staff in the Spanish-colonial visitor center, you can pick up a self-guided tour map or use your phone to scan QR codes for a virtual ranger tour and explore the extensive grounds, which include a stately Territorial-style hacienda, a chapel dating back to the 1700s, a farmyard and barn, and short walking trails through the woodlands. There's also an apple orchard and a pond that attracts all kinds of wildlife, from migrating waterfowl to occasional beavers and otters. It's easy to spend at least a couple of hours here without running out of engaging things to explore. ⊠ *253 County Rd. 41, Alcalde*

☎ 505/476–1165 ⊕ www.nmhistoricsites.org/los-luceros ⊠ $7 ⊙ Closed Mon. and Tues.

Vivác Winery

WINERY | "Vivác" means "high-altitude refuge," and that's a fitting name for this popular winery located at the junction on NM 68 (the Low Road) and NM 75 (which leads to the High Road). The family-owned vineyards and charming tasting room, with an adjacent patio, are surrounded by the dramatic sheer cliffs of the Rio Grande Gorge. The elegant, generally dry wines, feature a mix of mostly old-world grapes, including Dolcetto, Tempranillo, Cabernet Sauvignon, and Grüner Veltliner. The tasting room also sells artisanal chocolates, cheese-and-charcuterie plates, jewelry, and contemporary art. ⊠ 2075 NM 68, Dixon ☎ 505/579–4441 ⊕ www.vivacwinery.com.

Restaurants

Blue Heron Brewing Co.

$$ | **PIZZA** | On the Low Road to Taos just a five-minute drive from the center of Dixon, New Mexico's oldest woman-owned brewery dispenses not only nicely crafted ales—the crisp Rinconada Raspberry Rye and malty La Llorona Scottish Ale are great choices—but also tasty pizzas, salads, and desserts. Have a seat in the art-filled dining room, where you can also taste wine from the nearby La Chiripada Winery, or out on the cottonwood-shaded patio. **Known for:** rich darker beers (porters, stouts, Scottish ales); the Valle pizza, topped with chicharrones, smoked gouda, and green chiles; Kentucky bourbon–pecan pie. ⑤ Average main: $18 ⊠ 2214 NM 68, Dixon ☎ 505/579–9188 ⊕ www.blueheronbrews.com.

Shopping

Métier Studio Gallery

ART GALLERIES | Set inside a handsome and historic stone building in the center of town, this superb cooperative gallery is best known for the vibrant contemporary handweaving of its several fiber artists, but you'll also find beautifully crafted ceramics, jewelry, paintings, and more. ⊠ 202 NM 75, Dixon ☎ 505/542–9390 ⊕ www.metierweaving.com.

ALBUQUERQUE

Updated by
Lynne Arany

◎ Sights   🍴 Restaurants   🛏 Hotels   🛍 Shopping   🍸 Nightlife

★★★★☆   ★★★★☆   ★★★☆☆   ★★☆☆☆   ★★☆☆☆

WELCOME TO ALBUQUERQUE

TOP REASONS TO GO

★ **Dazzling views:** With mountains, volcanoes, and the Rio Grande in between, the city is an outdoor lover's dream. Hiking and biking trails abound, and you can paddle the Rio as well.

★ **Arts, heritage, and history:** From Native culture, flamenco, traditional arts, and Route 66's motor-court neon to the early railroad days, Albuquerque has galleries, museums, and performances that cover it all.

★ **Farm-fresh dining:** Savor traditional New Mexican specialties, vibrant growers' markets, and contemporary cuisine at a variety of dining establishments.

★ **Roadways to ruins (and pueblos today):** Explore nearby Petroglyph National Monument, then enjoy direct routes to the Jémez, Acoma, Laguna, and Zuni pueblos, and onward to Chaco Canyon.

★ **Hot air balloons:** There's the famous Hot Air Balloon Festival, of course, but with 360 days a year of blue sky, enjoy seeing them pop up—or take a ride yourself—year-round.

.

1 Old Town. A stroll back in time to the Spanish settlement on which ABQ was founded.

2 Downtown and EDo. A world-class group of art galleries and murals, with railroad-era architecture and the famous KiMo Theatre.

3 Barelas and South Valley. Home to historic adobe neighborhoods, the acclaimed National Hispanic Cultural Center, and the fabulous Rail Yard market.

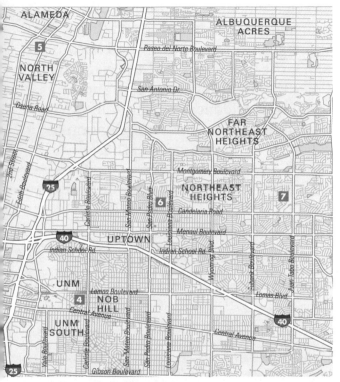

4 UNM and Nob Hill. A neighborhood shaped by Route 66 and the University of New Mexico.

5 Los Ranchos and North Valley. Along the Rio Grande Valley, where first Pueblo peoples, then the earliest Hispanic settlers, resided, lies the city's agrarian heart.

6 Uptown and Northeast Heights. A booming residential area that starts at Uptown (ABQ's shopping nexus) and rises east into the Heights, with great hiking and a breathtaking aerial tram.

7 East Side and West Side. Home to the National Museum of Nuclear Science & History (and the gateway to the Sandia Mountains) in the east and the famed Petroglyph National Monument in the west.

Perfectly set as the gateway to other New Mexico wonders like Chaco Canyon and the Gila Wilderness, Albuquerque's own rich history and dramatic terrain—desert volcanoes, unique cottonwood bosque along the broad banks of the river that flows through its very center, and a striking confluence of mountain ranges—have long captured the imagination of folks en route from here to there.

Today's smart traveler knows something special is afoot in this wonderfully diverse and charmingly quirky historic town halved by the Rio Grande. You'll want to plan on spending a day—or more—before venturing beyond. Vibrant art galleries, growers' markets, a fine wine and microbrewery scene, and world-class museums as well as superb nature trails and spectacular topography—and, of course, the seemingly endless blue sky and the joyous hot-air balloons that decorate it—make it a worthy destination of its own.

Centuries-old traces of Native American populations past and present abound throughout the Rio Grande Valley, and Albuquerque is no exception. Their trade routes are what drew the Spanish here; sections of what became their Camino Real are still intact. The little farming settlement was proclaimed "Alburquerque," after the Viceroy of New Spain—the 10th Duke of Alburquerque—in 1706. By the time Anglo traders arrived in the 1800s, that first "r" had been dropped, but that settlement, now known as Old Town, was still the heart of town. By the 1880s, with the railroad in place, the center of town moved east to meet it, in the Downtown we know today. Remnants of all linger still—and may readily be seen in the soft aging adobes in the North and South Valley, or the old Rail Yard buildings in Barelas.

Planning

When to Go

Albuquerque is sunny year-round and each season has its own appeal, but most locals will say fall is the best time to visit. On just about any day in late August through November, big balloons sail across the sharp blue sky and the scent of freshly roasting green chiles fills the air. Balloon Fiesta brings enormous crowds for nearly two weeks in early October (book hotels at this time as far in advance as possible). Shortly after, the weather's still great and hotel prices plummet. Albuquerque's winter days (generally 10°F warmer than those in Santa Fe) are usually mild enough for hiking, biking, and golf, or simply strolling around Old Town or Nob Hill. The occasional frigid spike in town usually thaws by morning yet Sandia Peak's ski area is hopping and barely an hour away. Spring brings winds, though plenty of sunshine, too, and hotel rates stay low until the summer crowds flock in. Hot but dry temps in mid-May through mid-July stay well below Phoenix-like extremes, but can hit the high 90s and hover there a bit, especially in June. This is followed by roughly six to eight weeks of cooler temperatures, a bit more humidity, and the spectacular late-afternoon cloud formations that herald the brief "monsoon" season. Keep in mind too, that whatever the time of year, the elevation here is just enough that visitors will want to take the usual precautions and prepare for a day or so to acclimate.

Planning Your Time

While some spots on your agenda will likely require car travel, Albuquerque does contain a handful of neighborhoods well suited to exploring on foot. When driving, you can get most anywhere in town in 20 minutes, barring a rush hour jam on the freeways or the Rio Grande bridges, and parking is rarely difficult. A helpful strategy for car days is to bunch together outlying attractions that interest you, perhaps hitting Vara or the Gruet Winery and the Balloon Museum the same day you venture to Petroglyph National Monument or ride the Sandia Peak Tram. Or combine your Tram day with a short hike in the foothills or a visit to the National Museum of Nuclear Science and History.

Walking neighborhoods—Downtown/EDo, Old Town, and UNM/Nob Hill—might take up a half-day each. If hiking, biking, or kayaking appeal, at least another half day or so is warranted. Keep in mind, too, the museums as well as the huge microbrewery and winery scenes that await—yet one more day in town can easily be filled. And if Albuquerque is your base in New Mexico, a day trip to Santa Fe on the Rail Runner (upper deck views are best late in the day) is an excellent option.

Getting Here and Around

AIR

Albuquerque International Sunport is the primary gateway to the state as well as the city. It's a well-designed and attractive art-filled facility that's just 5 miles southeast of Downtown and 3 miles south of UNM/Nob Hill. The city's ABQ Ride bus service runs a shuttle from the airport to Downtown's Alvarado Transportation Center, where you can connect with local bus routes as well as the Rail Runner Express train service to Santa Fe.

CONTACTS Albuquerque International Sunport. (ABQ). ⊠ *2200 Sunport Blvd. SE, Albuquerque* ☎ *505/244–7700* ⊕ *abqsunport.com.*

BIKE

With the creation of many lanes, trails, and dedicated bike paths (an impressive 400 miles worth), Albuquerque's city leaders are recognized for their bike-friendly efforts—a serious challenge given the committed car culture of its residents. The city's public works department produces the detailed Albuquerque Bicycle Map, which can be obtained free at most bike shops or viewed on their website. The Paseo del Bosque Trail, which follows along the Rio Grande Valley and runs flat for most of its 16-mile run, is one of the loveliest rides (or walks) in town.

Bike rentals (mountain, cruise, and e-bikes) are most reliably found in the Old Town area, which has good access to the Paseo del Bosque Trail.

CONTACTS Albuquerque Bicycle Map. ⊠ *Albuquerque* ☎ *505/768–2680* ⊕ *www.cabq.gov/bike.* **Paseo del Bosque Trail.** ⊠ *Albuquerque* ⊕ *www.cabq.gov/parksandrecreation/open-space/lands/paseo-del-bosque-trail.* **Routes Bicycle Tours & Rentals.** ⊠ *2113 Charlevoix St. NW, Old Town* ☎ *505/933–5667* ⊕ *www.routesrentals.com.*

BUS

If you're not planning to explore much beyond Old Town, Downtown, and Nob Hill (all on the old Route 66, or Central Avenue, corridor), the city's public bus system, ABQ Ride, is a practical option (while the bus network is extensive, it can be a slow go on other routes). Rapid Ride and the newer ART (Albuquerque Rapid Transit) lines ply Central Avenue through these neighborhoods every 15 minutes or so from early to midnight or later. You can download trip-planning apps or obtain a customized trip plan at the city's public bus website, ABQ Ride. There is no charge to ride the bus in Albuquerque, thanks to the city's Zero Fares pilot program.

The Alvarado Transportation Center (Downtown) is ABQ Ride's main hub and offers direct connections to the NM Rail Runner Express train service, as well as bus routes throughout the city. Buses accept bicycles at no additional charge, although space is limited. Bus stops are well marked and you can get arrival status updates on your smartphone.

CONTACTS ABQ Ride. ☎ *505/243–7433* ⊕ *www.cabq.gov/transit.*

CAR

While a bus might suffice for destinations along the Route 66/ Central Avenue corridor, to get a real feel for the Duke City's many treasures, a car is necessary. Getting around town is not difficult, and local roads are often quickest. The main highways through the city, north–south Interstate 25 and east–west Interstate 40, converge just northeast of Downtown and generally offer the speediest access to outlying neighborhoods and the airport. Rush-hour jams are common in the mornings and late afternoons, but they're still far less severe than in most big U.S. cities All the major car-rental agencies are represented at Albuquerque's Sunport airport; there are satellite locations around town as well.

Because it's a driving city, most businesses and hotels have free or inexpensive off-street parking, and it's easy enough to find metered street parking in many neighborhoods as well as affordable garages Downtown. Problems usually arise only when there's a major event in town, especially when it's at the University of New Mexico or in Nob Hill, Downtown, or in Old Town—you may want to arrive on the early side to get a space.

TAXI

Taxis are pretty much obsolete in Albuquerque; zTrip, Uber, and Lyft are your best bets for around-the-clock service. Given the considerable distances around town, car service of any kind can be relatively expensive; there may also be an airport fee. Given the limited car service options in town, it is always advisable to call ahead and reconfirm trips.

CONTACTS zTrip. ☎ *855/699–8747, 505/247–8888* ⊕ *www.ztrip. com.*

Thanks to the city's favorable air patterns, Albuquerque is famous for its hot-air balloon rides.

TRAIN

The New Mexico Rail Runner Express, a commuter-train line, provides a picturesque, hassle-free way to make a day trip to Santa Fe. From Albuquerque, these sleek bilevel trains run south for about 35 miles to the town of Belén (stopping in Isleta Pueblo and Los Lunas), and north about 65 miles on a scenic run right into the historic heart of Santa Fe, with stops in Bernalillo, Kewa Pueblo (Santo Domingo), and a few other spots. Albuquerque stops are Downtown (at the Alvarado Transportation Center, where the city's ABQ Ride bus hub is) and at the north end of town, at Montaño and Journal Center/Los Ranchos. On weekdays, the trains run about ten times per day, from about 4:30 am until 9 pm. Six trains usually run on Saturday and four on Sunday. Fares are zone-based (one-way from $2 to $8), but day passes are just $1 more; Albuquerque to Santa Fe is a 4-zone trip and a day pass is $9. All fares are discounted with an online purchase, and bicycles always ride free. Free connections to local bus service are available at most stations—keep your train ticket to get on.

CONTACTS New Mexico Rail Runner Express. ✉ *809 Copper Ave. NW, Albuquerque* ☎ *866/795–7245* ⊕ *www.riometro.org.*

Ballooning

If you've never been ballooning, you may picture a bumpy ride, where changes in altitude produce the queasy feeling you get in a tiny propeller plane, but the experience is far calmer than that. The balloons are flown by licensed pilots (don't call them operators) who deftly turn propane-fueled flames on and off, climbing and descending to find winds blowing the way they want to go—though Albuquerque is known for having a favorable air pattern known as "the box." There's no real steering involved, which makes the pilots' control that much more admirable. Pilots generally land balloons where the wind dictates, so chase vehicles pick you up and return you to your departure point. Even without door-to-door service, many visitors rank a balloon ride over the Rio Grande Valley as their most memorable experience.

Several reliable companies around Albuquerque offer tours. A ride costs about $100 to $200 per person.

Rainbow Ryders

BALLOONING | One of the longest-established balloon tours is with Rainbow Ryders, an official concession for the Albuquerque International Balloon Fiesta. Fly at sunrise (year-round) or sunset (November through February); a glass of Champagne awaits on your return. ⊠ *5601 Eagle Rock Ave. NE, West Side* ☎ *800/725–2477* ⊕ *www.rainbowryders.com.*

Hotels

With a few notable exceptions—Hotel Albuquerque, Hotel Chaco, and Hotel Parq Central, for example—Albuquerque's lodging options fall into two categories: national chain hotels and motels, and distinctive and typically historic inns and B&Bs.

If you are seeking charm, history, or both, Los Poblanos Inn in the North Valley is hands-down the top choice, while Hotel Parq Central in EDo and Downtown's Hotel Andaluz have history and, like Los Poblanos, design pizazz, too. True Modernist fans will be happy at the Sarabande B&B; for the latest and the sleekest, Hotel Chaco is for you. And, of the chains, the Best Western Rio Grande Inn in Old Town has a solid Southwestern feel and is fairly priced to boot. Wherever you stay in Albuquerque, you can generally find rates lower than the national average, and always lower than those in Santa Fe.

⇨ *Hotel and restaurant reviews have been shortened. For full information, visit Fodors.com. Hotel prices are for two people in a standard double room in high season, excluding 13%–14% tax. Restaurant prices are the average cost of a main course at dinner or, if dinner is not served, at lunch.*

What It Costs in U.S. Dollars			
$	$$	$$$	$$$$
HOTELS			
under $150	$150–$250	$251–$400	over $400
RESTAURANTS			
under $17	$17–$25	$26–$35	over $35

Restaurants

The Duke City has long been a place for hearty home-style cooking in big portions, and to this day that remains the spirit in its many authentic New Mexican restaurants. Today, Albuquerque is also firmly established as an innovative presence in farm-to-table dining, and that attitude for locally sourced ingredients influences many fine restaurants throughout the city. Of note here, too, is the city's significant Vietnamese population that has created a slew of excellent Vietnamese eateries. Indian, Japanese, Thai, Middle Eastern, and South American traditions are also spotted around town, making this New Mexico's best destination for global cuisine. Exemplary American standards—say, steak and chops or elevated old-school diner menus—are also well represented.

Whether in Nob Hill, Downtown, Old Town, the North Valley, or the Northeast Heights, the trick to dining well here is to bypass the miles of chain options, and perhaps even move beyond the ever-present "red or green" New Mexican diner's dilemma. A special meal may be had here at fancy and not-so-fancy places, and generally prices are lower than in Santa Fe or other major Southwestern cities.

Tours

ABQ Trolley Co. (AT&SF)

GUIDED TOURS | Narrated 100-minute open-air trolley trips are offered from April through October on a Best of ABQ City Tour (film shoot locations—including *Breaking Bad* and *Better Call Saul* sites—are always included). The 2½-hour Duke City Pedaler and 3½-hour Hopper guide riders to local brews. Trolleys depart from Old Town Plaza. ⊠ *Old Town Emporium, 204 San Felipe St. NW, Old Town* ☎ *505/200–2642* ⊕ *www.tourabq.com.*

Heritage Inspirations

GUIDED TOURS | These richly immersive culture and heritage in-town tours—via hike, e-bike, or walk—are great fun and deeply

The city's public art program is one of the oldest in the country.

informative too. Highlights include Bienvenidos de Albuquerque, ABQ Rio Grande & Farm, and Mezclas de Culturas (with lengths that span from two hours to a full day). ✉ *201 3rd St. NW, No. 1140, Downtown* ☎ *888/344–8687* ⊕ *www.heritageinspirations.com.*

NM Architectural Foundation

GUIDED TOURS | Superbly planned group architectural tours, usually annual, feature exemplary historic and contemporary sites. The online guide offers fabulous photos and in-depth detail on architectural destinations in Albuquerque and elsewhere in New Mexico. ✉ *Albuquerque* ⊕ *www.newmexicoarchitecturalfoundation.org.*

NM Jeep Tours

DRIVING TOURS | Led by respected backcountry and local history experts, NM Jeep Tours offers guided trips that start from Albuquerque and go as far as time (three-hour minimum) and permits allow. Itineraries (ruins, ghost towns, rock formations, and petroglyphs are just a few) are tailored to your interests and time frame. ☎ *505/633–0383* ⊕ *nmjeeptours.com.*

Public Art

SPECIAL-INTEREST TOURS | Started in 1978, Albuquerque's Public Art program is one of the oldest in the country, and the city is strewn with its wonders. Check the Local Maps and Tours section of the ABQ Public Art program's website to plot your route, and for murals around town, go to ⊕ *murosABQ.com.* ✉ *Albuquerque City Hall, 400 Marquette NW, Downtown* ☎ *505/768–3833* ⊕ *www. cabq.gov/publicart.*

Visitor Information

Visit Albuquerque operates tourism information kiosks at the airport (on the baggage-claim level) and in Old Town (⊠ *522 Romerto Street*). To see what's going on by date, go to ⊕ *www.abq365. com.*

CONTACTS Visit Albuquerque. ☎ *505/842–9918, 800/284–2282* ⊕ *www.visitalbuquerque.org.*

Old Town

Sights

★ ABQ BioPark
CITY PARK | FAMILY | The city's foremost outdoor draw, the BioPark comprises four distinct attractions: Aquarium, Botanic Garden, Zoo, and Tingley Beach. Verdant grounds are the setting for summer performances, the *River of Lights* brings crowds over the winter holidays, and exhibits like River Otters, Komodo Dragons, and the Sasebo Japanese Gardens have year-round appeal. The garden and aquarium are located together, just west of Old Town (admission gets you into both facilities) while the zoo is a short drive southeast, off 10th Street SW, and Tingley Beach (and its trout-stocked ponds) lies between. An electric shuttle connects them all. ⊠ *2601 Central Ave. NW, Old Town* ☎ *505/768–2000* ⊕ *www.abqbiopark.com* ⊠ *Tingley Beach and grounds free; Aquarium and Botanic Garden $14.50; Zoo $14.50; combination ticket for all attractions $22.*

★ Albuquerque Museum
ART MUSEUM | FAMILY | In a modern, light-filled space, the Albuquerque Museum serves up a brilliantly curated selection of contemporary art from the museum's own Southwestern artists–centric collections and world-class touring shows; it also presents illuminating shows with regionally topical themes. The must-see Common Ground galleries represent an important permanent collection of primarily 20th-century paintings, all by world-renowned artists with a New Mexico connection; a changing rotation of 19th- and 20th-century photographs from the museum's extensive local archive lines the museum's walkway halls. Other spaces dig even deeper into compelling aspects of Albuquerque and regional history.

Every holiday season, ABQ BioPark produces an annual walk-through light show called the *River of Lights*.

The Sculpture Garden contains more than 50 contemporary works by an internationally known roster of artists that includes Basia Irland and Fritz Scholder; Nora Naranjo-Morse's spiral land-art piece resonates deeply in a place defined by water and land-rights issues. Visitors may pick up a self-guided Sculpture Garden map or come for the free (with admission) docent-led tours at 11 am Wednesday and Saturday (March through November); docent-led tours of the galleries, also free, are held daily at 2 pm, year-round. ⊠ *2000 Mountain Rd. NW, Old Town* ☎ *505/243–7255 museum, 505/898–3915 Casa San Ysidro, 505/242–0434 shop, 505/242–5316 café* ⊕ *www.cabq.gov/museum* ⊠ *$4, free Sun. 9–1 and 1st Wed. of each month; Casa San Ysidro tours $6 (by advance reservation only)* ☉ *Closed Mon.*

American International Rattlesnake Museum
OTHER MUSEUM | FAMILY | Included in the largest collection of different species of living rattlers in the world are such rare and unusual specimens as an albino western diamondback and a melanistic (solid black) diamondback. From the outside the museum looks like just a plain old shop—aside from the friendly crew of tortoises who are usually there to greet you—but inside, the museum's exhibits, its engaging staff, and explanatory videos supply visitors with the lowdown on these venomous creatures. Did you know that they can't hear their own rattles and that the human death rate from rattlesnake bites is less than 1%? The mission here is to educate the public on the many positive benefits of rattlesnakes, and to contribute to their conservation. ⊠ *202 San Felipe St. NW,*

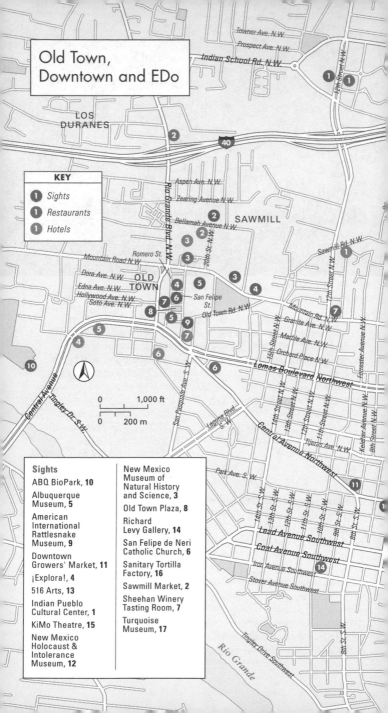

Old Town, Downtown and EDo

KEY

1 Sights

1 Restaurants

1 Hotels

LOS DURANES

SAWMILL

Towner Ave. N.W.

Prospect Ave. N.W.

Indian School Rd. N.W.

40

Aspen Ave. N.W.

Zearing Avenue N.W.

Bellamah Avenue N.W.

Mountain Road N.W.

Romero St.

Dora Ave. N.W.

OLD TOWN

Edna Ave. N.W.

Hollywood Ave. N.W.

Soto Ave. N.W.

San Felipe St.

Old Town Rd. N.W.

Sawmill Rd. N.W.

Mountain Rd. N.W.

Granite Ave. N.W.

Marble Ave. N.W.

Orchard Place N.W.

Lomas Boulevard Northwest

Central Avenue

Tingley Dr. S.W.

San Pasquale Ave. S.W.

Laguna Blvd. S.W.

Central Avenue Northwest

Tijeras Ave. N.W.

0   1,000 ft

0   200 m

Park Ave. S.W.

Lead Avenue Southwest

Coal Avenue Southwest

Iron Avenue Southwest

Stover Avenue Southwest

Tingley Drive Southwest

Rio Grande

Sights

ABQ BioPark, **10**

Albuquerque Museum, **5**

American International Rattlesnake Museum, **9**

Downtown Growers' Market, **11**

¡Explora!, **4**

516 Arts, **13**

Indian Pueblo Cultural Center, **1**

KiMo Theatre, **15**

New Mexico Holocaust & Intolerance Museum, **12**

New Mexico Museum of Natural History and Science, **3**

Old Town Plaza, **8**

Richard Levy Gallery, **14**

San Felipe de Neri Catholic Church, **6**

Sanitary Tortilla Factory, **16**

Sawmill Market, **2**

Sheehan Winery Tasting Room, **7**

Turquoise Museum, **17**

Restaurants

Antiquity, **5**

Artichoke Café, **11**

Bosque Baking Company, **14**

Church Street Café, **4**

Duran Central Pharmacy, **6**

Farina Pizzeria & Wine Bar, **12**

Golden Crown Panaderia, **7**

The Grove Café & Market, **13**

The Kosmos Restaurant, **8**

Range Café Old Town, **2**

Season's Rotisserie & Grill, **3**

Sixty-Six Acres, **1**

Slate Street Cafe, **9**

Villa Myriam Coffee, **10**

Hotels

Böttger Mansion of Old Town, **7**

Casas de Sueños, **6**

El Vado Motel, **4**

Embassy Suites by Hilton Albuquerque, **10**

Hotel Albuquerque at Old Town, **3**

Hotel Andaluz/Curio Collection by Hilton, **8**

Hotel Chaco, **2**

Hotel Parq Central, **9**

The Monterey Motel, **5**

Painted Lady Bed & Brew, **1**

just off southeast corner of Plaza, Old Town ☎ *505/242–6569* ⊕ *www.rattlesnakes.com* 🎫 *$8.95* ⊙ *Closed Sun. year-round and Mon. in Sept.–May.*

¡Explora!

SCIENCE MUSEUM | FAMILY | This imaginatively executed science museum—its driving concept is "Ideas You Can Touch"—is right across from the New Mexico Museum of Natural History and Science. ¡Explora! bills itself as an all-ages attraction (and enthralled adults abound), but there's no question that many of the innovative hands-on exhibits such as a high-wire bicycle and a kinetic sculpture display are geared to children. They offer big fun in addition to big science (and a good dose of art as well). While its colorful Bucky dome is immediately noticeable from the street, ¡Explora! also features a playground, theater, and a freestanding staircase that appears to "float" between floors. ⊠ *1701 Mountain Rd. NW, Old Town* ☎ *505/600–6072* ⊕ *www.explora.us* 🎫 *$10.*

Indian Pueblo Cultural Center

OTHER MUSEUM | FAMILY | Dedicated to the 19 Pueblo tribes in New Mexico, the multilevel semicircular layout of this museum was inspired by Pueblo Bonito, an astounding prehistoric ruin in Chaco Canyon, in northwestern New Mexico. Start by visiting their permanent exhibit space *We Are of This Place: The Pueblo Story*, which interprets the Pueblo people's legacy through carried-down traditions and remarkable pieces from their renowned holdings of fine Native American pottery, textiles, baskets, and other masterworks. Changing exhibits may feature close-ups of a particular artist, such as the colorful and gorgeously composed copper-plate prints of Santa Clara Pueblo painter Helen Hardin. Ceremonial dances are performed year-round on weekends; artisans (with their handcrafted wares available for purchase) are on site Tuesday through Sunday, and there are often arts-and-crafts demonstrations as well. ⊠ *2401 12th St. NW, Los Duranes* ☎ *505/843–7270* ⊕ *www.indianpueblo.org* 🎫 *$12* ⊙ *Closed Mon.*

New Mexico Museum of Natural History and Science

SCIENCE MUSEUM | FAMILY | The wonders at Albuquerque's most popular museum include the only Triassic exhibit in North America. Among some of the dinosaur rarities on display that were discovered right in New Mexico is the relatively youthful "Bisti Beast," a Cretaceous-period tyrannosaur found in the Four Corners area. A simulated volcano (with a river of bubbling hot lava visible through its glass floor) complements the geologic displays. Outer space gets its due here as well—changing exhibits have focused on Mars and the Perseverance lander—and the museum's planetarium is a state-of-the-art destination for dazzling constellation and other distant-space viewings. ✉ *1801 Mountain Rd. NW, Old Town* ☎ *505/841–2800* ⊕ *www.nmnaturalhistory.org* ✉ *Museum $8, DynaTheater $7, Planetarium $7; combined museum and planetarium or DynaTheater $10; all three $15* ⊘ *Closed Tues.*

★ Old Town Plaza

PLAZA/SQUARE | FAMILY | With the landmark 1793 San Felipe de Neri Catholic Church still presiding along the north side, tranquil Old Town Plaza is a pleasant place to sit on wrought-iron benches under a canopy of shade trees. Roughly 200 shops, restaurants, cafés, galleries, and several cultural sights in *placitas* (small plazas) and lanes surround the plaza. During fiestas, Old Town comes alive with mariachi bands and dancing señoritas; at Christmas it is lit with luminarias (the votive candles in paper bag lanterns known as *farolitos* up in Santa Fe). Mostly dating back to the late 1800s, styles from Queen Anne to Territorial and Pueblo Revival, and even Mediterranean, are apparent in the one- and two-story (almost all adobe) structures. ✉ *Old Town.*

★ San Felipe de Neri Catholic Church

CHURCH | FAMILY | Well over two centuries after it first welcomed worshippers, this lovely adobe structure is still active (mass is offered daily). A National Register of Historic Places site erected in 1793 (to replace Albuquerque's first Catholic church, which was founded here in 1706), its Spanish Colonial base was charmingly modified with a touch of Gothic Revival (note the spires) in the mid-19th century. Its tan stucco and fresh white trim stand out at the north end of Old Town's plaza, and while it has been expanded several times, a surprising amount of its original adobe walls (some 5 feet thick) and other features remain. Small gardens front and flank the church; the inside is a respite from the tourism bustle beyond its doorstep—the painting and iconography are simple and authentic, the atmosphere hushed. Next to it is a shop and small museum that displays relics (vestments, paintings, carvings) dating from the 17th century. Call ahead to arrange a tour. ■TIP➔ **There's a hidden treasure behind the church: inside the gnarled tree is a statue that some speculate depicts the Virgin Mary.** ✉ *2005 Plaza NW, Old Town* ☎ *505/243–4628* ⊕ *www.sanfelipedeneri.org* ✉ *Free.*

★ Sawmill Market

MARKET | FAMILY | A former lumber-yard building located by the one-time AT&SF Railway line in the city's old Sawmill district has been turned into a grand food hall that resonates with a sense of history and place. Some two dozen dining, shopping, and drinks vendors offer an eclectic range of high-quality (and, yes, higher priced) wares. A carefully honed selection of mostly independent enterprises, all embrace a definitively fresh and local ethos—some by way of Santa Fe, like Dr. Field Goods (an established spot with food-truck roots), and others talented transplants from afar (Flora and Flora Taco-to-Go). Whether poké, sushi, taters, or tapas, a lush dessert, or a savory cone, the same commitment to in-state growers, makers, and suppliers is apparent. Stroll around a bit and you can't help but appreciate the original architectural details (just gaze up at the fabulously restored wooden ceiling). Paxton's Taproom has a seasonal rotation of New Mexico–brewed beers, as well as a steady set of the state's best craft beers on tap (wines lean local as well as international). The cool Mobile Bar is ready to serve out on their grassy patio, where any food bought inside may be enjoyed as well. ⊠ *1909 Bellamah Ave. NW, Old Town* ☎ *505/563–4473* ⊕ *www.sawmillmarket.com.*

Sheehan Winery Tasting Room

WINERY | Sourcing his grapes from vineyards throughout the state, South Valley vintner Sean Sheehan welcomes serious local fans and visitors from afar to his Old Town tasting room—an inviting destination for those seeking the best in "old vine" wines in a convivial but intimate space. Lighter, brighter, and spicier components bring a special experience to tastings of the award-winning and notable favorites like a Cinsault Dry Rose and Cabernet Sauvignon Grand Reserve or the Riesling-based Cielo Dulce. ⊠ *303 Romero St. NW, Plaza Don Luis, Old Town* ☎ *505/508–1221* ⊕ *www.sheehanwinery.com/old-town-tasting-room* ✍ *Wine tastings $15 (5 wines in a set selection) or $20 (6 wines, guest's choice).*

 Restaurants

Antiquity

$$$ | **AMERICAN** | Within the thick adobe walls of this darkly lit, romantic space off the plaza in Old Town, patrons have been feasting on rich, elegantly prepared American classics for more than 50 years. This isn't the edgy, contemporary restaurant to bring an adventuresome foodie—Antiquity specializes in classics, from starters of French onion soup and Alaskan King crab cakes with a perfectly piquant remoulade sauce to main courses like Chicken Madagascar, Australian lobster tail with drawn butter, and black Angus New York strip-loin steak with horseradish sauce. **Known for:** old-world-style service; timeless menu; congenial buzz. ⑤ *Average main: $35* ⊠ *112 Romero St. NW, Old Town* ☎ *505/247–3545* ⊕ *www.antiquityrestaurant.com* ☉ *Closed Sun. and Mon. No lunch.*

Church Street Café

$$ | SOUTHWESTERN | This traditional adobe eatery features New Mexican–style family recipes, which happily feed streams of hungry tourists. Locals, too, are drawn here, especially for the alfresco dining in the lovely courtyard (and in the mosaic-bedazzled great room looking out to it), amid trellises of sweet grapes and flowers, and further enhanced by the occasional accompaniment of a classical and flamenco guitarist. **Known for:** chile rellenos stuffed with pork and cheese; historic tile and tin decorations; flower-filled courtyard seating. ⑤ *Average main: $17* ⊠ *2111 Church St. NW, Old Town* ☎ *505/247–8522* ⊕ *www.churchstreetcafe.com* ☽ *Closed Mon. No dinner Sun.*

★ Duran Central Pharmacy

$ | SOUTHWESTERN | FAMILY | A favorite of old-timers who know their way around a blue-corn enchilada (and know that Duran's deeply authentic New Mexican red is the chile to pick for it), this welcoming spot serves fine, freshly made and warm flour tortillas, too. Duran's harkens to the days when every drugstore had a soda fountain; it's got cold beer and a full kitchen now, serving up breakfast, lunch, and dinner, with your choice of counter stools, cozy tables, or the little shaded patio right off old Route 66. **Known for:** famous red chiles; friendly, fast service; retro charm with old-school pharmacy still on site. ⑤ *Average main: $12* ⊠ *1815 Central Ave. NW, Old Town* ☎ *505/247–4141* ⊕ *www.duransrx.com* ☽ *No dinner Sun.–Tues.*

Golden Crown Panaderia

$ | BAKERY | FAMILY | Tucked between Old Town and the Wells Park neighborhood, this aromatic, down-home-style bakery opens early but is especially well known for two things: its hearty green-chile bread and its hand-tossed (thin-crust) pizzas made with blue corn, peasant, or green-chile dough. You can also order hot cocoa, cappuccino, an award-winning local IPA or lager (or wine), some *biscochitos* (the official state cookie), fruit-filled empanadas, sandwiches, and a popular coffee milkshake. **Known for:** charming shaded patio; green-chile bread; 24/7 cookie ATM on site (credit card only). ⑤ *Average main: $15* ⊠ *1103 Mountain Rd. NW, Old Town* ☎ *505/243–2424* ⊕ *www.goldencrown.biz* ☽ *Closed Mon. and Tues.*

Range Café Old Town

$$ | AMERICAN | FAMILY | A local standby for any meal, the Range Café has a high comfort quotient with hearty dishes like their blue corn or fresh spinach enchiladas with black beans and arroz verde, biscuits and gravy, burgers, and the generously plated salmon-berry salad. Breakfast, served until 3 pm, has fans for its house-made green-chile turkey sausage and huevos rancheros. **Known for:** New Mexican and truckstop classics; sweet pecan rolls; colorful, funky decor. ⑤ *Average main: $17 ⊠ 1050 Rio Grande Blvd. NW, Old Town ☎ 505/508–2640 ⊕ www.rangecafe.com.*

Seasons Rotisserie & Grill

$$$ | AMERICAN | Upbeat and elegant, Seasons's pleasing arches, soothing palette, and open-kitchen plan draw diners for business lunches and dinner dates; oenophiles revel in its well-chosen cellar. Wood-fueled grills and pastas dominate the seasonally changing roster of dishes with tangy sauces (Atlantic salmon might be complemented with a dill crème fraîche; a creole jus for Cajun chicken; pork tenderloin brightened by a fig-bourbon blend). **Known for:** wood-grilled beef and seafood; creative vegetarian mains; lively rooftop scene. ⑤ *Average main: $28 ⊠ 2031 Mountain Rd. NW, Old Town ☎ 505/766–5100 ⊕ seasonsabq.com ⊗ No lunch. Closed Mon. and Tues.*

Sixty-Six Acres

$$ | ECLECTIC | A coolly modern glass-framed dining spot across from the Indian Pueblo Cultural Center, Sixty-Six Acres serves up satisfying locally sourced dishes that riff freely on New Mexican and Asian traditions. The generous bowls, grilled sandwiches, and salads here—from green-chile cheeseburgers to Korean chicken bites to salmon and Himalayan rice and farro with fresh spinach salad—are flavorful, often gluten-free, and make vegetarian dining easy. **Known for:** Southwestern style with an Asian twist; casual, convivial atmosphere; pet-friendly patio with mountain views. ⑤ *Average main: $20 ⊠ Avanyu Plaza, 2400 12th St. NW, Los Duranes ☎ 505/243–2230 ⊕ www.sixtysixacres.com ⊗ Closed Mon.*

 Hotels

Böttger Mansion of Old Town

$$ | B&B/INN | A National Register property built in 1912 in the American Foursquare style, Böttger Mansion offers thoughtfully refurbished rooms incorporating fine woodwork and other period details like a claw-foot tub, a lovely mural by the original owner's grandson, or a pressed-tin ceiling. **Pros:** off-street but still in the heart of Old Town; architectural gem; free parking. **Cons:** two-night minimum on most weekends; wood floors may creak; on-site cats not for everyone. ⑤ *Rooms from: $199 ⊠ 110 San Felipe St. NW, Old Town ☎ 505/539–2093 ⊕ www.bottger.com ⇥ 7 rooms ❏❶ Free Breakfast.*

Casas de Sueños

$$ | **B&B/INN** | This historic compound (it's a National Register property) of 1930s- and '40s-era adobe casitas is perfect if you're seeking seclusion and quiet, yet desire proximity to museums, restaurants, and shops. **Pros:** charming, quirky, and tucked away; some private patios; free parking. **Cons:** units vary in ambience and age—some are more enchanting than others; some high beds, claw baths, and tall steps—ask about accessibility; decor not for everyone. $ *Rooms from: $179* ⊠ *310 Rio Grande Blvd. SW, on the south side of Central Ave., Old Town* ☎ *505/767–1000* ⊕ *www.casasdesuenos.com* ⇩ *21 casitas* �’❙❉❙ *Free Breakfast.*

El Vado Motel

$$$ | **MOTEL** | Back in the day, El Vado was a prime Route 66 stay-over for those driving west (or back east), and now the 1937 vintage former motor court has been transformed into a desti-nation-worthy, fully modern motel, with a decor that winningly embraces mid century modernism. **Pros:** modern decor with a zippy and warm color scheme; outdoor lounging by the pool; on-site taproom and dining spots. **Cons:** limited parking, so guests may have to look on local streets; spillover sound from plaza-ar-ea events can reach rooms; pool on the small side. $ *Rooms from: $259* ⊠ *2500 Central Ave. SW, Old Town* ☎ *505/361–1667* ⊕ *www.elvadoabq.com* ⇩ *22 rooms* ❙❉❙ *No Meals.*

Hotel Albuquerque at Old Town

$$$ | **HOTEL** | This 11-story Heritage Hotels & Resorts property over-looking Old Town has historic Territorial-style touches across its inviting facade, and attention is paid throughout its public spaces to New Mexican artisan craftwork, from Nambe Pueblo–designed metalwork to Navajo rugs. **Pros:** understated room decor with pleasing Southwestern flavor; lovely gardens that surround dining patio and outdoor pool; mountain view rooms available. **Cons:** air-conditioning units can be loud; in-room furnishings sufficient but spare; $20 amenity fee for all. $ *Rooms from: $359* ⊠ *800 Rio Grande Blvd. NW, Old Town* ☎ *505/843–6300, 866/505–7829* ⊕ *www.hotelabq.com* ⇩ *188 rooms* ❙❉❙ *No Meals.*

Hotel Chaco

$$$$ | **HOTEL** | A special commitment to New Mexico shines through in this dedicated study of Chaco Canyon as an inspiration for one of Albuquerque's most popular hotels; it uses materials meant to evoke the fine stone chinking that comprise most of the 9th- to 12th-century structures found at that deeply compelling ancient Puebloan site. **Pros:** contemplative outdoor lounge; deep appreciation of New Mexico's arts and heritage in every detail; full spa and 24/7 fitness center. **Cons:** oddly fortress-like entrance; $35

resort fee (includes parking); joint-use pool is on (adjacent) Hotel Albuquerque site. $ *Rooms from: $469* ✉ *2000 Bellamah Ave. NW, Old Town* ☎ *505/246–9989, 855/997–8208 reservations only* ⊕ *www.hotelchaco.com* ➦ *118 rooms* ¶❍¶ *No Meals.*

The Monterey Motel

$ | **MOTEL** | With its streamlined modern decor and tasteful palette, the fully renovated and upscale Monterey, like neighboring El Vado Motel, is one Route 66-vintage motel that—luckily for travelers seeking a more unique stay today—outlasted the trend of turning motels into chains. **Pros:** fun lounge and patio areas for all guests; free parking; unique design. **Cons:** management not on site 24/7; street noise can travel; not all bathrooms are ensuite. $ *Rooms from: $149* ✉ *2402 Central Ave. SW, Old Town* ☎ *505/243–3554* ⊕ *www.themontereymotel.com* ➦ *27 rooms* ¶❍¶ *No Meals.*

Painted Lady Bed & Brew

$$ | **B&B/INN** | On a quiet side street on the fringe of Albuquerque's Sawmill-Wells Park districts, a particular personality is revealed in this low-slung historic adobe: while it decidedly favors fans of the ever-growing craft brew scene, it also offers comfortably appointed suites that have been thoughtfully modernized from their original early 1900s construction. **Pros:** garden seating enhanced with murals and locally hand-forged metalwork; cool history; two afternoon beers free. **Cons:** creative furnishings vary in appeal; two-night stay may be required; beer beats breakfast (no meal offered). $ *Rooms from: $210* ✉ *1100 Bellamah Ave. NW, Old Town* ☎ *505/200–3999* ⊕ *www.breakfastisoverrated.com* ➦ *2 suites* ¶❍¶ *No Meals.*

 Performing Arts

★ Tablao Flamenco

FOLK/TRADITIONAL DANCE | Flamenco music and dance speak to something in Albuquerque's soul, and for folks new to the tradition or yearning for a taste, this venue—with food and wine to match—is the perfect spot to kindle that flame. In an intimate, appropriately sultry setting, enjoy the four-course prix fixe menu offered with evening performances or small bites with the Sunday matinee. Arrive early, and be dazzled by the world-class artists performing here. ✉ *Hotel Albuquerque at Old Town, 800 Rio Grande Blvd. NW, Old Town* ☎ *505/222–8797* ⊕ *www.tablaoflamenco.org.*

Old Town has the city's largest concentration of one-of-a-kind retail shops.

🛍 Shopping

El Vado Market

MARKET | FAMILY | Just across from the BioPark, shaded outdoor seating on El Vado Motel's plaza is surrounded by a cluster of locally committed shopkeepers and food purveyors. A good meal option is Buen Provecho, inspired by Costa Rican traditional cooking, or enjoy a *cerveza* (beer) from the El Vado Taproom. Stroll just beyond the plaza to a cluster of local vendors on the complex's outer periphery (Southwest Cactus Shop has not only the expected succulents, but a well-selected range of southwest-themed hand-stamped cards, earrings, clever metal birds, and more), or a little further east on Central Avenue to Kaufman's Coffee & Bagels (freshly made on site) or Swan Song, a retro-ware recycler. ⊠ *2500 Central Ave. SW, Old Town* ☎ *505/361–1667* ⊕ *www.elvadoabq. com* ⊗ *Buen Provecho closed Mon.; Southwest Cactus closed Mon. and Tues.; Kaufman Coffee & Bagels closed Tues.*

⭐ Grey Dog Trading/Zuni Fetish Museum

CRAFTS | This shop carries a very special selection of fetishes, along with kachina dolls, baskets, and a small grouping of vintage and contemporary Native American jewelry and pottery, for the beginning and seasoned collector. The shop's owner, Yvonne Stokes, is well respected in this field, and presents work from all 19 pueblos as well as Hopi and Navajo pieces. Changing exhibits focus on one tradition—stone carvers, for example—and hone in on the work of one artist and perhaps that of the artist's family as well. Gorgeous hand-carved Ye'i figures by contemporary Navajo artist Sheldon Harvey are here, as are his wonderful abstraction paintings. Enter the Zuni Fetish Museum from within the gallery; an unusually fine range of historic Zuni-crafted fetishes awaits, along with those by other Native artisans. Transitions in style and theme are well-documented here, as are trends in materials and form. Visits to both the store and the museum are by advance appointment only. ⊠ *Plaza Hacienda, 1925 Old Town Rd. NW, Old Town* ☎ *505/243–0414* ⊕ *www.greydogtrading.com.*

★ Old Town Antiques

ANTIQUES & COLLECTIBLES | Take a moment in this neat and quiet shop to appreciate the very particular eye of its owner, Connie Fulwyler, who, while not at all intrusive, will gladly relay the backstory of any piece here. Her offerings center on 19th- and 20th-century art and history (Anglo, Mexican, and Native American), with a touch of "odd science" and politics: find a winsome piggy bank rendered in 1940s–50s Tlaquepaque glazeware, an original Harrison Begay gouache painting, vintage Taxco sombrero cufflinks, 1813 political engravings, early-20th-century Santo Domingo bowls, a Gilbert Atencio serigraph used for a menu cover, rare books and paper ephemera, and more. ⊠ *416 Romero St. NW, Old Town* ☎ *505/842–6657* ⊕ *oldtownantiquesabq.com.*

Santisima

OTHER SPECIALTY STORE | Meeting Johnny Salas, Santisima's spirited owner, is part of the fun of visiting this Old Town shop. It sells mostly artwork and objects that celebrate New Mexican santos traditions and Día de los Muertos across the globe. ⊠ *328 San Felipe St. NW, # F, Old Town* ☎ *505/246–2611.*

Downtown and EDo

You may plan to visit Downtown—or its northward extension, Wells Park—mostly for the arts and brews scene (⊕ *abqartwalk. com* posts a monthly update), but take a closer look. Along Central Avenue, there's not only the Pueblo Deco dazzler KiMo Theatre, but a prime trail of architectural details (peppered with modern murals and mosaics) dating back to the railroad era. The same Gold Avenue stretch, from First Street SW to Eighth Street SW, has its own riches: the Venetian Gothic Revival Occidental Insurance Building (No. 305), the mid-century landmark Simms Building (No. 400), and the U.S. Historic Courthouse (No. 421).

As for EDo (East Downtown, First Street SW east to I-25), on Central, the old main library (a Spanish-Pueblo Revival wonder inside and out) and the one-time railroad hospital (now the fabulous Parq Central Hotel) are but two highlights. But there's more: wander out along Broadway and find a growing walkable universe of maker shops, good bites, brews, and art galleries; side streets reveal a wealth of residential Victorian buildings.

Sights

Downtown Growers' Market

MARKET | FAMILY | Toe-tapping music and the freshest of fresh produce—and surely the delicious shade created by the towering cottonwoods here in Robinson Park—have folks gathering every Saturday morning from April through October. This sweet respite on the western fringe of Downtown also hosts city crafts makers—high-quality wares range from fine block-printed linens to small-batch soaps and creative ceramics—and purveyors of baked goods. Or simply pick up a hot (or cold) brew and enjoy a stroll. ✉ *Robinson Park, Central Ave. at 8th St. NW, Downtown* ⊕ *www. downtowngrowers.org* ⊗ *Closed Nov.–Mar.*

★ 516 Arts

ART GALLERY | World-class contemporary art dominates the changing shows at this multilevel nonprofit that holds a special place in the New Mexico art scene. Visually compelling collaborations with an international set of museums and artists cross media boundaries, and often explore issues that are not only dear to the hearts and minds of this multicultural, environmentally diverse state, but resonate globally. The installations here are always top-notch, the works displayed are of the highest quality, the ideas—whether expressed in video, prints, sculpture, diodes, or paint—provocative. ✉ *516 Central Ave. SW, Downtown* ☎ *505/242–1445* ⊕ *www.516arts.org* ☒ *Free* ⊗ *Closed Sun. and Mon.*

★ KiMo Theatre

PERFORMANCE VENUE | Decorated with light fixtures made from buffalo skulls (the eye sockets glow amber in the dark), traditional Navajo symbols, dazzling tilework, and nine spectacular Western-theme wall murals by Carl Von Hassler, the 1927 Carl Boller–designed movie palace represents Pueblo Deco at its apex. The 660-seat KiMo (refurbished with its original balcony, hand-painted ceilings, and restored marquee) would be a standout anywhere. Former Albuquerque resident Vivian Vance of *I Love Lucy* fame once performed on the stage; today you're more likely to catch Mary Chapin Carpenter or the Wallflowers, a ballet, flamenco

Albuquerque's most historic theater is the Pueblo Deco masterpiece, the KiMo Theatre.

performance, or a film- or book-festival event. Guided tours are occasionally offered. ✉ *423 Central Ave. NW, at 5th St., Downtown* ☎ *505/768–3522 theater, 505/228–9857 box office* ⊕ *www.cabq.gov/kimo.*

New Mexico Holocaust & Intolerance Museum
HISTORY MUSEUM | This small but moving 1932-vintage storefront museum packs plenty of punch with its poignant exhibits that document genocide and persecution throughout history, with a special emphasis on the Holocaust and World War II. Exhibits also include *The African American Experience* and others touch on child slave labor. ✉ *616 Central Ave. SW, Downtown* ☎ *505/247–0606* ⊕ *www.nmholocaustmuseum.org* ✉ *$6* ⊘ *Closed Mon. and Tues.*

★ Richard Levy Gallery
ART GALLERY | A stellar roster of artists with an international following (many New Mexico–based) show at this airy gallery that would be right at home on either coast. Its clean lines are perfect for displaying important contemporary pieces from photographers (Natsumi Hayashi, Hiroshi Sugimoto), multimedia artists (Mary Tsiongas, Eric Tillinghast, John Baldessari), metal-work sculptors (Emi Ozawa), and printmakers (Alex Katz, Ed Ruscha), as well as works from global initiatives like ISEA 2012: Machine Wilderness and 2009's LAND/ART New Mexico. ✉ *514 Central Ave. SW, Downtown* ☎ *505/766–9888* ⊕ *www.levygallery.com* ✉ *Free* ⊘ *Closed Sun.–Wed.*

Sanitary Tortilla Factory

ARTS CENTER | At a nexus of Downtown's coffee-beer-arts scene, Sanitary Tortilla is an exemplary adaptive reuse project. Now housing artist studios and gallery spaces, the eponymous onetime tortilla and chile go-to for politicos and locals of all stripes provides a cleverly curated counterpoint to the 516 Arts–Richard Levy arts nexus down on Central. Occasional outdoor installations (like Pastel FD's Botanical mural project, a collaboration with 516) complement the intriguing, often topical, shows inside. ⊠ *401–403 2nd St. SW, Downtown* ☎ *505/228–3749* ⊕ *sanitarytortillafactory.org* 🎫 *Free* ⊙ *Closed Sat.–Wed. except for events or by appointment.*

Turquoise Museum

OTHER MUSEUM | **FAMILY** | Located in a formerly residential "castle" replete with Victorian chandeliers, the Turquoise Museum casts fresh light on the beauty, mythology, and physical properties of turquoise, a semiprecious but adored gemstone that many people associate with the color of New Mexico's skies. Displays show how turquoise forms, the importance of individual mines, and uses of the stone by Native Americans in prehistoric times. The museum's proprietors, the Lowry family, are longtime traders with deep knowledge of the gem; if you retain nothing else, remember that only turquoise specified as "natural" is the desirable, unadulterated stuff. A small gift shop sells historic and contemporary pieces. Tickets for entry and tours are only available online. ⊠ *400 2nd St. SW, Downtown* ☎ *505/433–3684* ⊕ *www.turquoisemuseum.com* 🎫 *$20* ⊙ *Closed Sun.*

 Restaurants

Artichoke Café

$$$ | **CONTEMPORARY** | Locals praise this smartly contemporary EDo stalwart for its attentive service and French, American, and Italian dishes often prepared with organic ingredients. Seasonal specials might include strip steak with Southwestern sides; a zesty, vegetarian house-made ravioli; and Mary's Farm chicken with a Peruvian rub. **Known for:** pleasing gallery-style decor; occasional off days; high-end local favorite. 💲 *Average main: $34* ⊠ *424 Central Ave. SE, EDo* ☎ *505/243–0200* ⊕ *www.artichokecafe.com* ⊙ *Closed Sun. No lunch.*

Bosque Baking Company

$ | **BAKERY** | Beautiful loaves—Old World Rye, South Valley Sourdough, Sunflower Seed Multigrain, and Rustic Baguettes—beckon at the open-kitchen storefront location of Bosque Baking. Tucked away in an historic neighborhood on the western edge of Downtown, it's helmed by Jim Mecca, the best bread baker in town.

Known for: the best bread in town; savory and sweet empanadas; amazing cookies. $ *Average main: $5* ⊠ *922 Coal Ave. SW, Downtown* ☎ *505/234–6061* ⊕ *bosque-baking-co.business.site* ⊘ *Closed Sun.–Tues. No dinner.*

★ Farina Pizzeria & Wine Bar

$$ | PIZZA | A stellar spot for truly artisanal thin-crust pizza, Farina draws loyal crowds inside an old-school former EDo grocery store with hardwood floors, exposed-brick walls, a pressed-tin ceiling, and simple rows of wooden tables along with a long, inviting bar. This spirited place serves up exceptional pizzas with tastily charred crusts and imaginative toppings; the Salsiccia, with sweet-fennel sausage, roasted onions, and mozzarella, has plenty of fans. **Known for:** award-winning pizza and Italian favorites; contemporary art-filled atmosphere; creative pizza toppings. $ *Average main: $25* ⊠ *510 Central Ave. SE, EDo* ☎ *505/243–0130* ⊕ *www.farinapizzeria.com* ⊘ *Closed Sun. No lunch Sat.*

★ The Grove Café & Market

$ | CAFÉ | This airy, modern EDo neighborhood favorite features locally grown, seasonal specials at reasonable prices. Enjoy such fresh, quality treats as Grove Pancakes with fresh fruit, crème fraîche, local honey, and real maple syrup; a Farmers Salad with roasted golden beets, Marcona almonds, goat cheese, and lemon-on-basil vinaigrette; or an aged Genoa salami sandwich with olive tapenade, arugula, and provolone on artisanal sourdough bread. **Known for:** culinary market with specialty goods; quick-moving line to order; easy, relaxed atmosphere. $ *Average main: $13* ⊠ *600 Central Ave. SE, EDo* ☎ *505/248–9800* ⊕ *www.thegrovecafemarket.com* ⊘ *Closed Mon. No dinner.*

★ The Kosmos Restaurant

$ | AMERICAN | In an old brick Wells Park-area factory building that has a long history as an alternative art space, Kosmos is where you go for a fun beer and a *very* good bite. You might try the crispy beer-battered fish-and-chips or a chimichurri-sauced grilled steak sandwich (get it with their spiral Spudnik fires). **Known for:** creative dishes across the American spectrum; comfortably arty decor with an inspired handmade feel; well-chosen craft beer menu. $ *Average main: $16* ⊠ *1715 5th St. NW, Downtown* ☎ *505/369–1772* ⊕ *www.kosmosabq.com* ⊘ *Closed Sun.–Tues.*

Slate Street Cafe

$$ | ECLECTIC | A high-energy, high-ceilinged dining room with a wine bar and modern lighting, this stylish restaurant sits amid pawn shops and bail-bond outposts on a quiet, unprepossessing side street Downtown. Once inside, you'll find a sophisticated, colorful space serving memorable, modern renditions of classic road fare, such as a seared salmon club and a green chile chicken sandwich; their brown bag fish-and-chips is a longtime crowd fave. **Known for:** Thursday night wine tastings; excellent fish-and-chips; sleek but comfortable business meeting spot. ⑤ *Average main: $17* ⌧ *515 Slate St. NW, Downtown* ☎ *505/243–2210* ⊕ *www.slatestreetcafe.com* ⊘ *Closed Mon. No dinner.*

★ Villa Myriam Coffee

$ | **CAFÉ** | A visit to Villa Myriam is always satisfying, not just for the uber-fresh coffee drinks on offer and its crisply contemporary design, but for the sense of discovery—tucked away as it is in this emerging early 20th-century warehouse area not far from the train tracks. Tasty teas and sandwiches are also served. **Known for:** comfy, contemporary seating; freshly roasted Colombian beans (on-site!); flavorful spins on small-bite snacks. ⑤ *Average main: $7* ⌧ *573 Commercial St. NE, Downtown* ☎ *505/336–5652* ⊕ *www. vmcoffee.com* ⊘ *Closed weekends.*

Hotels

Embassy Suites by Hilton Albuquerque

$$ | **HOTEL** | **FAMILY** | This all-suites high-rise with a contemporary design sits on a bluff alongside Interstate 25, affording guests fabulous views of the Downtown skyline (and the open desert beyond) to the west, and the Sandia Mountains to the east. **Pros:** convenient location adjacent to Interstate 25, near the Interstate 40 interchange; free hot breakfast and nightly cocktails; fitness center and indoor pool. **Cons:** suites attract families as well as business travelers; showing its age, so must request a renovated floor; views limited on lower floors. ⑤ *Rooms from: $155* ⌧ *1000 Woodward Pl. NE, Downtown* ☎ *505/245–7100, 800/362–2779* ⊕ *www.hilton.com* ⇙ *261 suites* ⭕ *Free Breakfast.*

Hotel Andaluz/Curio Collection by Hilton

$$ | **HOTEL** | Opened in 1939 by Conrad Hilton and now on the National Register of Historic Places, this 10-story Southwestern Territorial–style boutique hotel incorporates the Spanish Moorish elements of the original Hilton design in its dramatic interior decor. **Pros:** historic aesthetic enhanced with tech-forward perks; nice view from the Ibiza terrace lounge; great on-site dining. **Cons:** in-room lighting may be a bit dim for some; valet parking fee; fitness center access is across street. ⑤ *Rooms from: $227* ⌧ *125 2nd St. NW, Downtown* ☎ *505/242–9090* ⊕ *www.hotelandaluz. com* ⇙ *107 rooms* ⭕ *No Meals.*

★ Hotel Parq Central

$$ | HOTEL | A decidedly imaginative adaptation, the landmark Parq Central occupies a striking Moravian tile-trimmed three-story former AT&SF Railroad employees' hospital that dates to 1926. **Pros:** on the National (and State) Register of Historic Places; smartly designed rooms with sound-blocking windows; wonderfully landscaped back patio. **Cons:** parking (free) can be sparse when Apothecary Lounge is hopping; noise might travel to rooms nearest the Lounge; free airport shuttle shuttle not always available. $ *Rooms from: $190* ⊠ *806 Central Ave. SE, Downtown* ☎ *505/242–0040* ⊕ *www.hotelparqcentral.com* ↪ *74 rooms* ⦿ *Free Breakfast.*

Nightlife

Effex Night Club

DANCE CLUBS | Albuquerque's sizable LGBTQ+ community—and anyone else seeking a jumping dance scene—flocks to Effex, a vibrant, centrally located, multi-level nightclub with a huge rooftop bar and an even larger downstairs dance floor. Also inside is SideEffex, a small but sufficient gastropub. ⊠ *420 Central St. SW, Downtown* ☎ *505/842–8870* ⊕ *www.effexabq.com.*

JUNO Brewery + Cafe + Art

BREWPUBS | Beer and art still mingle successfully at this Wells Park destination, great for anyone looking for a good brew and tapas or panini. Even better, Ian LeBlanc's exuberant metal sculpture works steadfastly preside over the outdoor patio seating. Indoors, artwork and clever design details enhance a visit to this special craft brewery, where Mexican-style 505 Lager and a developing line of English-style beers (and occasional music- and dance-based events) are featured. ⊠ *1501 1st St. NW, Downtown* ☎ *505/219–3938* ⊕ *www.junopub.com.*

Thirsty Eye Brewing Company

BREWPUBS | Mixing art and brews, as Thirsty Eye does, is not unique for Albuquerque, but it's certainly welcome. As is the neighborhood atmosphere here, where craft beers are king (their own brews—El Ojo Rojo and Citrus Buzz—are regular faves, plus there's a tempting selection of seasonals and guest taps) and its indoor/outdoor set-up allows for live music weekly. Often the art on display is tied into a show at Exhibit/208 next door (the smart-eyed curator, Kim Arthun, is also a partner at Thirsty); openings, held jointly, might be accompanied by pizza made fresh on the back patio. ⊠ *206 Broadway Blvd. SE, EDo* ☎ *505/639–5831* ⊕ *www.thirstyeyebrew.com.*

🎭 Performing Arts

★ Chatter

CONCERTS | Holding sway at 10:30 am Sunday morning, the Chatter chamber ensemble's classical-to-modern music program draws a devoted crowd of regulars. Free cappuccino and a spoken-word performance round out the one-hour shows. Expect the best of local and guest performers—Santa Fe Opera stars have been known to pop in during the season. Arrive early, as the seating is open and limited; it's best to buy tickets ahead of time online. Check online as well for their special first Friday "Late Works" evening programs at 9 pm and the Chatter Cabaret series at the Albuquerque Museum on occasional Sundays at 5 pm throughout the year. ⊠ 912 3rd St. NW, Downtown ⊕ www.chatterabq.org ☜ $16.50.

FUSION

ARTS CENTERS | Housed in the 100-seat Cell Theatre, FUSION Theatre Company has been central to the professional theatrical scene here ever since its 2001 founding. Building on its acclaimed annual "Seven Works" short-works play festival, FUSION has doubled down with creative initiatives that serve its deep commitment to community, from art shows and AMP Concerts productions to film screenings and more. Set in a historic railroad-industrial area (on the city's developing Rail Trail), FUSION's programming takes place in the Cell, their 708 performance/gallery space, and the 1,200-seat outdoor Meadow facility. ⊠ 700–708 1st St. NW, Downtown ☎ 505/766–9412 ⊕ www.FUSIONnm.org.

🛍 Shopping

★ The Man's Hat Shop

HATS & GLOVES | An Albuquerque mainstay since 1946, and here on Central since 1964, the Man's Hat Shop is where anyone, man or woman, who needs just the right hat, with just the right fit, will find what they're looking for—whether that's fedora, porkpie, Cossack-style, coonskin, or, of course, top-of-the-line Western felt or straw. Owner Stuart Dunlap clearly loves his business—as do costume designers from the state's expanding film industry—and will help guide you among some 5,000 styles to a new chapeau that suits, or modify one you already have. ⊠ 511 Central Ave. NW, Downtown ☎ 505/247–9605 ⊕ www.themanshatshop.com.

Town & Ranch

OTHER SPECIALTY STORE | Another inspired endeavor from the design-forward folks at Los Poblanos Inn, Town & Ranch smartly offers a side-by-side tasting Lounge (for its on-site distillery's "new

At the National Hispanic Cultural Center, you can see many cultural performances including some from Ehecatl Aztec dancers.

Western" dry gins) and a supplies shop, where you can stock up a picnic basket, refill your lotion bottles, or buy a local vintage and have it poured for you next door. ⊠ *1318 4th St. NW, Downtown* ☎ *505/808–1715* ⊕ *www.lospoblanos.com/shop/town-and-ranch.*

Barelas and South Valley

The historic Barelas neighborhood, to the south of Downtown, features the must-see National Hispanic Cultural Center and the Rail Yards Market. Bounded by the Rio Grande bosque trails and the revitalizing rail district, this mostly residential neighborhood centers on 4th Street SW (a section of old Route 66) and is one of Albuquerque's oldest; it has shops and services—and earlier 20th-century architecture—that appear to have enjoyed a pause in time. Barelas gradually gives way to the broad South Valley. While perhaps somewhat rough-around-the-edges, the South Valley's deep agrarian roots may be seen in the burgeoning local farm and winery scene. Other highlights are the historic remnants found along the pre-freeway byways, as well as the developing Valle de Oro National Wildlife Refuge.

Sights

★ National Hispanic Cultural Center
ARTS CENTER | FAMILY | A showpiece for the city, and a showcase for Hispanic culture, this beautifully designed space contains a

vibrant art museum, multiple performance venues, a restaurant, a fresco-lined Torreón (tower) depicting the span of Hispanic (and pre-Hispanic) history, a 10,000-volume genealogical research center and library, and an education center. Its acoustically superb Roy E. Disney Center for Performing Arts and smaller Albuquerque Journal Theatre host ballet and flamenco performances, a bilingual film series, traditional Spanish and New Mexican music, the famed world music festival ¡Globalquerque!, Opera Southwest, and more. Exhibits at its museum include works by local artists as well as internationally known names and often feature traditional and contemporary craftwork. ⊠ *1701 4th St. SW, Barelas* ☎ *505/246–2261* ⊕ *www.nhccnm.org* ⊠ *$6, Torreón tour $2* ⊙ *Closed Mon.*

★ Rail Yards Market & Wheels Museum
MARKET | **FAMILY** | Vibrant with growers and maker wares, the sprawling Sunday market here (May from October, 10–2) is a fine excuse to explore this wondrous, light-filled, almost cathedral-like space, said to have been the largest steam locomotive repair facility in the country in its heyday. The early 20th century Atchison, Topeka & Santa Fe buildings here, built on the Atlantic & Pacific originals from the 1880s, put you at the center of how Downtown (or New Town, as it was then known)—and modern Albuquerque—came to be. The market occupies the 1917 Blacksmith Shop. ⊠ *777 1st St. SW, Barelas* ☎ *505/246–2926 AT&SF 2926, 505/243–6269 museum, 505/600–1109 market* ⊕ *www.railyardsmarket.org* ⊠ *Free* ⊙ *Market closed Nov.–Apr.; museum closed Fri.* ☞ *Best to call ahead for hours.*

🍴 Restaurants

Barelas Coffee House
$ | **SOUTHWESTERN** | **FAMILY** | This eatery may look like a set in search of a script, but it's the real deal: folks come from all over the city to sup in the longtime New Mexican–style chile parlor in a historic Route 66 neighborhood south of Downtown. You may notice looks of quiet contentment on the faces of its many dedicated diners as they dive into their bowls of Barelas's potent red chile. **Known for:** local hangout with patio seating; old-fashioned hospitality; chicharrones and huevos rancheros supreme. ⑤ *Average main: $10* ⊠ *1502 4th St. SW, Barelas* ☎ *505/843–7577* ⊕ *www.facebook.com/thebarelascoffeehouse* ⊙ *Closed Sun. No dinner.*

Nightlife

★ ¡Globalquerque!

LIVE MUSIC | FAMILY | Usually an annual affair in late September, ¡Globalquerque! is a dazzling two-day multistage (indoors and out) world music festival that firmly places Albuquerque on the global music map. The National Hispanic Cultural Center has been a perfect home for it since it launched in 2005. In addition to three evening performances, a full day is devoted to (free) family-focused programming. ⊠ *National Hispanic Cultural Center, 1701 4th St. SW at Ave. César Chavez, Barelas* ☎ *505/724–4771* ⊕ *www. globalquerque.org.*

Activities

Valle de Oro National Wildlife Refuge

BIRD-WATCHING | FAMILY | This 570-acre refuge area, an easy 15-minute drive from Downtown, welcomes visitors who can wander the developing nature trails as they try and spot the more than 229 species of birds that come through the diverse Rio Grande floodplain habitats—wetlands, bosque, and more—found here. Its Visitor Center has rangers on hand along with interpretive displays (a calendar of seasonal events is also part of their programming). Take a walk on the 2½-mile Bosque Loop Trail (but be aware, shade may be scarce) and enjoy the vast, sweeping views in all directions (perhaps imagining those who once trod the 16th-century Camino Real de Adentro trail that ran through here from Mexico), or simply settle into one of the Adirondack chairs out back of the Visitor Center and watch the red-wing blackbirds, egrets, and showy dragonflies flit across the peaceful pond there. ⊠ *7851 2nd St. SW, Barelas* ☎ *505/248–6667* ⊕ *www.fws.gov/refuge/ valle_de_oro* 🎫 *Free* ☉ *Visitor Center closed Sun. and Mon.*

UNM and Nob Hill

Established in 1889, the University of New Mexico (UNM) is the state's leading institution of higher education. Its outstanding galleries and museums are open to the public free of charge. The university's predominately Pueblo Revival–style architecture is noteworthy, particularly the beautifully preserved 1938 west wing of Zimmerman Library, which houses the superb Center for Southwest Research and changing topical exhibits, and the Alumni Chapel, both designed by John Gaw Meem, a Santa Fe–based architect whose mid-20th-century work became a template for new campus buildings for years to come. Newer structures, such as Antoine Predock's George Pearl Hall, are distinctive in their own right. Numerous contemporary sculptures also make this campus worth a stroll; Bruce Nauman's 1988 *The Center of the Universe* is a destination in itself. Stop at the campus Welcome Center to pick up self-guided campus art and architecture tour maps.

The campus's easterly spread leads directly into the heart of Nob Hill and a quintessential assortment of Route 66 and art deco–influenced buildings. The vintage motels and gas stations with neon signage have housed a shifting landscape of galleries, microbreweries, cafés, furnishing shops, and more. The circa-1947 Nob Hill Business Center sits right on old Route 66 (Central Avenue); sandwiched between Carlisle Boulevard and Amherst Drive SE, this is the heart of the neighborhood and where it first began. Anchored by fine local stalwarts Mariposa Gallery and IMEC, Amherst Drive between Central and Silver is a good block to peruse; once on Silver, the stretch between Bryn Mawr and Wellesley Drive SE is another good pocket. Other noteworthy businesses—from some of the city's best restaurants to offbeat shops, the venerable Guild indie cinema, and a mix of professional and student hangouts—run right along Central, both a few blocks east of Carlisle, and to the west, back toward UNM.

Sights

★ Isotopes Park
SPORTS VENUE | FAMILY | Watching the Isotopes (a sparkling Triple A affiliate of the Colorado Rockies) at this sweet 13,279-seat ballpark is always great fun, and with the New Mexico United pro soccer team playing here now as well, there's yet more opportunity to join a rousing crowd while the setting sun vividly colors the Sandias to the east. The 'Topes season runs April through September while the United play March or April through October. ⊠ *1601 Ave. César Chavez, University of New Mexico* ☎ *505/924–2255* ⊕ *www.abqisotopes.com* ☎ *Ticket prices vary* ☉ *Closed Nov.–Feb.*

Maxwell Museum of Anthropology
OTHER MUSEUM | Tapping a significant collection of Southwestern artifacts and archival photos, the Maxwell's engaging shows encompass three fascinating fields: archaeology, cultural anthropology, and evolutionary anthropology. As the first public museum in Albuquerque (established in 1932), its influence has grown over the years, but its compact space ensures that exhibits are scaled to the essentials. ⊠ *University of New Mexico, 500 University Blvd. NE, at northwest end of campus, University of New Mexico*

Greater Albuquerque

CORRALES

ALAMEDA

Alameda Blvd.

Paseo del Norte Blvd.

2

NORTH VALLEY

TAYLOR RANCH

Montaño Road

Rio Grande

Coors Boulevard

Rio Grande Blvd.

6

2

5

Osuna Road

3 **3**

Montaño Road

7

NEAR NORTH VALLEY

8

Rio Grande Blvd.

Candelaria Rd.

2nd Street

Edith Boulevard

LOS DURANES

Luecero Dr.

Menaul Boulevard

SAWMILL

40

40

Coors Blvd.

OLD TOWN

WELLS PARK

Mountain Rd.

Lomas Blvd.

Tingley Dr.

UNM

Central Avenue

DOWNTOWN and EDo

Central Ave.

9

10

Central Avenue

Bridge Blvd.

5

11

UNM SOUTH

Old Coors Drive

Arenco Drive

BARELAS

13

4

12

14

Sage Road

25

Arenal Road

4th Street

Broadway Blvd.

Yale Boulevard

ARENAL

Isleta Boulevard

Sunset Road

SOUTH VALLEY

Rio Grande

2nd Street

Sunport

University

✈ Albuquerque International Sunport

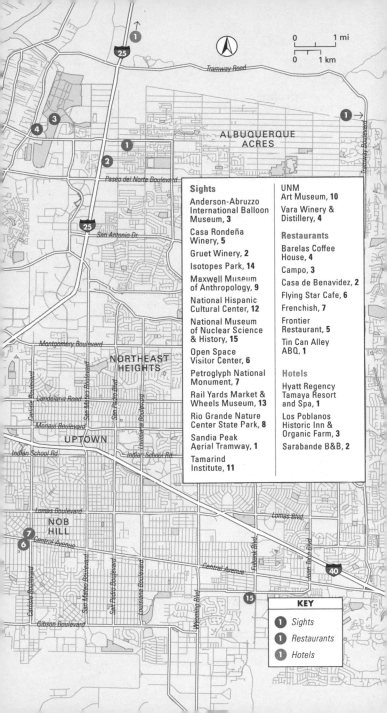

Sights

Anderson-Abruzzo International Balloon Museum, **3**

Casa Rondeña Winery, **5**

Gruet Winery, **2**

Isotopes Park, **14**

Maxwell Museum of Anthropology, **9**

National Hispanic Cultural Center, **12**

National Museum of Nuclear Science & History, **15**

Open Space Visitor Center, **6**

Petroglyph National Monument, **7**

Rail Yards Market & Wheels Museum, **13**

Rio Grande Nature Center State Park, **8**

Sandia Peak Aerial Tramway, **1**

Tamarind Institute, **11**

UNM Art Museum, **10**

Vara Winery & Distillery, **4**

Restaurants

Barelas Coffee House, **4**

Campo, **3**

Casa de Benavidez, **2**

Flying Star Cafe, **6**

Frenchish, **7**

Frontier Restaurant, **5**

Tin Can Alley ABQ, **1**

Hotels

Hyatt Regency Tamaya Resort and Spa, **1**

Los Poblanos Historic Inn & Organic Farm, **3**

Sarabande B&B, **2**

KEY

1 *Sights*

1 *Restaurants*

1 *Hotels*

☎ 505/277–4405 ⊕ maxwellmuseum.unm.edu ✉ Free ⊗ Closed Sun. and Mon.

Tamarind Institute

ART GALLERY | This world-famous institution played a major role in reviving the fine art of lithographic printing, which involves working with plates of traditional stone and modern metal. Tamarind certification is to a printer what a degree from Juilliard is to a musician. A small gallery within the modern facility exhibits prints and lithographs by well-known masters like Jaune Quick-to-See Smith, Jim Dine, Judy Chicago, Kiki Smith, and Ed Ruscha, as well as up-and-comers in the craft. Guided tours (reservations essential) are conducted the first Friday of every quarter at 1:30. ✉ *2500 Central Ave. SE, University of New Mexico* ☎ *505/277–3901* ⊕ *tamarind.unm.edu* ✉ *Free* ⊗ *Closed Sun. and Mon.*

★ UNM Art Museum

ART MUSEUM | This museum features magnificent 20th- and 21st-century prints, as well as photos and paintings that rival the finest collections throughout the Southwest. Changing exhibits cull from more than 30,000 archived pieces, which include groundbreaking works by modernist giants such as Bridget Riley, Richard Diebenkorn, and Elaine DeKooning. Photography—from the likes of Ansel Adams, Patrick Nagatani, and Beaumont Newhall—is a particular strength, and provocative shows have featured immense prints, complemented with video projections and a range of mixed-media installations. ✉ *University of New Mexico Center for the Arts, 203 Cornell Dr. NE, University of New Mexico* ☎ *505/277–4001* ⊕ *artmuseum.unm.edu* ✉ *Free* ⊗ *Closed Sun.–Tues.*

 **Restaurants**

Flying Star Cafe

$ | **CAFÉ** | A staple in the city, each outpost of this locally owned order-at-the-counter-first café suits its neighborhood (some have patios and allow pets). At the original spot here in Nob Hill, the university crowd digs into a creative mix of American and New Mexican dishes (plus several types of wine and beer). **Known for:** all-day breakfast; late-night dessert; creative specials and solid basics. ⑤ *Average main: $16* ✉ *3416 Central Ave. SE, Nob Hill* ☎ *505/255–6633* ⊕ *www.flyingstarcafe.com.*

Frenchish

$$$ | **BISTRO** | Innovative, flavorful, fun, and, indeed, French-ish, the renowned culinary team of Nelle Bauer and James Beard Award-semifinalist Jennifer James shines at this modern spot with a seasonally specific bistro menu (with *vins* and bubblies to match). *Plats principaux* might include their perfectly turned New Mexico beef steak frites, an elevated salade niçoise, or "day boat" halibut; perennial faves like their Frenchie burger, famous devilish egg, and a very popular carrot dog balance the menu. **Known for:** twists on French classics; reservations recommended (via phone); walk-ins may sit at congenial chef's counter. ⑤ *Average main: $33* ⊠ *3509 Central Ave. NE, Nob Hill* ☎ *505/433–5911* ⊕ *www. frenchish.co* ⊙ *Closed Sun.–Tues. No lunch.*

Frontier Restaurant

$ | CAFÉ | FAMILY | This definitive student hangout—it's directly across from UNM and has been since 1971—is open seven days from 5 am until late, and hits the spot for inexpensive diner-style American and New Mexican chow. A notch up from a fast-food joint, the chile's good (vegetarian and non), the breakfast burritos are fine (the burgers are, too), and who can resist a hot, melty oversize Frontier cinnamon sweet roll? **Known for:** hours to suit both early birds and night owls; killer cinnamon sweet rolls; roadside attraction–style decor. ⑤ *Average main: $10* ⊠ *2400 Central Ave. SE, at Cornell Dr. SE, University of New Mexico* ☎ *505/266–0550* ⊕ *www.frontierrestaurant.com.*

Nightlife

Bosque Brewing Public House

BREWPUBS | Striking nature photographs line this popular, modernly rustic pub (an early location of a growing state-wide empire), which offers memorable ales like their Scotch-style Scotia and the award-winning Pistol Pete's 1888 as well as IPAs, hard seltzers, and ciders year-round. There are also seasonal specialties like Elephants on Parade (a raspberry-tempered wheat ale), traditional cocktails and wine, and reasonably priced savory snacks to accompany them all. Their brewmaster has made Bosque a multi-time National IPA Challenge Champion. ⊠ *106 Girard Blvd. SE, Suite B, Nob Hill* ☎ *505/508–5967* ⊕ *www.bosquebrewing.com.*

★ Canteen Brewhouse

BREWPUBS | Come to this longtime, low-key destination for brew fans for live music Sunday afternoons (and most Thursday nights). Picture casual picnic seating (indoors and out, where there's plenty of shade) and a sweet choice of IPAs (try the Flashback), a good red ale, a steady brown (Pecos Trail), or a briskly cold 2016 World Beer Cup–winning High Plains Pils. Don't miss the Canteen's hard ciders, wines, and seasonal selections as well. ⊠ *2381 Aztec Rd. NE, University of New Mexico* ☎ *505/881–2737* ⊕ *canteenbrewhouse.com.*

★ Outpost Performance Space

LIVE MUSIC | This outstanding venue programs an inspired, eclectic slate of genres, from local *nuevo* folk to techno, jazz, and traveling East Indian beats. Some big names—especially from the jazz world—show up at the compact, comfortable space (perfect for serious listeners), which is a key player in bringing the world-class New Mexico Jazz Festival to the state every September. ⊠ *210 Yale Blvd. SE, University of New Mexico* ☎ *505/268–0044* ⊕ *www.facebook.com/outpostperformancespace.*

🎭 Performing Arts

★ Popejoy Hall

ARTS CENTERS | Of the three notable performance halls in UNM's Center for the Arts, Popejoy Hall, with just under 2,000 seats, is the city's go-to for the New Mexico Philharmonic, blockbuster Broadway touring shows, dance performances, concerts, comedy acts, and lectures. Rodey Theatre, a smaller, 420-seat house in the same complex, stages experimental and niche works throughout the year while Keller Hall, a 274-seater with superb acoustics, is the perfect home for the much-acclaimed annual John Donald Robb Composers' Symposium for new music (in spring) and the university's excellent chamber music program. ⊠ *University of New Mexico Center for the Arts, 203 Cornell Dr. NE, University of New Mexico* ✥ *Enter from Central Ave. SE* ☎ *505/277–4569 tickets, 505/277–9771 customer service* ⊕ *www.popejoypresents. com.*

🛍 Shopping

IMEC

JEWELRY & WATCHES | A sliver of a shop that feels like an art gallery, IMEC (International Metalsmith Exhibition Center) carries an unusual range of jewelry and craftwork by a nationally renowned group of metal and glass artisans. Many are New Mexico based, like Luis Mojica, who does stunning work in sterling, resin, and mother-of-pearl, and Mary Kanda, whose intricate glass-bead pieces are richly colored. ⊠ *101 Amherst Dr. SE, Nob Hill* ☎ *505/265–8352* ⊕ *www.shopimec.com.*

★ Kei & Molly Textiles

OTHER SPECIALTY STORE | With joyful designs composed in the spirit of traditional woodblock prints, whimsical pure cotton flour-sack dish towels—and yardage, napkins, potholders, and more—roll off the silk-screen presses here (don't miss their special misprint sales). While the perfectly soft and absorbent towel fabric is imported from Pakistan, the themes and attitude are purely local and New Mexico-inspired. View the printing process from their retail shop, where you will also find an irresistible selection of finely made hand-hewn products from other sustainably focused makers with keen eyes for design. The colorfully felted Flying Dragon children's mobiles (Nepal) are delightful, and the pewter animal magnets from Roofoos in Oregon are pretty cool too. ✉ *4400 Silver Ave. SE, Suite A, Nob Hill* ☎ *505/268–4400* ⊕ *www. keiandmolly.com.*

Mariposa Gallery

CRAFTS | Contemporary fine crafts, including jewelry, sculptural glass, ceramics, and fiber arts can be found at this longtime Albuquerque gallery. In town since 1974, a smart and changing selection of high-quality wares by local artisans has been a constant. Special exhibits focus on established artists (such as extraordinary mixed-media metalwork by Cynthia Cook and provocative pieces by collagist Suzanne Sbarge) and worthy newcomers. ✉ *3500 Central Ave. SE, Nob Hill* ☎ *505/268–6828* ⊕ *www.mariposa-gallery.com.*

Los Ranchos and North Valley

Many Albuquerque attractions lie north of Downtown, Old Town, and the University of New Mexico. Quite a few, including the Casa Rondeña winery and the Rio Grande Nature Center, are clustered in a contiguous stretch that comprises two of the city's longest-settled areas: the lush cottonwood-lined North Valley and Los Ranchos de Albuquerque, along the Rio Grande. Early Spanish settlers made their homes here, building on top of even earlier Pueblo homesteads. Historic adobe houses abound. The Montaño Road Bridge crosses through the area, making a sublime gateway to the West Side.

Sights

Anderson-Abruzzo International Balloon Museum

OTHER MUSEUM | FAMILY | This dramatic museum celebrates the city's legacy as the hot-air ballooning capital of the world. The fun, massive facility is named for Maxie Anderson and Ben Abruzzo, who pioneered ballooning here and were part of a team of three aviators who made the first manned hot-air balloon crossing of the Atlantic Ocean in 1978. Filling the airy museum space are several fully inflated historic balloons, and both large- and small-scale replicas of gas balloons and zeppelins. You'll also see vintage balloon baskets, china and flatware from the ill-fated *Hindenburg* and an engaging display on that tragic craft, and dynamic exhibits that trace the history of the sport, dating back to the first balloon ride, in 1783. ⊠ *9201 Balloon Museum Dr. NE, off Alameda Blvd. NE, North Valley* ☎ *505/768–6020* ⊕ *www.cabq.gov/balloonmuseum* 🖾 *$6, free Sun. 9–1 and 1st Fri. every month (except Oct. during Balloon Fiesta)* ⊗ *Closed Mon.*

Casa Rondeña Winery

WINERY | Perhaps the most stunning of Albuquerque's wineries, Casa Rondeña was designed to resemble a Tuscan villa, with its green-tile roof and verdant grounds laced with shade trees, fountains, and of course, vineyards. Though a true patina of age has yet to develop (the winery was founded in 1995 by vintner John Calvin), this is a most pleasant place for sipping. Respect for the centuries-old heritage of wine in the state is shown through their very drinkable "1629" red blend (made from Tempranillo, Syrah, and Cabernet grapes, it's a nod to the Spaniards who carried the first vines here in that year). A vintage oak fermentation sits in the great hall where tastings are conducted. ⊠ *733 Chavez Rd. NW, between Rio Grande Blvd. and 4th St. NW, Los Ranchos de Albuquerque* ☎ *505/344–5911* ⊕ *www.casarondena.com* 🖾 *Tastings (4 wines) $14.*

★ Rio Grande Nature Center State Park

NATURE PRESERVE | **FAMILY** | Along the banks of the Rio Grande, this 270-acre refuge in an especially tranquil portion of the bosque (about midway up on the Paseo del Bosque trail) is the nation's largest cottonwood forest. There are numerous walking and biking trails that wind into the 53-acre Aldo Leopold Forest and down to the river. Bird-watchers come to view all manner of migratory waterfowl, but especially the sandhill cranes that swoop in in late fall. Constructed half above ground and half below the edge of a pond, the park's interpretive Rio Grande Nature Center—a distinctive Antoine Predock design—has viewing windows and speakers that broadcast the sounds of the birds you're watching; frogs, ducks, and turtles may be seen (and heard) as well. ⊠ *2901 Candelaria Rd. NW, North Valley* ☎ *505/344–7240* ⊕ *www.rgnc. org* 🖾 *$3 per vehicle, grounds free.*

 Restaurants

★ Campo

$$$$ | **ECLECTIC** | With pink light rising on the Sandias and lavender fields aglow, dining at Los Poblanos—its menu wholly committed to finely prepared dishes made from organic and locally sourced ingredients—can be a transcendent experience thanks to the pastoral setting of Albuquerque's historic North Valley. The seasonal menu is a tantalizing mix of distinctive farm-to-table flavors crossed with Southwestern cooking traditions that together have been become the basis for Rio Grande Valley cuisine. **Known for:** top-notch farm-to-table dining (reservations a must); inspired decor with fun Bar Campo up front; brilliant outdoor seating with superb views. $ *Average main: $36* ⊠ *Los Poblanos Historic Inn & Organic Farm, 4803 Rio Grande Blvd. NW, Los Ranchos de Albuquerque* ☎ *505/338–1615* ⊕ *www.lospoblanos.com.*

Casa de Benavidez

$ | **SOUTHWESTERN** | The fajitas at this welcoming local spot with a romantic garden patio are a favorite here, and are served-up in generous portions. The burger wrapped inside a sopaipilla is another specialty, as are the chimichangas packed with beef. **Known for:** breakfast on the shaded patio; meat-based red and green chiles; friendly atmosphere in a traditional adobe. $ *Average main: $10* ⊠ *8032 4th St. NW, Los Ranchos de Albuquerque* ☎ *505/898–3311* ⊕ *www.casadebenavidez.com* ☾ *Closed Sun. No dinner Sat.*

 # Hotels

★ Hyatt Regency Tamaya Resort and Spa

$$$ | **RESORT** | Set spectacularly on 550 pristine acres on the Santa Ana Pueblo (just north of Albuquerque, near Bernalillo), Tamaya awaits those seeking a culturally rich and even spiritually revivifying respite. **Pros:** great amenities like outdoor heated pools, horseback riding, and free bikes; lovely backroads drive from historic Albuquerque and Corrales; convenient base for traveling on to Chaco Canyon. **Cons:** on the pricey side; additional daily resort fee; breakfast not included. $ *Rooms from: $325* ⊠ *1300 Tuyuna Trail, Santa Ana Pueblo* ☎ *505/867–1234* ⊕ *tamaya.regency.hyatt.com/en/hotel/home.html* ⇱ *350 rooms* ⦿❘ *No Meals.*

★ Los Poblanos Historic Inn & Organic Farm

$$$ | **B&B/INN** | **FAMILY** | Designed in the 1930s by the renowned Pueblo Revival architect John Gaw Meem, Los Poblanos stands today as a quintessential element of Albuquerque's North Valley and its pastoral soul. **Pros:** visitor well-being is paramount; lovely gardens and landscape stonework; guests-only Library Bar and afternoon tea at La Quinta. **Cons:** peacocks may startle (and consequently screech); breakfast not included except with package plans; pricey. $ *Rooms from: $384* ⊠ *4803 Rio Grande Blvd. NW, Los Ranchos de Albuquerque* ☎ *505/985–5000* ⊕ *www.lospoblanos.com* ⇱ *45 rooms* ⦿❘ *No Meals.*

★ Sarabande B&B

$$ | B&B/INN | While the name of this soothing, Modernist compound is inherited from the prior owners, the current setup blends a respect for its Southwestern roots with a refreshing commitment to a high-end midcentury modern aesthetic (a rarity in these parts). **Pros:** casita-like feel; delicious breakfast; pastoral hideaway with a serene seasonal lap pool. **Cons:** seven-day cancellation notice required (longer during Balloon Fiesta); property manager not on site 24/7 (but reachable by phone/text); two-night minimum may be required. $ *Rooms from: $250* ✉ *5637 Rio Grande Blvd. NW, Los Ranchos de Albuquerque* ☎ *505/348–5593* ⊕ *www. sarabandebnb.com* ⇥ *5 rooms* �‖ *Free Breakfast.*

 # Shopping

★ Bookworks

BOOKS | This North Valley stalwart has been reviving readers' spirits for many a year in a cozy neighborhood setting. A committed independent seller, Bookworks fairly prides itself on service, and booklovers from all corners flock here for its fine stock of regional coffee-table books, a well-culled selection of modern fiction and nonfiction, architecture and design titles, well-chosen calendars and cards, and a (small) playground's worth of kids' books. Regular signings and readings draw some big guns to this compact treasure. ✉ *4022 Rio Grande Blvd. NW, Los Ranchos de Albuquerque* ☎ *505/344–8139* ⊕ *www.bkwrks.com.*

★ Eldora Craft Chocolate

CHOCOLATE | Ramble north on this rural stretch of Edith Boulevard and your reward is not only a bit of Albuquerque history en route (the old Camino Real ran along Edith), but the unexpected wonder that is Eldora Chocolate. The actual chocolate making happens here, too, and the many shop's many awards attest to owner Steve Prickett's attention to quality and the nuances of the chocolate bean. This is true artisanal chocolate—any aficionado is sure to learn something special about their 70% Tanzanian, say, and tastings are offered freely. ✉ *8114 Edith Blvd. NE, North Valley* ☎ *505/433–4076* ⊕ *www.eldorachocolate.com.*

★ The Farm Shop at Los Poblanos

OTHER SPECIALTY STORE | FAMILY | A destination on its own, the wonderful Farm Shop at the renowned Los Poblanos Inn carries a distinctive selection of books, culinary gadgets, fine crafts from local makers (jewelry, textiles, ceramics), the same soothing and perfectly scented lavender lotions and soaps found in the inn's guestrooms, and a considerable variety of artisan jams, vinegars, and sauces. For takeaway sustenance, the inn's Campo kitchen whips up crisply crusted breads, sandwiches, coffee, tea, and cakes. ⊠ *Los Poblanos Historic Inn & Organic Farm, 4803 Rio Grande Blvd. NW, Los Ranchos de Albuquerque* ☎ *505/938–2192* ⊕ *www.lospoblanos.com.*

Uptown and Northeast Heights

Once in the Northeast Heights you are approaching the foothills of the Sandia Mountains, with upscale neighborhoods that surprise with the sudden appearance of piñon and ponderosa. Trips to this area can easily be combined with more north-central venues like the Balloon Museum and local microbreweries, or the National Museum of Nuclear Science & History, which, once you've made it into the foothills, is due south. The Uptown area is closer to the center of town, and shopping and restaurants are its main attractions.

Sights

Gruet Winery

WINERY | First-time visitors may be forgiven for a bit of concern as they approach Gruet's brick chalet-inspired building, set as it is just off the highway. The setting inside and out in its garden seating area, however, better befits one of the nation's most acclaimed producers of sparkling wines. Famous in France since the 1950s, the Gruet (pronounced *grew*-ay) family began production here in 1984 (some of its vineyards—all in-state—are as close as Santa Ana Pueblo, and may be viewed along Interstate 25, just north of Bernalillo). And while it's changed hands since, it still earns kudos for its Methode Champenoise (which employs traditional Champagne-making methods), as well as for its Pinot Noirs, Rosés, and Chardonnays. ⊠ *8400 Pan American Fwy. NE (I–25), off northbound I–25 frontage road, between Paseo del Norte and Alameda Blvd., Northeast Heights* ☎ *505/821–0055* ⊕ *www. gruetwinery.com* 🍷 *Tastings $16.*

★ Sandia Peak Aerial Tramway

VIEWPOINT | **FAMILY** | One of the world's longest aerial tramways, here tramway cars climb nearly three miles up the steep western face of the Sandias, giving you a dazzling close-up view (whatever the season) of the imposing rock formations and wind-blown wilderness. From the observation deck at the 10,378-foot summit, you can scan some 11,000 square miles of spectacular scenery, including desert, volcanos, mountains, and more. A graceful hawk or an eagle soaring above or mountain lions roaming the cliffs below may also be spotted. An exhibit room at the top surveys the area's wildlife; a few steps away is Ten 3, where fine dining and a casual eatery and lounge await (reservations required), or you can access the Sandia Peak ski area.

It's much colder and windier at the summit than at the tram's base, so pack a jacket. Tram cars leave from the base at regular intervals for the 15-minute ride to the top. Purchase tickets (all round-trip) up to 24 hours advance online (or in-person on the day of); the parking fee is included. ⊠ *10 Tramway Loop NE, Far Northeast Heights* ☎ *505/856–1532* ⊕ *www.sandiapeak.com* ☞ *$33; $3 parking fee.*

Vara Winery & Distillery

WINERY | Partial to wines and spirits that share a distinctive Spanish heritage, Vara announces itself rather subtly, with just a discreet sign at its main road turn-off. But stunning views along with its tap room, shop, and distillery await. Head inside or enjoy the shaded patio seating while a tasting flight of its award-winning sparkling Silverhead Brut (cava or rosado), whites (a delicious Albariño), and *vino tintos,* like their Tempranillo (or spirits like their High Desert Gin or Paso Uno Brandy), make their way to you. A full tapas menu (and sometimes paella) is available during their evening dining hours; charcuterie boards are on tap for tasting flights. ⊠ *315 Alameda Blvd. NE, Northeast Heights* ☎ *505/898–6280* ⊕ *www.varawines.com* ☞ *Tastings $14* ☉ *No tastings Mon.*

🍴 Restaurants

Tin Can Alley ABQ

$ | **ECLECTIC** | **FAMILY** | A stack-up of mural-painted shipping containers houses a Santa Fe Brewing Co. taproom, an arcade, and a changing set of Albuquerque-based food vendors (Guava Tree Cafe's warm-pressed Caribbean sandwiches, Cake Fetish, and Amore pizza are some highlights). But it's really about the views and indoor-outdoor hangout nooks here. **Known for:** excellent desert views; outdoor spaces perfect for group hang-outs; variety of dining options. ⑤ *Average main: $10* ⊠ *6110 Alameda Blvd. NE, Northeast Heights* ☎ *505/208–0508* ⊕ *www.tincanalleyabq.com.*

🛍 Shopping

Bien Mur Indian Market Center

CRAFTS | The Sandia Pueblo-run Bien Mur Indian Market Center showcases regional Native American rugs, jewelry, and crafts of all kinds. It is a good place to get familiar with the distinct styles found at each of the 19 pueblos here (as well as that by Diné, or Navajo, artists), and you can be certain about the authenticity of purchases made here as well. ⊠ *100 Bien Mur Dr. NE, off Tramway Rd. NE east of I–25, Northeast Heights* ☎ *505/821–5400* ⊕ *www.bienmur.art.*

Page 1 Books

BOOKS | One of the city's best independent bookstores, Page 1 is a singular find for its mix of rare and used books shelved to entice the serious browser, while also offering a deep selection of literature, fiction and nonfiction, print ephemera, books for kids, and gifts for the book lover. Count on astute staff recommendations, as well as a regular roster of book signings, poetry readings, and children's events. ⊠ *5850 Eubank Blvd. NE, Northeast Heights* ☎ *505/294–2026* ⊕ *www.page1book.com.*

East Side and West Side

South of Interstate 40 and the Northeast Heights, the East Side bridges the older and historic parts of Route 66 with pockets of strip-shopping centers (especially along Eubank Boulevard) and some newer development of an upscale nature. But you are at the gateway to multiple mountain chains here—the Sandias, as well as the rewarding byways of the Manzano Mountains—and before you consider heading out to them, you will want to make time for the decidedly destination-worthy National Museum of Nuclear Science & History.

Farther west, the fastest-growing part of Albuquerque lies on a broad mesa high above the Rio Grande Valley. The West Side is primarily the domain of new suburban housing developments and strip malls, some designed more attractively than others. Somewhat controversially, growth on the West Side has crept up all around the archaeologically critical Petroglyph National Monument. Not far from the Monument's trails is the very special Open Space Visitor Center, a migrating sandhill crane population's winter home. The center is adjacent to another archaeological site of interest, Piedras Marcadas Pueblo, which features interpretive displays within. Allow a 20-minute drive from Old Town and the North Valley to reach either (and about the same time to travel between them).

 Sights

★ National Museum of Nuclear Science & History

HISTORY MUSEUM | **FAMILY** | Previously known simply as the National Atomic Museum, this brilliant Smithsonian affiliate traces the history of the atomic age and how nuclear science has dramatically influenced the course of modern history. Exhibits include replicas of Little Boy and Fat Man (the bombs dropped on Japan at the end of World War II), a compelling display about the difficult decision to drop atomic bombs, and a look at how atomic culture has dovetailed with pop culture. One particular highlight is the restored 1942 Plymouth that was used to transport the plutonium core of "the Gadget" (as that first weapon was known) down from Los Alamos to the Trinity Site for testing. ⊠ *601 Eubank Blvd. SE, a few blocks south of I–40, East Side* ☎ *505/245–2137* ⊕ *www.nuclearmuseum.org* ⌑ *$15.*

★ Open Space Visitor Center

NATURE SIGHT | FAMILY | Sandhill cranes make their winter home here or stop for a snack en route to the Bosque del Apache, just south in Socorro. The outdoor viewing station opens onto the site's expansive field, which faces out to the Sandia Mountains; the hush—aside from the occasional flock circling above (look for them from mid-October through February)—is restorative. Complementing the experience inside are changing art and photography exhibits, an interpretative display on the adjacent 14th- to 15th-century Piedras Marcadas Pueblo ruins, and well-informed guides. ⊠ *6500 Coors Blvd. NW, West Side* ☎ *505/768–4950* ⊕ *www.cabq.gov/openspace* ⊘ *Closed Sun. and Mon.*

Petroglyph National Monument

INDIGENOUS SIGHT | FAMILY | Beneath the stumps of five extinct volcanoes, this park encompasses more than 25,000 ancient Native American rock drawings inscribed on the 17-mile-long West Mesa escarpment overlooking the Rio Grande Valley. For centuries, Native American hunting parties camped at the base, chipping and scribbling away. Archaeologists believe most of the petroglyphs were carved on the lava formations between 1100 and 1600, but some images at the park may date back as far as 1000 BC. Accessible in three separate (and mostly shade-free—bring water and a hat!) sections, each is a short drive from the helpful Visitor Center, where rangers will supply maps and help you determine which trail is best for the time you have. ⊠ *Visitor Center, 6001 Unser Blvd. NW, West Side* ☎ *505/899–0205* ⊕ *www.nps. gov/petr* ⌑ *Free.*

Chapter 9

TAOS

Updated by
Ariana Kramer

👁 **Sights**   🍴 **Restaurants**   🛏 **Hotels**   🛍 **Shopping**   🍸 **Nightlife**

★★★★★   ★★★★☆   ★★★★☆   ★★★☆☆   ★★★☆☆

WELCOME TO TAOS

TOP REASONS TO GO

★ **Cultural sophistication:** Taos supports an astonishing array of cultural experiences, from powwows and chamber music to off-grid rock concerts and literary arts festivals.

★ **Ancient roots:** The Tiwa-speaking peoples of Taos and Picuris Pueblos have lived here continuously for more than one thousand years, alongside other Indigenous peoples such as the Ute, Apache, and Navajo. In the late 1500s, Spanish explorers came to the area and began to settle it in the 1600s, eventually building the town of Taos and surrounding villages.

★ **Expansive views:** Few panoramas in the Southwest can compare with that of the 13,000-foot Sangre de Cristo Mountains soaring over the adobe homes of Taos, and beyond that, the endless high-desert mesa that extends for miles to the west.

★ **Outdoor adventures:** Birdwatching, wildlife viewing, scenic river rafting, fishing, hiking, and camping opportunities abound, and the world-famous Taos Ski Valley and family-oriented Sipapu Ski Resort offer snow sports for all abilities.

1 Historic Downtown Taos. Home to Taos Plaza, the historic area of the town of Taos that continues to serve as a vibrant community and commercial center.

2 The Southside and Ranchos de Taos. A low-key stretch of highway with some lovely eateries and hotels along with several agricultural communities and the famous Ranchos Plaza.

3 El Prado. An unincorporated area northwest of the Plaza that features some lovely restaurants and hotels, along with gorgeous views of the Taos mountains.

4 Taos Pueblo. A sovereign nation, and a UNESCO World Heritage site, that's one of the must-see sights in the area.

5 The Mesa. The high desert area west of downtown Taos famous for its clear night skies and expansive views.

6 Arroyo Seco. A charming, historic village with a collection of interesting galleries, shops, and restaurants.

7 Taos Ski Valley. A world-class ski resort and the gateway to hiking in Taos's highest alpine habitat.

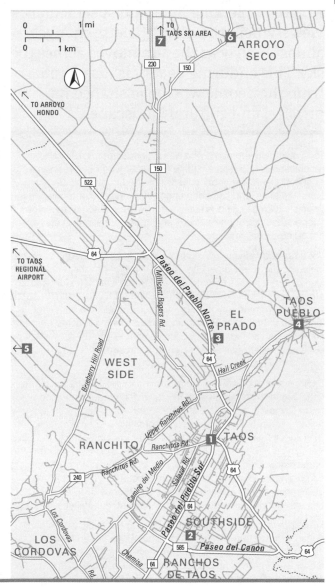

0   1 mi
0   1 km

TO
TO TAOS SKI AREA **7**   **6**   ARROYO
SECO

230   150

TO ARROYO
HONDO

150

522

TO TAOS
REGIONAL
AIRPORT

64

Paseo del Pueblo Norte

Millicent Rogers Rd.

EL
PRADO

TAOS
PUEBLO
4

3

64

Hail Creek

← **5**

WEST
SIDE

Brushberry Hill Road

Upper Ranchitos Rd.

RANCHITO

Ranchitos Rd.   **1**   TAOS

Ranchitos Rd.

240

Camino del Medio

Salazar Rd.

64

Paseo del Pueblo Sur

SOUTHSIDE

2

585   Paseo del Cañon   64

Los Cordovas

LOS
CORDOVAS

Chamisa

Rd.

64   RANCHOS
DE TAOS

Set on an undulating mesa at the base of the Sangre de Cristo Mountains, Taos is a place of piercing light and spectacular views, where the desert palette changes almost hourly as the sun moves across the sky. This enduring beauty is inseparable from the people who have shaped its physical and cultural landscapes.

Taos is actually the name of a Nation (population 1,196), a town (population 6,442), and a county (population 34,580). It's home to one of the oldest continuously inhabited communities in North America, and has been under the influence of Indigenous, Spanish, Mexican, and American governance. Each of these has shaped the community's values and appearance into layers of intriguing complexity.

For thousands of years, Indigenous people have called Taos home, including the Ute, Comanche, Kiowa, Navajo, Apache, and Puebloan communities. The famous Taos Pueblo is a multistory adobe structure that was built from earth mixed with water and wood harvested from nearby forests. Northern Tiwa is the ancestral language of both Taos Pueblo and Picuris Pueblo (located near the southern part of Taos County). Today most residents of these two pueblos speak English, and often Spanish and other languages, in addition to Tiwa.

Explorers for the Spanish Crown arrived in the 1500s, and Spaniards began to settle the area the following century, bringing with them Catholicism and Iberian agricultural ways. They fought, and mixed, with their Indigenous neighbors and over time established many adobe villages on land grants given by the Spanish and Mexican governments. The ancestors of today's Indo-Hispano communities built the adobe town and surrounding villages of Taos, combining Puebloan and Iberian architectural influences. Their descendants have created a vibrant community over the centuries, navigating many historical, political, and cultural changes.

Fur trappers and mountain men, including the scout Kit Carson, began to arrive in the 1700s. In the late 1800s, when New Mexico was still a territory, a group of European-trained American painters led by Bert Phillips and Ernest Blumenschein came to Taos. In 1915, they created the Taos Society of Artists. East Coast socialite

Mabel Dodge Luhan viewed Taos as a utopian community, and started a salon here the 1920s, inviting artists, writers, and thinkers such as Georgia O'Keeffe, Ansel Adams, D. H. Lawrence, Willa Cather, and Carl Jung to visit her new home. Later on, Helene Wurlitzer became a significant, and unassuming, patron of the arts in the 1940s. The residency program she started continues to attract artists of all types to Taos today. A number of excellent museums document the town's esteemed artistic history and showcase contemporary artists.

Modern-day Taos artists include Taos Pueblo's haute couture fashion designer Patricia Michaels; traditional *enjarradora* (adobe finisher) turned painter Anita Rodriguez; ceramicist and photographer Michael Gorman (nephew of artist R. C. Gorman); and multimedia artist Sasha vom Dorp, who visualizes the interactions between sound, light, and water. Taos is also rich in music, literary arts, dance, theater, and the healing arts.

Sustainable living has always been synonymous with the traditionally rooted communities of Taos. This attracted a large number of young people from the counterculture of the 1960s and 1970s who were looking for a more satisfying way of life. Taos continues to appeal to creative and free-spirited people with an interest in land-based, sustainable ways of living. There's a solar-powered radio station, and the county is powered largely by solar energy through its electric cooperative. Taos is also a center for green building technologies, including Mike Reynold's Earthships.

Finally, opportunities for outdoor adventures abound in the Rio Grande National Monument, Carson National Forest, and Bureau of Land Management public lands. Taos is truly an ideal place to visit for those aiming to slow down and embrace a distinct regional blend of culture, cuisine, outdoor activities, creative expression, and natural beauty.

Planning

When to Go

With more than 300 days of sunshine annually, Taos typically yields pleasant—if sometimes chilly—weather year-round. The typical summer high season brings warm days (upper 80s) and cool nights (low 50s), as well as frequent afternoon thunderstorms. A packed arts and festival schedule in summer means hotels and B&Bs sometimes book up well in advance, lodging rates are high, restaurants are jammed, and traffic anywhere near the plaza can slow to a standstill. Early spring can be quite windy, but late spring and fall are stunning and favor mild days and cool nights, fewer visitors, and more reasonably priced accommodations. In winter, especially during big years for snowfall, skiers arrive en masse but tend to stay close to the slopes and only venture into town for an occasional meal or shopping trip.

Planning Your Time

Whether you've got an afternoon or a week in the area, begin with a visit to Taos Pueblo, then follow with a visit to the Hacienda de los Martinez and the San Francisco de Asis Church in Ranchos to gain an appreciation for the Spanish settlers who built the town of Taos and its surrounding villages. Next, stroll around Taos Plaza, the John Dunn Shops, and Bent Street, taking in the galleries, crafts shops, and boutiques, plus nearby museums, including the Harwood and Taos Art Museum. Outlying attractions include the Millicent Rogers Museum, the village of Arroyo Seco, the Rio Grande Gorge Bridge, and the Earthship Visitor Center. Finally, a stay in Taos is not complete without spending some quality time outdoors, whether that's a siesta on a shaded patio, a stroll along the Rio Grande, or a hike in the mountains.

Getting Here and Around

AIR

Albuquerque International Sunport, about 130 miles away and a 2½-hour drive, is the nearest major airport to Taos. The small Santa Fe Municipal Airport, a 90-minute drive, also has daily service from Dallas, Denver, and Phoenix. Alternatively, as Taos is one of the gateway towns to New Mexico if coming from Colorado, some visitors fly into Denver (five hours north) or Colorado Springs (four hours). Taos Municipal Airport, 12 miles west of town, serves private planes, as well as public charters from Burbank, San Diego, Dallas, and Austin.

AIRPORTS Albuquerque International Sunport. (ABQ). ✉ *220 Sunport Blvd. SE, Airport* ☎ *505/244–7700* ⊕ *www.abqsunport.com.* **Santa Fe Regional Airport.** (SAF). ✉ *121 Aviation Dr., Santa Fe* ☎ *505/955–2900* ⊕ *www.santafenm.gov/airport.* **Taos Regional Airport.** (SKX). ✉ *24662 U.S. 64, El Prado* ☎ *575/758–4995* ⊕ *www.taosgov. com/149/Airport.*

AIRPORT TRANSFERS

For getting to and around the Taos area, your best bet is to drive by car. Rental cars are readily available in Santa Fe and Albuquerque airports (options in Taos are more limited). North Central RTD provides free bus service between Taos and Santa Fe, including a stop at Santa Fe's train station, from which you can catch the New Mexico Rail Runner train to Albuquerque (and then a free bus to the airport). NCRTD also runs to the Taos Ski Valley during the winter season. NCRTD also now offers an on-demand service for trips outside of their usual schedule. Other options are Taos Rides shuttle and charter service, and Tripcarma, a locally owned rideshare service for getting to and around the area.

SHUTTLE CONTACTS North Central Regional Transit District.
☎ 505/629–4725 ⊕ www.ncrtd.org.

BIKE

Many Taos-area roads are steep and hilly, and very few have marked bicycle lanes. Be extremely careful while cycling in traffic. The West Rim Trail offers a fairly flat but view-studded 9-mile ride that follows the Rio Grande Gorge's west rim from the Rio Grande Gorge Bridge to near the Taos Junction Bridge. There are also nice trails on the East Rim, to the south of Taos. Be advised that mountain biking in the Talpa foothills is not looked upon favorably by many local residents. Please be respectful when accessing or cycling on public lands. Cultural use of these areas pre-date the existence of the United States.

CAR

A car is your most practical means both for reaching and getting around Taos. The main route from Santa Fe is via U.S. 285 north to NM 68 north, also known as the Low Road, which winds between the Rio Grande and rocky cliffs before rising to a sweeping view of the mesa and river gorge. You can also take the spectacular and vertiginous High Road to Taos, which takes longer but offers a wonderfully scenic ride—many visitors come to Taos via the Low Road, which is more dramatic when driven south to north, and then return to Santa Fe via the High Road, which has better views as you drive south. From Denver, it's a five-hour drive south via Interstate 25, U.S. 160 west (at Walsenburg), and CO 159 to NM 522—the stretch from Walsenburg into Taos is quite scenic. Be advised that in snow season you may need four-wheel drive to get to some parts of Taos.

TAXI

Taxi service is virtually nonexistent in Taos. For local transportation needs, try Tripcarma, a rideshare service run by Taos residents.

CONTACTS Tripcarma. ⊠ *208 Paseo Del Pueblo Sur, Taos* ⊕ *www. tripcarma.com.*

Hotels

Taos is a well-honed tourist destination with an abundant supply of hospitality. Hotels are mostly congregated in Historic Downtown Taos, with hotels and motels along NM 68 (Paseo del Pueblo), most of them on the south side of town, that suit every need and budget; rates vary little between big-name chains and smaller establishments. Make advance reservations and expect higher rates during ski season (usually from late December to early April, and especially for lodgings on the north side of town, closer to the ski area) and in the summer. The Taos Ski Valley has a number of condos and rental units, but unless you're in town expressly for skiing or perhaps hiking in summer, it's too far from Taos proper to be a convenient base for exploring the rest of the area. The area's many B&Bs offer some of the best values, when you factor in typically hearty full breakfasts, personal service, and, often, roomy casitas with private entrances.

⇨ *Hotel and restaurant reviews have been shortened. For full information, visit Fodors.com. Lodging prices are for two people in a standard double room in high season, excluding 12%–13% tax. Dining prices are the average cost of a main course at dinner or, if dinner is not served, at lunch.*

What It Costs in U.S. Dollars			
$	$$	$$$	$$$$
HOTELS			
under $150	$150–$250	$251–$400	over $400
RESTAURANTS			
under $17	$17–$25	$26–$35	over $35

Restaurants

For a relatively small, remote town, Taos has a sophisticated and eclectic dining scene. Enjoy authentic New Mexican and Mexican dishes, as well as creative regional and international cuisine utilizing mostly local ingredients. In addition, several very good cafés and coffeehouses are perfect for a satisfying breakfast or lunch.

River Rafting

The Taos Box, at the bottom of the steep-walled canyon far below the Rio Grande Gorge Bridge, is the granddaddy of thrilling white water in New Mexico and is best attempted by experts only—or on a guided trip—but the river also offers more placid sections such as through the Orilla Verde Recreation Area (one of the two main parcels of the Rio Grande del Norte National Monument), just south of Taos in the village of Pilar, and the Rio Grande Gorge Visitor Center, a font of information on outdoor recreation in the region. Spring runoff is the busy season, from late March through June, but rafting companies conduct tours from early March to as late as November. Shorter two-hour options usually cover the fairly tame section of the river.

CONTACTS Los Rios River Runners. ✉ *Taos* ☎ *575/776–8854* ⊕ *www.losriosriverrunners.com.* **New Mexico River Adventures.** ✉ *Taos* ☎ *800/983–7756* ⊕ *www.newmexicoriveradventures.com.* **Rio Grande Gorge Visitor Center.** ✉ *2873 NM 68, Pilar* ☎ *575/751–4899* ⊕ *www.blm.gov/visit/orilla-verde-recreation-area.*

Visitor Information

CONTACTS Taos Ski Valley Chamber of Commerce. ✉ *10 Thunderbird Rd., Taos Ski Valley* ☎ *800/517–9816* ⊕ *www.taosskivalley.com.* **Taos Chamber of Commerce/ Taos Visitor Center.** ✉ *1139 Paseo del Pueblo Sur, Taos* ☎ *800/732–8267* ⊕ *www.taos.org.*

Historic Downtown Taos

The historic Taos Plaza is the central focal point of the town of Taos. Established in 1796, the plaza began as a quadrangle for a Spanish fortlike settlement. Merchants and traders traveled from all over the West to display their wares on the plaza. Today, Taos Plaza continues to be a gathering place for the local community and visitors. Dozens of independent shops and galleries, along with several notable restaurants, hotels, and museums, can be found in and around the plaza. The plaza itself is a bit overrun with souvenir shops, but you only need to walk a block in any direction—especially north and east—to find more unique offerings. Important upgrades to the town's infrastructure are taking place throughout 2024 in the Plaza and the main road through town, but businesses are still open, and access is available, so please don't be deterred by the construction.

The Harwood Museum of Art is the former home of Taos painter Burt Harwood and one of the town's best museums.

 Sights

E. L. Blumenschein Home and Museum

HISTORIC HOME | For an introduction to the history of the Taos Society of Artists, visit the residence of Ernest L. Blumenschein, one of the founding members. One of the rooms in the adobe-style structure dates from 1797. On display are the art, antiques, and other personal possessions of Blumenschein and his wife, Mary Greene Blumenschein, who also painted, as did their daughter Helen. Several of Ernest Blumenschein's vivid oil paintings hang in his former studio, and works by other early Taos artists are also on display. ⊠ *222 Ledoux St., Plaza and Vicinity* ☎ *575/758–0505* ⊕ *www.taoshistoricmuseums.org* 🖅 *$10.*

★ Harwood Museum of Art

ART MUSEUM | Just two blocks from Taos Plaza, the Harwood Museum of Art is an essential destination for all art lovers. The beautifully renovated Pueblo Revival-style adobe compound has served as a center for the arts and culture in New Mexico for more than 100 years and once housed the town's library. With nine galleries and a collection of more than 6,500 objects, the Harwood exhibits works that range from colonial Hispanic artists and the Taos Society of Artists to post-World War II modernists and cutting-edge contemporary artists. The Harwood is also home to the world-famous Agnes Martin Gallery and an impressive collection by renowned *santero* (religious icon artist) Patrociño Barela, not to mention robust educational programming with outstanding

films, lectures, and concerts in its state-of-the-art auditorium.
✉ *238 Ledoux St., Plaza and Vicinity* ✛ *One block south of Historic Taos Plaza* ☎ *575/758–9826* ⊕ *www.harwoodmuseum.org* 🏷 *$10* 🕑 *Closed Mon. and Tues.*

★ Historic Taos Plaza

PLAZA/SQUARE | FAMILY | The bustling center of downtown Taos, the Plaza is also filled with some of the town's most important history. The first European explorers of the Taos Valley came here in a 1540 expedition, and Spanish settlements began to be established in the 1600s. In 1796, the King of Spain gave the Don Fernando de Taos land grant to 63 Hispanic families—the most significant settlement in the area second only to Taos Pueblo. It was then developed into two plazas: one was a thriving business district for the early colony, while the second, a walled residential plaza, was constructed a few hundred yards behind it.

A gruesome, but important, historic chapter took place at Taos Plaza in 1847, during the Mexican-American War. The Taos Rebellion, or Taos Revolt, was an effort by the Indo-Hispano and Taos Pueblo communities to resist the American invasion of Northern New Mexico, resulting in the murder of newly-appointed Governor Charles Bent and other Americans and a massacre at Taos Pueblo by the U.S. Army. Following a jury trial at the Taos County Courthouse weighted to favor the American view, a number of local men were declared guilty and publicly executed by hanging on Taos Plaza. Be sure to visit the old Taos County Courthouse on the north side of the Plaza, the site of these convictions. A series of dramatic murals depicting the use and misuse of the law were painted on its walls in the 1930s by Taos artists. Luckily for modern-day visitors, today's plaza is the home to summer fiestas, family-friendly concerts, and other community events, and houses gift shops, galleries, and restaurants. ✉ *Plaza and Vicinity* ⊕ *www. taos.org/what-to-do/landmark-sites/taos-plaza.*

Inger Jirby Gallery

ART GALLERY | This popular gallery displays Jirby's whimsical, brightly colored landscape paintings. Her work is bold and colorful, and largely dedicated to her favorite subject: the Taos landscape. She was born in Kiruna, Sweden (north of the Arctic Circle), and it was there she learned to paint, influenced by Swedish artists who had studied with Impressionists. Be sure to stroll through the lovely sculpture garden. ✉ *207 Ledoux St., Plaza and Vicinity* ☎ *575/758–7333* ⊕ *www.jirby.com.*

Kit Carson Park & Cemetery

CITY PARK | FAMILY | This centrally located town park is a good place to rest or get active. Landscaped with mature trees and lilacs that

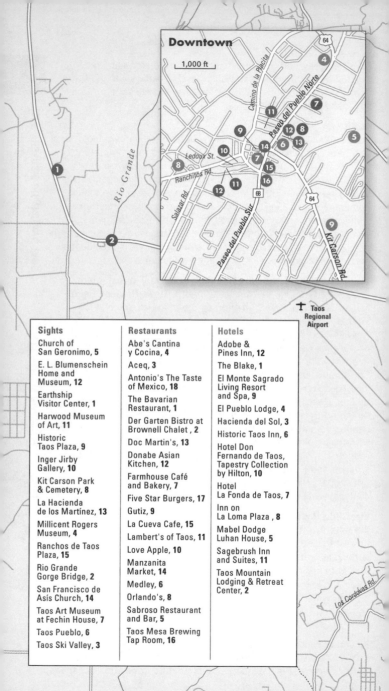

Downtown

1,000 ft

Taos
Regional
Airport

Sights

Church of
San Geronimo, **5**

E. L. Blumenschein
Home and
Museum, **12**

Earthship
Visitor Center, **1**

Harwood Museum
of Art, **11**

Historic
Taos Plaza, **9**

Inger Jirby
Gallery, **10**

Kit Carson Park
& Cemetery, **8**

La Hacienda
de los Martínez, **13**

Millicent Rogers
Museum, **4**

Ranchos de Taos
Plaza, **15**

Rio Grande
Gorge Bridge, **2**

San Francisco de
Asís Church, **14**

Taos Art Museum
at Fechin House, **7**

Taos Pueblo, **6**

Taos Ski Valley, **3**

Restaurants

Abe's Cantina
y Cocina, **4**

Aceq, **3**

Antonio's The Taste
of Mexico, **18**

The Bavarian
Restaurant, **1**

Der Garten Bistro at
Brownell Chalet , **2**

Doc Martin's, **13**

Donabe Asian
Kitchen, **12**

Farmhouse Café
and Bakery, **7**

Five Star Burgers, **17**

Gutiz, **9**

La Cueva Cafe, **15**

Lambert's of Taos, **11**

Love Apple, **10**

Manzanita
Market, **14**

Medley, **6**

Orlando's, **8**

Sabroso Restaurant
and Bar, **5**

Taos Mesa Brewing
Tap Room, **16**

Hotels

Adobe &
Pines Inn, **12**

The Blake, **1**

El Monte Sagrado
Living Resort
and Spa, **9**

El Pueblo Lodge, **4**

Hacienda del Sol, **3**

Historic Taos Inn, **6**

Hotel Don
Fernando de Taos,
Tapestry Collection
by Hilton, **10**

Hotel
La Fonda de Taos, **7**

Inn on
La Loma Plaza , **8**

Mabel Dodge
Luhan House, **5**

Sagebrush Inn
and Suites, **11**

Taos Mountain
Lodging & Retreat
Center, **2**

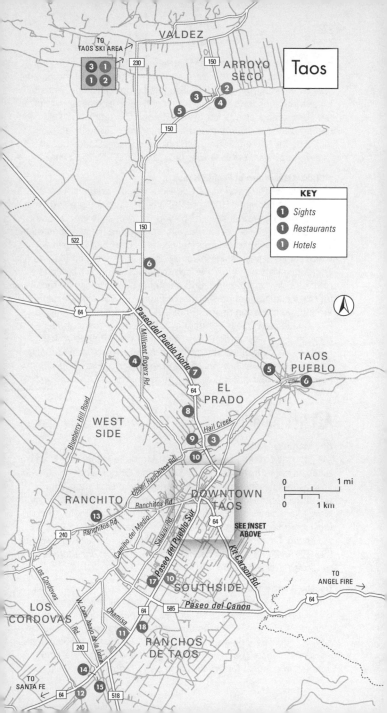

Taos

KEY
- Sights
- Restaurants
- Hotels

VALDEZ

TO TAOS SKI AREA

ARROYO SECO

230

150

522

64

150

Paseo del Pueblo Norte

Millicent Rogers Rd.

WEST SIDE

Blueberry Hill Road

Hail Creek

EL PRADO

TAOS PUEBLO

RANCHITO

Upper Ranchitos Rd.

Ranchitos Rd.

240

Camino del Medio

Salazar Rd.

DOWNTOWN TAOS

SEE INSET ABOVE

Paseo del Pueblo Sur

Kit Carson Rd.

64

SOUTHSIDE

TO ANGEL FIRE

LOS CORDOVAS

Los Cordovas

W. Cam. Abajo de la Loma

Chamisa

585

Paseo del Canon

64

240

64

518

RANCHOS DE TAOS

TO SANTA FE

0   1 mi
0   1 km

bloom in the springtime, it has facilities for baseball, soccer, basketball, tennis, and a .75-mile track towards the east of the park as well as trails throughout for walking and jogging. The perfect site for summer concerts and outdoor family films and other events, the 19-acre park also holds the Kit Carson Cemetery, the final resting place for many famous (and infamous) Taos characters including Kit Carson, Padre Martinez, and Mabel Dodge Luhan. ⊠ *211 Paseo del Pueblo Norte, Taos* ☎ *575/737–2626* 🖼 *Free.*

★ Taos Art Museum at Fechin House

ART MUSEUM | The interiors of this extraordinary adobe house and studio, built between 1927 and 1933 by Russian émigré and artist Nicolai Fechin, are a marvel of carved Russian-style woodwork and furniture as well as Southwest architecture. Fechin constructed them to showcase his daringly colorful paintings, intricate wood carvings and cabinetry, and coppersmith work on fixtures. The house now contains the Taos Art Museum, which exhibits a rotating collection of some 600 paintings by more than 50 Taos artists, including founders of the original Taos Society of Artists, among them Joseph Sharp, Ernest Blumenschein, Bert Phillips, E. I. Couse, and Oscar Berninghaus. Be sure to take a stroll through the lovely gardens, and a peek in the gift shop which houses exquisite pieces by contemporary jewelers among many attractive items. ⊠ *227 Paseo del Pueblo Norte, Plaza and Vicinity* ☎ *575/758–2690* ⊕ *www.taosartmuseum.org* 🖼 *$10* ⊙ *Closed Mon.*

Restaurants

Doc Martin's

$$$ | **SOUTHWESTERN** | Located in the Historic Taos Inn, Doc Martin's takes its name from the building's original owner, a physician who saw patients in the rooms that are now the dining areas. The beautiful, centrally located restaurant serves authentic Northern New Mexico cuisine. **Known for:** delicious chiles rellenos; fresh, local ingredients; extensive wine list. 💲 *Average main: $26* ⊠ *Historic Taos Inn, 125 Paseo del Pueblo Norte, Plaza and Vicinity* ☎ *575/758–2233* ⊕ *www.taosinn.com/restaurant/doc-martins* ⊙ *Closed Tues. and Wed. No lunch.*

Donabe Asian Kitchen

$$ | **ASIAN** | Chef-owner Marshall Thompson has overseen some of the town's top kitchens as well as a popular noodle cart, and Donabe is his own Asian restaurant that serves delightful and satisfying food. The kitchen specializes in a wide variety of Japanese, Korean, Chinese, Thai, and Vietnamese dishes, with meat and vegetarian options. **Known for:** impressive range of Asian dishes;

fresh, locally sourced ingredients; historic building with art gallery. $ *Average main: $25* ✉ *133 Paseo del Pueblo Norte, Plaza and Vicinity* ☎ *575/751–9700* ⊕ *www.donabetaos.com* ☺ *Closed Tues. and Wed.*

La Cueva Cafe

$ | MEXICAN | FAMILY | This casual Mexico–meets–New Mexico eatery is run by Mexico-born couple Juana and Horacio Zarazua, who have built a devoted following working in some of the best restaurants in town. Their specialty is regional Mexican food, including ceviche, chipotle shrimp tacos, and several other seafood dishes, plus chiles rellenos, chicken mole enchiladas, and some familiar New Mexico-style standbys. **Known for:** authentic Mexican and New Mexican menu; friendly, family-owned establishment; gluten-free menu. $ *Average main: $15* ✉ *135 Paseo del Pueblo Sur, Plaza and Vicinity* ☎ *575/758–7001* ⊕ *www.lacuevacafe.com* ☺ *Closed Sun.*

★ Lambert's of Taos

$$$$ | CONTEMPORARY | Superb service, creative cuisine, and an utterly romantic setting inside a historic adobe house just a short walk north of the plaza define this Taos landmark that's been a go-to for special meals since 1988 (it was previously located a few blocks away). A seasonally changing menu presents elegant contemporary American cuisine brushed with influences from around the world. **Known for:** elegant dining experience; casual upstairs bar lounge; excellent wine list. $ *Average main: $40* ✉ *123 Bent St., Plaza and Vicinity* ☎ *575/758–1009* ⊕ *www.lambertsoftaos. com* ☺ *Closed Tues. and Wed.*

Manzanita Market

$ | AMERICAN | Located on the north side of the Historic Taos Plaza, this spacious and airy restaurant bills itself as a community café, a reference to its locally sourced foods from farms that use sustainable methods. The menu rotates seasonally among veggie bowls, grass-fed meat sandwiches, and hearty soups made from bone broth. **Known for:** local, organic foods; bustling but friendly ambience; great smoothies and ice cream. $ *Average main: $9* ✉ *103 North Plaza, Plaza and Vicinity* ☎ *575/613–4808* ⊕ *www. manzanitamarket.net* ☺ *Closed Mon. No dinner.*

Taos Mesa Brewing Tap Room

$ | PIZZA | You don't have to be a craft beer fan to enjoy this convivial taproom a brief walk south of the plaza, although it is a terrific place to sample a crisp ruby-red Amarillo Rojo red ale or a robust Black Widow porter. Pizza lovers will also appreciate this spot, which serves delicious, generously topped pies out of a wood-fired oven. **Known for:** locally brewed beers; easy, no-fuss pub pizza menu; large space with different seating areas. $ *Average main: $15* ✉ *201 Paseo del Pueblo Sur, Plaza and Vicinity* ☎ *575/758–1900* ⊕ *www.taosmesabrewing.com* ◷ *Closed Wed.*

Hotels

El Monte Sagrado Living Resort and Spa

$$$$ | **RESORT** | This elite boutique resort is part of New Mexico's Heritage Hotels & Resorts brand and features beautifully manicured grounds, valet parking, an indoor swimming pool and hot tub, and a full-service spa. **Pros:** luxurious resort experience; on-site restaurant, bar, and spa services; close to plaza with beautiful mountain views. **Cons:** posh atmosphere somewhat incongruous with an authentic experience of Taos; steep prices; half-mile walk to the plaza is slightly uphill. $ *Rooms from: $700* ✉ *317 Kit Carson Rd., Plaza and Vicinity* ☎ *855/846–8267 reservations* ⊕ *www.elmontesagrado.com* ⇥ *84 rooms* ⦿ *No Meals.*

El Pueblo Lodge

$$ | **HOTEL** | **FAMILY** | This well-maintained adobe-style hotel with a fun retro sign out front and the feel of an old-school Route 66 motel is a real gem. **Pros:** nice hot tub and fitness room; on-site laundry service; central location. **Cons:** family-friendly vibe might not allow for quiet retreat; off busy main road; Southwestern decor may not suit everyone's taste. $ *Rooms from: $180* ✉ *412 Paseo del Pueblo Norte, Plaza and Vicinity* ☎ *575/758–8700, 800/433–9612* ⊕ *www.elpueblolodge.com* ⇥ *50 rooms* ⦿ *Free Breakfast.*

Historic Taos Inn

$$$ | **B&B/INN** | Located just north of Taos Plaza, this celebrated property is a local landmark, with its Spanish-colonial architecture, including decorative alcoves in rooms, lending a warm, distinctive aesthetic to the four buildings, including the upscale Helen's House, which contains some of the fanciest rooms. **Pros:** legendary bar and excellent restaurant; authentic Southwestern character and rich history; unbeatable location in the heart of Historic Downtown Taos. **Cons:** highly active social scene not for everyone; some rooms are very small; noise from traffic on the main road. $ *Rooms from: $300* ✉ *125 Paseo del Pueblo Norte, Plaza and Vicinity* ☎ *575/758–2233* ⊕ *www.taosinn.com* ⇥ *45 rooms* ⦿ *No Meals.*

Hotel La Fonda de Taos

$$ | **HOTEL** | This handsomely updated and elegant historic property (there's been a hotel on this location since 1820) is ideal if you wish to be in the heart of the action—it's directly on the plaza.

Pros: great central location; fascinating history; romantic ambience. **Cons:** occasional noise from plaza events; not suitable for families; some rooms are quite small. $ *Rooms from: $220* ⌂ *108 S. Plaza, Plaza and Vicinity* ☎ *575/758–2211* ⊕ *www.lafondataos.com* ⊋ *25 rooms* ❖ *No Meals* ☞ *No children under 8 allowed.*

Inn on La Loma Plaza

$$ | B&B/INN | Surrounded by thick walls, this early 1800s Pueblo Revival building—and the surrounding gardens—capture the spirit and style of Spanish-colonial Taos. **Pros:** dietary accommodations for breakfast available; short walk from Taos Plaza; charming decor. **Cons:** lots of stairs; could use some updates throughout; on a busy street. $ *Rooms from: $180* ⌂ *315 Ranchitos Rd., Plaza and Vicinity* ☎ *800/530–3040* ⊕ *www.vacationtaos.com* ⊋ *12 rooms* ❖ *Free Breakfast.*

★ Mabel Dodge Luhan House

$ | B&B/INN | Located one mile from Taos Plaza, this National Historic Landmark was once home to the heiress who drew illustrious writers and artists to Taos, including D. H. Lawrence and Georgia O'Keeffe, and is now an eccentric and beautiful adobe estate that borders Taos Pueblo land and offers an authentic window into the community. **Pros:** quiet, rural setting; delicious breakfasts served in dining hall with views; reasonably priced. **Cons:** lots of stairs and uneven paths; can hear music from the occasional outdoor concert during summer season; located at far end of a narrow, dead-end road. $ *Rooms from: $135* ⌂ *240 Morada La., Plaza and Vicinity* ☎ *575/751–9686* ⊕ *www.mabeldodgeluhan.com* ⊋ *21 rooms* ❖ *Free Breakfast.*

Nightlife

★ Adobe Bar

BARS | This legendary bar at the Historic Taos Inn has free live music (please tip the musicians), epic margaritas, and a packed dance floor. Talented acts range from singer-songwriters to fiery flamenco dancers. It's also a favorite spot for happy hour—there's a great menu of appetizers and cocktails, and the patio is a lovely place to sit and people-watch on warm evenings. ⌂ *Historic Taos Inn, 125 Paseo del Pueblo Norte, Historic Downtown* ☎ *575/758–2233* ⊕ *www.taosinn.com/restaurant/adobebar.*

★ The Alley Cantina

BARS | Housed in the oldest adobe structure in downtown Taos, this friendly spot has live jazz, folk, rock, and blues music, as well as shuffleboard, pool, and board games for those not inclined to dance. The bar stays open until midnight (the kitchen closes at

9 pm) making it one of the only late-night spots in town. ✉ *121 Teresina La., Historic Downtown* ☎ *575/758–2121* ⊕ *www.alley-cantina.com.*

The Lounge by Rolling Still

BARS | This women-owned, family-run cocktail bar serves up tasty bites and gluten-free drinks made from locally distilled vodka infusions made by Rolling Still. Enjoy outdoor seating on the vibrant, social patio, which often features live music, or find a more intimate table inside. ✉ *110 Paseo Del Pueblo Norte, Historic Downtown* ☎ *575/613–0326* ⊕ *www.rollingstill.com/the-lounge.*

★ Parcht Bottleshop + Bites

WINE BARS | Known for its tasty artisanal cheese and charcuterie boards and an excellent selection of craft beers and wines, this intimate wine bar is a lovely place for a treat with your sweetheart or a gathering of friends. It's nestled below the Gorge Bar and Grill on the east side of Taos Plaza. ✉ *103 E. Plaza, Plaza and Vicinity* ☎ *575/758–1994* ⊕ *www.parcht.com.*

 Performing Arts

Taos Center for the Arts

ARTS CENTERS | **FAMILY** | Since 1953, when the Taos Center for the Arts was founded by a group of working artists, TCA has been a leader in arts collaboration and partnership. With a 275-seat theater (the largest indoor auditorium in town) and two galleries, TCA curates culturally relevant films, art exhibitions, and live performances by creatives of local, regional, and international renown. ✉ *Taos Community Auditorium, 145 Paseo del Pueblo Norte, Historic Downtown* ☎ *575/758–2052* ⊕ *www.tcataos.org.*

★ Taos Chamber Music Group

CONCERTS | Since 1993, this esteemed group of musicians has performed traditional—Bach, Beethoven, Brahms—and contemporary chamber music concerts. Performances are generally held in the Arthur Bell Auditorium (at the Harwood Museum of Art) and are vivid thanks to the state-of-the-art sound design. ☎ *575/770–1167* ⊕ *www.taoschambermusicgroup.org.*

Shopping

Coyote Moon

CRAFTS | With a great selection of expertly crafted New Mexican, Mexican, and South American folk art, paintings, and block prints, Coyote Moon sells delightful pieces for every budget. The colorful shop also carries unique silver jewelry by owner Luis Garcia and by Pueblo, Zuni, and Navajo artists. ✉ *John Dunn Shops, 120-C Bent St., Plaza and Vicinity* ☎ *575/758–4437* ⊕ *www.johnd-unnshops.com/project/coyote-moon.*

★ Robert L. Parsons Fine Art

CRAFTS | This is one of the best sources of early Taos art-colony paintings, antiques, and authentic antique Navajo blankets. Inside you'll find originals by such luminaries as Ernest Blumenschein, Bert Geer Phillips, Oscar Berninghaus, Joseph Bakos, and Nicolai Fechin. ✉ *131 Bent St., Plaza and Vicinity* ☎ *575/751–0159* ⊕ *www.parsonsart.com.*

Starr Interiors

ANTIQUES & COLLECTIBLES | Run by the Starr family, this colorful shop has been around since 1974. Walk in and delight your senses with their gorgeous collection of Zapotec Indian rugs and hangings, brightly painted Oaxacan animals and masks, and other folk art and furnishings. ✉ *117 Paseo del Pueblo Norte, Plaza and Vicinity* ☎ *575/758–3065* ⊕ *www.starr-interiors.com.*

★ Taos Blue

CRAFTS | For more than 30 years, this fine handcrafts gallery on the northeast corner of Bent Street has featured exquisite one-of-a-kind pieces by a gifted stable of artists. Here you can find textiles, rugs, wall hangings, fine jewelry, paintings, sculptures, decorative and functional ceramics, and Zuni carvings. ✉ *101 Bent St., Plaza and Vicinity* ☎ *575/758–3561* ⊕ *www.taosblue.com.*

The Southside and Ranchos de Taos

The early Spanish settlers were agrarian, and many families continue to till the fertile land south of Taos, an area anchored by the Ranchos de Taos Plaza and its iconic San Francisco de Asis Church memorialized by Georgia O'Keeffe and photographer Ansel Adams. The main approach into Taos from the south on NM 68 is lined with gas stations and chain stores, but there are some distinctive hotels and eateries as well.

Sights

★ La Hacienda de los Martínez

HISTORIC HOME | One of the most impressive surviving Spanish Colonial houses in the Southwest, the Hacienda was built between 1804 and 1820 on the west bank of the Rio Pueblo and served as a community refuge during Comanche and Apache raids. Its thick walls, which have few windows, surround two central courtyards. Don Antonio Severino Martínez was a farmer and trader; his hacienda was the final stop along El Camino Real (the Royal Road), the trade route the Spanish established between Mexico City and New Mexico. The restored period rooms here contain textiles, spiritual art, and fine handcrafted pieces from the early 19th century. Be sure to stop in the gift shop, which features many renowned Taos artists, books on the region, and more. Visit in June for the hacienda's American mountain man event, or in September for their well-loved trading fair. ⊠ *708 Hacienda Way, off Ranchitos Rd. (NM 240), Southside* ☎ *575/758–1000* ⊕ *www. taoshistoricmuseums.org* ✑ *$10.*

Ranchos de Taos Plaza

PLAZA/SQUARE | On the south end of Taos, the Ranchos de Taos Plaza is the site of the oldest Spanish village in Taos Valley. Built as a fortified settlement for protection, it was finished in the late 1770s. The famous adobe San Francisco de Asis church sits in the center of the plaza, and around its perimeter are adobe buildings that once housed the earliest Spanish settlers of the area. Some of these historic residences have been converted into shops, galleries, and restaurants that can be visited by the public. Others are returning back to the earth from which they were formed. The Ranchos Plaza lies within a larger area that was designated as a Traditional Historic Community in 2022, under the official name "Las Comunidades del Valle de los Ranchos Traditional Historic Community." ⊠ *Southside* ⊕ *www.ranchosdetaosna.com.*

★ San Francisco de Asís Church

CHURCH | A National Historic Landmark, this is a beloved destination among the faithful, as well as for artists, photographers, and architectural buffs. The active Catholic church regularly celebrates Mass, contains numerous Hispanic religious artifacts, and is open to the public for visiting. Be sure to show respect for house of worship norms. The building's shape is a surprise with rounded, sculpted buttresses. Construction began in 1772 and today its mud-and-straw adobe walls are replastered by hand every year in an annual event. The "Ranchos Church" with its massive earthen walls and undulating lines is an awe-inspiring sight that Georgia O'Keeffe painted and Ansel Adams photographed many times. Group tours provided by the church historian can be scheduled in advance. The famous *Shadow of the Cross* painting is preserved in a nearby building and is also worth seeing. ⊠ *60 St. Francis Pl., Ranchos de Taos* ☎ *575/758–2754* ⊕ *www.sfranchos.org.*

Restaurants

Antonio's The Taste of Mexico

$ | **MEXICAN** | Chef Antonio Matus has been delighting diners in the Taos area for many years with his authentic, boldly flavorful, and beautifully plated regional Mexican cuisine. In this intimate art-filled restaurant with a slate courtyard, Matus focuses more on regional Mexican than New Mexican fare. **Known for:** red-chile pork posole; chile en nogada; tres leches cake. ⑤ *Average main: $15* ⊠ *1379 Paseo del Pueblo Sur, Southside* ☎ *575/758–2599* ☾ *Closed weekends.*

Five Star Burgers

$ | **BURGER** | A standout amid the strip of mostly unmemorable fast-food restaurants along Paseo del Pueblo on the south side of town, this airy, high-ceiling contemporary space—part of a regional chain with locations in Albuquerque as well—serves stellar burgers using hormone-free Angus beef from respected Harris Ranch; turkey, veggie, Colorado lamb, bison, and salmon burgers are also available. You can also choose from an assortment of novel toppings, including fried eggs, wild mushrooms, grilled onions, and crispy jalapeños. **Known for:** green-chile cheeseburgers; various protein bowls; delicious sweet potato fries. ⑤ *Average main: $12* ⊠ *1032 Paseo del Pueblo Sur, Southside* ☎ *575/758–8484* ⊕ *www.5starburgers.com.*

Hotels

★ Adobe & Pines Inn

$ | **B&B/INN** | This 1830s adobe hacienda is set on a beautiful 3-acre property that features native plants and an acequia. **Pros:** quiet rural location with beautiful gardens; cleaned with eco-friendly, nontoxic products; unique, beautifully decorated rooms. **Cons:** a bit of a drive south of the plaza; least expensive rooms are a bit small; mountain views somewhat limited. ⑤ *Rooms from: $135* ⊠ *4107 NM 68, Ranchos de Taos* ☎ *575/751–0947, 800/723–8267* ⊕ *www.adobepines.com* ⇌ *8 rooms* ⏿ *Free Breakfast.*

Hotel Don Fernando de Taos, Tapestry Collection by Hilton

$$ | **HOTEL** | Part of a portfolio of unique hotels with local personalities, Hotel Don Fernando is backed by the reliability and value of the Hilton brand. **Pros:** local lodging backed by global brand; beautiful contemporary Southwestern art and decor; ideal venue for weddings, meetings, and social events. **Cons:** not within walking distance of the plaza; noise from the main road; located near a busy intersection. ⑤ *Rooms from: $220* ⊠ *1005 Paseo del Pueblo*

Sur, Southside ☎ *575/751–4444* ⊕ *www.hilton.com/en/hotels/ tsmtmup-hotel-don-fernando-de-taos* ⌂ *126 rooms* ⦿ *No Meals.*

Sagebrush Inn and Suites

$$ | HOTEL | Georgia O'Keeffe once lived and painted in a third-story room of the original inn; these days it's not as upscale—or expensive—as many other lodging options in Taos, and most rooms are in a newer building, but it has a shaded patio with large trees, a serviceable restaurant, and a collection of antique Navajo rugs. **Pros:** popular bar with live music and dancing; nice grounds to wander around; charming Southwestern decor. **Cons:** not within walking distance of Taos Plaza; noise from the main road; conference venue can attract large groups. ⑤ *Rooms from: $200* ⊠ *1508 Paseo del Pueblo Sur, Southside* ☎ *575/758–2254* ⊕ *www.sagebrushinn.com* ⌂ *156 rooms* ⦿ *No Meals.*

Shopping

★ Chimayo Trading Del Norte

CRAFTS | This family-run gallery of nearly 6,000 square feet specializes in Native American art and jewelry, Pueblo pottery, Mata Ortiz pottery, Navajo rugs, and fine art. Located in the Ranchos de Taos Plaza next to the San Francisco de Asís Church, its historic architecture has the feel of an old trading post. Inside, you can browse through an astonishing collection of contemporary and traditional regional art that includes gorgeous jewelry, baskets, and Native American beadwork. ⊠ *1 St. Francis Church Pl., Ranchos de Taos* ☎ *575/758–0504* ⊕ *www.chimayotrading.com.*

Activities

★ Taos Valley Overlook Trails

HIKING & WALKING | FAMILY | Part of the Rio Grande del Norte National Monument, this trail system is a spectacular place to stop and get your bearings as you approach Taos from the south on Highway 68. With 20 miles of trails, the area is popular with locals and visitors and suitable for hiking, dog-walking, wildlife watching, and bicycling. The views of Taos Valley are breathtaking and trails lead from the highway to the rim of the Rio Grande Gorge. From here you can follow the Slide Trail down to the river, or walk along the rim. If you're lucky, you might glimpse some of the wild bighorn sheep or river otters who have been successfully reintroduced into the area. ⊠ *Southside* ✛ *The Overlook trail parking lot is located on the west side of the road near mile marker 36* ☎ *575/758–8851* ⊕ *www.blm.gov/visit/taos-valley-overlook-trails.*

El Prado

As you drive north from Taos toward Arroyo Seco and points north or west, you'll first take the main thoroughfare, Paseo del Pueblo Norte (U.S. 64) through the small village of El Prado, a mostly agrarian area that's notable for having several of the area's best restaurants, sights, and shops.

Sights

★ Millicent Rogers Museum

ART MUSEUM | More than 7,000 pieces of spectacular Native American and Hispanic art, many of them from the private collection of the late Standard Oil heiress Millicent Rogers, are on display here. Among the pieces are baskets, blankets, rugs, kachina dolls, carvings, tinwork, paintings, rare religious artifacts, and, most significantly, jewelry (Rogers, a fashion icon in her day, had a deep appreciation for the turquoise-and-silver artistry of Native American jewelers). Other important works include the pottery and ceramics of Maria Martinez and other potters from San Ildefonso Pueblo (north of Santa Fe). Docents conduct guided tours by appointment, and the museum hosts lectures, films, workshops, and demonstrations. The two-room gift shop has exceptional jewelry, rugs, books, and pottery. ⊠ *1504 Millicent Rogers Rd., off Paseo del Pueblo Norte, just south of junction with NM 150, El Prado* 🕾 *575/758–2462* ⊕ *www.millicentrogers.org* 🍽 *$15* 🕙 *Closed Wed. in Nov.–Mar.*

🍴 Restaurants

★ Farmhouse Café and Bakery

$ | **AMERICAN** | **FAMILY** | The best seats at this charming café are outside on the patio, surrounded by gardens and wind sculptures with sweeping views of the mountains and Taos Pueblo's beautiful buffalo pasture. The flavorful breakfasts and lunches use ingredients sourced from local farms and ranches, and the bakery turns out decadent made-from-scratch carrot cakes, scones, cinnamon rolls, and other treats, many of them gluten-free. **Known for:** house-baked pies, cakes, and scones; locally sourced, farm-fresh produce; vegetarian, local bison, and grass-fed beef burgers. 🆂 *Average main: $14* ⊠ *1405 Paseo del Pueblo Norte, El Prado* 🕾 *575/758–5683* ⊕ *www.farmhousetaos.com* 🕙 *No dinner.*

★ Gutiz

$ | **FUSION** | This ambitious and consistently terrific spot for lunch and breakfast (served all day) blends French and Spanish culinary influences. Favorite breakfast dishes include eggs Benedict and their signature French toast made from freshly baked bread while lunch specialties feature a green chile sausage bowl, pollo borracho, and sandwiches served on homemade French bread. **Known for:** friendly staff; handcrafted chocolate truffles; cheerful atmosphere with local art on display. ⑤ *Average main: $14* ⊠ *812B Paseo del Pueblo Norte, El Prado* ☎ *575/758–1226* ⊕ *www.gutiztaos.com* ⊘ *Closed Mon. and Tues. No dinner.*

★ Love Apple

$$ | CONTEMPORARY | It's easy to drive by the small adobe former chapel that houses this delightful farm-to-table restaurant a short drive north of Taos Plaza, but slow down—you don't want to miss the culinary magic of chef Andrea Meyer. She uses organic, mostly local ingredients in the preparation of simple yet sophisticated creations like homemade sweet-corn tamales with red-chile mole, a fried egg, and crème fraîche, and tacos (using homemade tortillas) filled with grilled antelope, potato-Gruyère gratin, and parsley gremolata. **Known for:** boldly flavored, locally sourced cuisine; romantic setting inside former chapel; cash-only policy. ⑤ *Average main: $20* ⊠ *803 Paseo del Pueblo Norte, El Prado* ☎ *575/751–0050* ⊕ *www.theloveapple.net* ▭ *No credit cards* ⊘ *Closed Mon. and Tues. No lunch.*

★ Medley

$$ | MODERN AMERICAN | Set in a rustic-chic roadhouse on the scenic road between El Prado and Arroyo Seco that adjoins one of the area's best wineshops, Medley is an excellent choice for a gathering of friends or a romantic night out. You could make a meal of one of their outstanding salads and soups or order a few shareable small plates such tuna tartare tostadas, mac-and-cheese with roasted Hatch chiles, or ratatouille en croûte. **Known for:** elaborate and satisfying small plates; terrific mountain views from patio; extensive wine and cocktail list. ⑤ *Average main: $23* ⊠ *100 NM 150, El Prado* ☎ *575/776–8787* ⊕ *www.medleytaos.com* ⊘ *Closed Sun. and Mon.*

★ Orlando's

$ | MEXICAN FUSION | FAMILY | This family-run, local favorite is likely to be crowded during peak hours, while guests wait patiently to devour perfectly seasoned favorites such as *carne adovada* (red chile–marinated pork), blue-corn enchiladas, and scrumptious fish tacos. You can eat in the colorful and cozy dining room or outside on the umbrella-shaded front patio. **Known for:** famous avocado pie for dessert; colorful, festive atmosphere; authentic New Mexican and Mexican dishes. ⑤ *Average main: $15* ⊠ *1114 Don Juan Valdez*

La., El Prado ☎ *575/751–1450* ⊕ *www.facebook.com/Orlandos-NewMexicanCafe* ⊗ *Closed Sun. and Mon.*

 Hotels

Hacienda del Sol

$$ | B&B/INN | Art patron Mabel Dodge Luhan bought this house about a mile north of Taos Plaza in the 1920s and lived here with her husband, Tony Luhan, while building their main house; most of the rooms contain Pueblo-style fireplaces, Southwestern handcrafted furniture, and original artwork—a few have Jacuzzi tubs. **Pros:** stunning mountain views; private retreat setting; some excellent restaurants within walking distance. **Cons:** traffic noise from the main road; some rooms are less private than others; 1-mile walk to the plaza. $ *Rooms from: $180* ⊠ *109 Mabel Dodge La., El Prado* ☎ *575/758–0287, 866/333–4459* ⊕ *www.taoshaciendadelsol.com* ⇆ *12 rooms* ⊙ *Free Breakfast.*

 Shopping

Casa Cristal Pottery

CRAFTS | Located 2½ miles north of the Taos Plaza, Casa Cristal has a huge stock of stoneware, serapes, clay pots, Native American carvings, fountains, sweaters, ponchos, clay fireplaces, Mexican blankets, tiles, piñatas, and blue glassware from Guadalajara. You'll feel like you've arrived at a Mexican market, and that's because many of their crafts hail from south of the border (though there are regional New Mexican and Native American crafts to be found, too). Shipping is available for some of the more delicate or larger pieces you don't want to carry home. ⊠ *1306 Paseo del Pueblo Norte, El Prado* ☎ *575/758–1530.*

Taos Pueblo

The Pueblo is the ancient, beating heart of Taos. A short drive northeast of the plaza, Taos Pueblo consists of a living community with residences, fields, farms, schools, historical structures, churches, and graveyards, as well as 93,000 acres of Pueblo homeland. It is the site of religious practices that predate the formation of the United States and continue today. As a living community with its own etiquette and decorum, guests should be sure to follow all guidelines and requests provided by the Pueblo government or Pueblo residents. No visit to Taos is complete without spending time at this UNESCO World Heritage site.

Taos Pueblo is the largest collection of multistory pubelo dwellings in the United States.

Sights

Church of San Geronimo

CHURCH | The Church of San Geronimo, or St. Jerome (the patron saint of Taos Pueblo), was completed in 1850 and is the fourth church to stand at Taos Pueblo. The original church, built in 1627, was destroyed in 1640 by the Pueblo people in protest of Spanish attempts to missionize them. After this, the Taos people left their village and did not return until 1660, when they were persuaded by Governor Lopez de Mendizibal to come back. The second church was then built, but it was destroyed in 1680 during the Pueblo Revolt when Pueblo Natives throughout the region united in a successful effort to force the Spanish to leave the area. A third church was begun by Spanish Franciscans after they returned to Taos twelve years later. This church, finished by 1726, stood until 1847. At that point, during the Taos Rebellion (aka Taos Revolt), U.S. soldiers attacked what they believed were the men who had killed Governor Bent and other Americans. In reality, most of these men had fled to the mountains and the people inside the church were mainly women and children. The ruins of this third church can be seen today, and have become a cemetery site to the left of the Pueblo's public entrance. The fourth church that stands today on the Pueblo's plaza was built in 1850. With its smooth symmetry, stepped portal, and twin bell towers, the church is a popular subject for photographers and artists. ⊠ *Taos Pueblo, Taos Pueblo* ☎ *575/758–9208.*

★ Taos Pueblo

INDIGENOUS SIGHT | FAMILY | For nearly 1,000 years, the mud-and-straw adobe walls of Taos Pueblo have sheltered Tiwa-speaking Native Americans. A United Nations World Heritage site, the multi-story Pueblo is the largest of its kind. The Pueblo's main buildings, a north house and a south house, are believed to have been built between 1000 and 1450. Taos Pueblo has retained 95,000 acres of its original homeland. Forty-eight thousand acres of this was won back from the U.S. government through Taos Pueblo's historic legal fight for the return of Blue Lake. Tribal custom allows no electricity or running water in the two houses of the ancient Pueblo, where varying members (roughly 150) of Taos Pueblo live full-time. An additional 1,900 or so live in homes outside of the ancient pueblo. The pueblo also has schools, cemeteries, a health center, farms and fields, buffalo pastures, powwow grounds, and many religious dwellings including traditional kivas and the Catholic Church of San Geronimo.

Although the population is predominantly Catholic, the people of Taos Pueblo also maintain their original religious traditions. The public is invited to certain ceremonial and social dances held throughout the year: highlights include the Feast of Santa Cruz (May 3); Taos Pueblo Pow Wow (mid-July); Santiago and Santa Ana Feast Days (July 25 and 26); San Geronimo Days (September 29 and 30); Procession of the Virgin Mary (December 24); and Deer Dance or Matachines Dance (December 25). While you're at the pueblo, respect all rules and customs, which are posted prominently. There are some restrictions on personal photography. Guided tours are available daily and are the best way to start your visit. Tours are led Taos Pueblo community members and provide insight into both the history and present-day life of the Pueblo. ✉ *120 Veterans Hwy., Taos Pueblo* ☎ *575/758–1028* ⊕ *www. taospueblo.com* ✎ *$25.*

Shopping

★ House of Water Crow and Red Coral Flower

CRAFTS | Located directly to the left of the church as you walk into the Pueblo's open plaza, this shop of the talented Bernal family frequently updates what is sold, but there is always a beautiful collection of handmade, original pieces of jewelry, turquoise inlay wood wall hangings, and other unique items. In addition, the Dawn Butterfly Cafe serves a full menu of specialty coffees and beverages. Proceeds from the shop's sales go to the Coral Dawn and Paul J. Bernal Center for Arts and Literature. ✉ *Taos Pueblo*

✛ *Located at Taos Pueblo, directly to the west of the Church of San Geronimo* ☎ *575/770–5852.*

The Mesa

Taos is hemmed in by the Sangre de Cristo Mountains on the east, but to the west, extending from downtown clear across the precipitously deep Rio Grande Gorge (and the famous bridge that crosses it), the landscape is dominated by sweeping wide-open spaces. The west side of the town, sometimes called the Mesa, is largely residential and makes for a scenic shortcut around the sometimes traffic-clogged plaza (from Ranchos de Taos, just follow NM 240 to Blueberry Hill Road to complete this bypass).

 ## Sights

Earthship Visitor Center

OTHER ATTRACTION | FAMILY | Now found all over the world, the unique off-grid design of an Earthship home got its start in Taos. Local architect Michael Reynolds started the movement in 1969, motivated to create affordable housing that utilized waste materials such as tires, soda cans, and beer bottles that would otherwise end up in the landfill. Reynolds fought to create and establish the Sustainable Testing Site Act in the New Mexico state legislature in 2007. Learn about this fascinating architecture and its potential at the Earthship Visitor Center. The informative, self-guided tour is highly recommended. Guided tours are available for those seeking a more in-depth understanding, as are overnight stays in an Earthship rental. There is also an Earthship Academy with online and in-person educational opportunities. ⊠ *2 Earthship Way, West Side* ✛ *2 miles west of Rio Grande Gorge Bridge* ☎ *575/613–4409* ⊕ *www.earthshipglobal.com* 🎟 *$8.*

★ Rio Grande Gorge Bridge

BRIDGE | It's a dizzying experience to see the Rio Grande 650 feet underfoot, where it flows at the bottom of an immense, steep rock canyon. In summer the reddish rocks dotted with green scrub contrast brilliantly with the blue sky, where you might see a hawk lazily floating in circles. The bridge is one of the highest suspension bridges in the country. Hold on to your camera and eyeglasses when looking down. Many days just after daybreak, hot-air balloons fly above and even inside the gorge. There's a campground with picnic shelters and basic restrooms on the west side of the bridge. ⊠ *U.S. 64, 8 miles west of junction NM 522 and 150, El Prado.*

Nightlife

★ Taos Mesa Brewing

BREWPUBS | FAMILY | This fabulously unusual pub and microbrewery is located just a few miles east of the Rio Grande Gorge Bridge, across the highway from the regional Taos airport. In a high-ceilinged, eco-friendly building with soaring windows, you can sample exceptionally well-crafted Scottish Ale, Black Widow Porter, and Kolsch 45. Step outside to sit on the expansive patio and take in the amazing mountain and mesa views. Two outdoor stages present the best in live musical entertainment, frequently drawing large and enthusiastic crowds to enjoy regional and international artists. Tasty burgers, fries, salads, and desserts are served too. ⊠ *20 ABC Mesa Rd., Mesa* 🕾 *575/758–1900* ⊕ *www.taosmesabrewing.com.*

Arroyo Seco

With stunning, close-up views of the Taos mountains, this old Spanish agricultural village of about 1,700 has attracted a number of outdoor enthusiasts and creative types over the years. Established in 1834 by local Spanish farmers and ranchers, Arroyo Seco has today become a secluded, artsy escape from the sometimes daunting summer crowds and commercialism of the Taos Plaza. You reach the tiny commercial district along NM 150, about 5 miles north of the intersection with U.S. 64 and NM 522 (it's about 9 miles north of the plaza). The drive is part of the joy of visiting, as NM 150 rises steadily above the Taos Valley, offering panoramic views of the Sangre de Cristos—you pass through Arroyo Seco en route to the Taos Ski Valley. Though small, there are a handful of excellent restaurants in the village, several galleries, and some one-of-a-kind shops.

🍴 Restaurants

Abe's Cantina y Cocina

$ | MEXICAN FUSION | This family-owned, family-run establishment is a cultural landmark of Arroyo Seco. Named after proprietor Abe Garcia, the place has been in operation since the 1940s and serves as a community focal point. **Known for:** friendly small-town ambience; homemade tamales; good selection of beer. $ *Average main: $9* ⊠ *489 NM 150, Arroyo Seco* 🕾 *575/776–8643* ⊗ *Closed Sun. No dinner.*

The village of Arroyo Seco has plenty of charming shops and restaurants.

Aceq

$$ | **MODERN AMERICAN** | Head to this cozy bistro tucked behind some galleries in Arroyo Seco's charming little business district for superb, reasonably priced farm-to-table food with a decidedly global bent. The menu changes often to take advantage of seasonal ingredients, with excellently prepared dishes such as polenta tartine, arroz con puerco, and Thai peanut rice bowls. **Known for:** locally sourced farm-to-table ingredients; great beer, wine, and cocktail lists; small space so reservations are recommended. $ *Average main: $25* ⊠ *480 NM 150, Arroyo Seco* ☎ *575/776–0900* ⊕ *www.aceqrestaurant.com.*

★ Sabroso Restaurant and Bar

$$$ | **MODERN AMERICAN** | Sophisticated, innovative cuisine and outstanding wines are served in this 150-year-old adobe hacienda, where you can also relax in lounge chairs near the bar, or on a delightful patio surrounded by plum trees. The contemporary American menu changes regularly to take advantage of locally sourced meats and seasonal ingredients. **Known for:** fireplace-warmed dining room; live music; popular happy hour. $ *Average main: $29* ⊠ *470 NM 150, Arroyo Seco* ☎ *575/776–3333* ⊕ *www.sabrosotaos.com* ⊙ *Closed Tues. No lunch.*

Hotels

★ Taos Mountain Lodging & Retreat Center

$ | B&B/INN | FAMILY | This locally run bed and breakfast is set on ten acres in a beautiful riverside, rural setting with breathtaking views looking up to El Salto Peak. **Pros:** walking distance to center of Arroyo Seco; peaceful ambience; in-house integrative medicine services available. **Cons:** upstairs accommodations require stairs; shared bathrooms; older property. ⑤ *Rooms from: $100* ✉ *15 El Salto Rd., Arroyo Seco* ☎ *575/776–8940* ⊕ *www.taosmountain-lodging.com* ⤳ *6 rooms* ⦿ *Free Breakfast.*

Shopping

Arroyo Seco Mercantile

ANTIQUES & COLLECTIBLES | Packed to the rafters with a varied assortment of 1930s linens, handmade quilts, candles, organic soaps, vintage cookware, hand-thrown pottery, decorated crosses, and souvenirs, this colorful shop is a highlight of shopping in the charming village of Arroyo Seco. ✉ *488 NM 150, Arroyo Seco, Taos* ☎ *575/776–8806* ⊕ *www.secomerc.com.*

★ Rottenstone Pottery

CERAMICS | This locally owned pottery store features expertly designed glazed plates, bowls, cups, vases, pitchers, and more. Handmade and fired in a wood kiln, each piece is a work of art, making this a great place to shop for gifts that are both useful and beautifully one-of-a-kind. ✉ *486 NM 150, Arroyo Seco* ☎ *575/770–6183* ⊕ *www.rottenstonegallery.com.*

Taos Ski Valley

Skiers and snowboarders travel to this legendary ski area from all over the world for the thrill of its steep slopes. But it's not just for expert skiers; there is fun to be had for all ages and skill levels. For summer visitors, Taos Ski Valley offers hiking, biking, and scenic chairlift rides. There's also an active calendar of events, including ski competitions, guest lectures, outdoor parties, and fireworks shows.

Sights

Taos Ski Valley

SKIING & SNOWBOARDING | **FAMILY** | Started in the mid-1950s by Ernie and Rhoda Blake, Taos Ski Valley has been synonymous with legendary skiing ever since. The Blakes fashioned their ski village after the Swiss slopes that Ernie learned to ski on. The family-run resort was known for its quaint, friendly hospitality and its tight-knit community. In 2013, the Blake family sold the resort to billionaire Louis Bacon, and under the new leadership, the resort has been significantly reinvented, with ongoing construction that has expanded lift service, rebuilt the central village, and more. The historic Hotel St. Bernard has been torn down, and a larger, re-envisioned St. Bernard is being constructed at the base of the slopes, with completion expected by late 2025. These days you can find excellent skiing in Taos, with a culture akin to Aspen or Vail. There are still a few establishments left from the old days, and they are worth seeking out to experience the flavor of the original Taos Ski Valley's hospitality. ⊠ *116 Sutton Pl., Taos Ski Valley* ☎ *888/388–8457* ⊕ *www.skitaos.com* 🎫 *Lift tickets from $90.*

 Restaurants

The Bavarian Restaurant

$$$ | **GERMAN** | Located near the trailhead of Williams Lake/Wheeler Peak and at the base of Lift 4, this ski-in ski-out restaurant offers excellent, contemporary Bavarian-inspired cuisine. Try a warm pretzel and mustard, or one of several varieties of bratwurst with a stein of Bavarian beer. **Known for:** large deck facing Kachina Peak; authentic German dishes; imported German beers. $ *Average main: $26* ⊠ *100 Kachina Rd., Taos Ski Valley* ☎ *575/776–8020* ⊕ *www.skitaos.com/things-to-do/bavarian.*

★ Der Garten Bistro at Brownell Chalet

$$ | **AMERICAN** | **FAMILY** | This family-owned chalet and bistro is run by Christoff Brownell and Asia Golden; Christoff grew up at the ski valley and knows the mountain like the back of his hand while Asia is a farmer and chef. Der Garten serves farm-to-table, mostly organic food from local farmers and ranchers. **Known for:** made from scratch dishes with organic ingredients; friendly, family-run restaurant; luxurious on-site accommodations. $ *Average main: $18* ⊠ *Brownell Chalet, One Thunderbird Rd., Taos Ski Valley* ☎ *575/204–8784* ⊕ *www.brownellchalet.com* ☉ *Closed Thurs., Wed., Easter–June, and mid-Oct.–early Dec. No dinner Tues.*

Hotels

The Blake

$$$$ | **RESORT** | This luxury boutique hotel just steps from the resort's lifts has quickly developed a reputation as the swankiest accommodation in the Taos region. **Pros:** steps from the main lift; sizable rooms and plenty of amenities; beautiful views of the mountain. **Cons:** a 30-minute drive from Taos; feeling of remoteness if you're not outdoorsy; lobby is only modestly sized. ⑤ *Rooms from: $575* ⊠ *116 Sutton Pl., Taos Ski Valley* ☎ *575/776–5335 reception, 855/208-4988 reservations* ⊕ *www.skitaos.com/theblake* ⇨ *80 rooms* � Ⓞ *No Meals.*

Activities

Wheeler Peak

HIKING & WALKING | Part of a designated wilderness area of Carson National Forest, this iconic mountain summit—New Mexico's highest, at 13,161 feet—can only be reached by a rigorous hike or horseback ride. Only very experienced hikers should tackle this strenuous trail all the way to the top, but for a moderately challenging and still very rewarding hike, you take the trail to the halfway point, overlooking the shores of rippling Williams Lake. Numerous other rewarding hikes of varying degrees of ease and length—along the road to the ski valley and around the village area—make this a popular place to hike. ⊠ *Parking area for trailhead is along Kachina Rd. by the Bavarian lodge, Taos Ski Valley* ☎ *575/758–6200* ⊕ *www.fs.usda.gov/main/carson/home.*

Williams Lake Trail

HIKING & WALKING | **FAMILY** | This is a popular trail with visitors and locals alike. Before hiking, contact the Carson National Forest Office for information on the latest trail conditions; they rank this trail as "easy to intermediate" in difficulty level. It's important to note that the Williams Lake Trail and its surrounding forest is not a park, but a federally designated wilderness area and is not staffed with rangers or facilities. The well-trodden hiking trail is two miles (one-way) and climbs from 10,200 feet to 11,100 feet in elevation. It leads you to a remote alpine lake that is not huge, but is quite lovely. Towering above Williams Lake is Wheeler Peak, the highest peak in New Mexico. ⊠ *Taos Ski Valley* ✛ *Near end of Kachina Rd. Trailhead parking lot is well-signed* ☎ *575/758–6200 Carson National Forest Office* ⊕ *www.fs.usda.gov.*

Index

Photo Credits

Front Cover: John Dambik/Alamy Stock Photo [**Description:** Iaia Museum of Contemporary Native Arts, Santa Fe, New Mexico]. **Back cover, from left to right:** Sumikophoto/Dreamstime. Douglas Knight/Shutterstock. Mathieulemauff/Dreamstime. **Spine:** Patrick Civello/Shutterstock. **Interior, from left to right:** Genevieve Russell/Tourism Santa Fe (1). Anita Warren-Hampson/Shutterstock (2-3). **Chapter 1: Experience Santa Fe:** Sean Pavone/iStockphoto (6-7). Chris Corrie/Santa Fe Tourism (8-9). Doug Merriam/SantaFeTourism (9). Stephen B. Goodwin/Shutterstock (9). Americanspirit/Dreamstime (10). Jeffrey M. Frank/Shutterstock (10). Helio San Miguel/Turquoise Trail (10). Ppeterson6030/Dreamstime (10). Donald Riddle Images (11). Kate Russell, courtesy of Meow Wolf (11). Sumikophoto/Shutterstock (12). Byron Flesher/Zane Bennett Gallery (12). Andriy Blokhin/Shutterstock (12). Ffooter/Dreamstime (13). Georgia O'Keeffe Museum (13). Shizuko Alexander/iStockphoto (14). Robert Reck/Santa Fe Tourism (14). Gabriella Marks/SWAIA (14). Gimas/Shutterstock (14). Seth Roffman/SantaFeTourism (15). Sumikophoto/Dreamstime (15). Greg Meland/iStockphoto (20). New Mexico True (20). New Mexico True (20). Brent Hofacker/Shutterstock (20). Carlosrojas20/iStockphoto (21). Wendy McEahern/Shiprock Santa Fe (22). Wendy McEahern/Shiprock Santa Fe (22). Gabriella Marks/SWAIA (22). MichaelMou85/Shutterstock (22). Addison Doty/Lyn A. Fox Fine Pueblo Pottery (23). Genevieve Russell/Tourism Santa Fe (24). Brenda Kelley/Tourism Santa Fe (24). NPS Photo (24). Judy Kohn (24). Blake Jorgensen/Taos Ski Valley (25). **Chapter 3: The Plaza and Downtown Santa Fe:** Swdesertlover/Dreamstime (51). Efrain Padro/Alamy (58). Swdesertlover/Dreamstime (62). William Cushman/Shutterstock (65). Wendy McEahern/Shiprock Santa Fe (72). Nagel Photography/Shutterstock (77). **Chapter 4: The East Side with Canyon Road and Museum Hill:** Fotoluminate LLC/Shutterstock (81). Museum of International Folk Art (88). Jay Goebel/Alamy (90). **Chapter 5: The Railyard District:** Csfotoimages/iStockphoto (97). Pmphoto/Dreamstime (102). Genevieve Russell/StoryPortrait Media (111). **Chapter 6: Greater Santa Fe:** Genevieve Russell/Tourism Santa Fe (113). Harvey O Stowe/Shutterstock (117). Santa Fe Tourism (118). Roschetzky Photography/Shutterstock (131). **Chapter 7: Side Trips from Santa Fe:** Helio San Migue/Rio Grande Valley (133). Helio San Migue/MadridOldCoalTownMuseum (138). V Pyle/Shutterstock (151). Raymond Douglas Ewing/Shutterstock (156). Nick Fox/Shutterstock (159). **Chapter 8: Albuquerque:** Kit Leong/Shutterstock (165). Blairwacha/Shutterstock (172). Helio San Migue/Albuquerque Historical Society (175). Richard Lakin/Xinhua/River of Lights at ABQ BioPark Botanic Garden (177). Sean Pavone/Shutterstock (187). Maijaliisa/Dreamstime (190). Efrain Padro/Alamy (196). **Chapter 9: Taos:** CrackerClips/iStockphoto (213). John Elk III/Alamy (222). Dan Kaplan/Shutterstock (238). Nolichuckyjake/Shutterstock (242). **About Our Writers:** All photos are courtesy of the writers except for the following: Andrew Collins, courtesy of Fernando Nocedal.

*Every effort has been made to trace the copyright holders, and we apologize in advance for any accidental errors. We would be happy to apply the corrections in the following edition of this publication.

Fodor's InFocus SANTA FE

Publisher: Stephen Horowitz, *General Manager*

Editorial: Douglas Stallings, *Editorial Director;* Jill Fergus, Amanda Sadlowski, *Senior Editors;* Brian Eschrich, Alexis Kelly, *Editors;* Angelique Kennedy-Chavannes, *Assistant Editor;* Yoojin Shin, *Associate Editor*

Design: Tina Malaney, *Director of Design and Production;* Jessica Gonzalez, *Senior Designer;* Jaimee Shaye, *Graphic Design Associate*

Production: Jennifer DePrima, *Editorial Production Manager;* Elyse Rozelle, *Senior Production Editor;* Monica White, *Production Editor*

Maps: Rebecca Baer, *Senior Map Editor;* Mark Stroud (Moon Street Cartography), *Cartographer*

Photography: Viviane Teles, *Director of Photography;* Namrata Aggarwal, Neha Gupta, Payal Gupta, Ashok Kumar, *Photo Editors;* Jade Rodgers, *Photo Production Intern*

Business and Operations: Chuck Hoover, *Chief Marketing Officer;* Robert Ames, *Group General Manager*

Public Relations and Marketing: Joe Ewaskiw, *Senior Director of Communications and Public Relations*

Fodors.com: Jeremy Tarr, *Editorial Director;* Rachael Levitt, *Managing Editor*

Technology: Jon Atkinson, *Executive Director of Technology;* Rudresh Teotia, *Associate Director of Technology;* Alison Lieu, *Project Manager*

Writers: Lynne Arany, Natalie Bovis, Andrew Collins, Ariana Kramer

Editor: Amanda Sadlowski

Production Editor: Monica White

Copyright © 2024 by Fodor's Travel, a division of MH Sub I, LLC, dba Internet Brands.

Fodor's is a registered trademark of Internet Brands, Inc. All rights reserved. Published in the United States by Fodor's Travel, a division of Internet Brands, Inc. No maps, illustrations, or other portions of this book may be reproduced in any form without written permission from the publisher.

4th Edition

ISBN 978-1-64097-664-1

ISSN 2333-7958

All details in this book are based on information supplied to us at press time. Always confirm information when it matters, especially if you're making a detour to visit a specific place. Fodor's expressly disclaims any liability, loss, or risk, personal or otherwise, that is incurred as a consequence of the use of any of the contents of this book.

SPECIAL SALES

This book is available at special discounts for bulk purchases for sales promotions or premiums. For more information, e-mail SpecialMarkets@fodors.com.

PRINTED IN CANADA

10 9 8 7 6 5 4 3 2 1

MIX
Paper from responsible sources
FSC www.fsc.org FSC® C016245

About Our Writers

First lured to New Mexico for its rich cultural heritage and an archaeology career, **Lynne Arany** was soon firmly in thrall to this stunning state and its Mexico neighbor. A frequent contributor to *Fodor's New Mexico* and *Fodor's New York City* guides and other travel series, among them *Access: New York City* and *Born to Shop,* she is the co-author of *Little Museums* and *The Reel List,* as well as consulting editor for the acclaimed *New Mexico: A Guide for the Eyes.* She has also written for the *New York Times* and *New Mexico* magazine. She updated the Albuquerque chapter this edition.

Natalie Bovis is an award-winning mixologist, best-selling cocktail book author, and co-founder of OM Chocolate Liqueur. She is also an avid solo traveler whose adventures include on the Camino de Santiago in Spain and wandering through mountains and rainforest in Nepal. She teaches cooking, cocktail, and writing classes, created the national TACO WARS competition, and produces culinary events. She updated the Santa Fe chapters this edition.

Former Fodor's staff editor **Andrew Collins** is based in Mexico City but spends a good bit of the year traveling throughout the United States, especially northern New Mexico, where he formerly resided. A long-time contributor to more than 200 Fodor's guidebooks, he's also a regular contributor to The Points Guy travel website. He's also written for dozens of mainstream and LGBTQ+ publications, and he teaches travel writing and food writing for New York City's Gotham Writers Workshop. You can find more of his work at ⊕ AndrewsTraveling.com, and follow him on Instagram at @TravelAndrew. He updated the Experience, Travel Smart, and Side Trips From Santa Fe chapters this edition.

Ariana Kramer is a freelance writer focused on ecology and culture. She grew up in Taos County and has been privileged to travel across the borders of nations within her small hometown, around the Americas, and across the world. She believes that guest-host reciprocity is one of the oldest and most important forms of culture. Her favorite travel experiences have occurred when she has been invited into the homes and hearts of the people she has visited, and when she has been able to gift them a meaningful song, story, or meal in return. She updated the Taos chapter this edition.